The
Incontinental Divide

Christina Crall-Reed

Copyright © 2017 by Christina Crall-Reed

All rights reserved. No part of this publication may be reproduced, used in any manner, stored in a retrieval system or transmitted in any form whatsoever without prior written permission, except in the case of brief quotations embodied in critical articles and reviews.

Based on real events in the life of the author some depictions herein may have been altered for privacy, continuity of story or for comedic effect.

This is a memoir, not science.

The recollections and opinions expressed herein are those of the author and are subject to change.

ISBN 978-1-97450-480-0
ISBN 1-974-50480-8

Design and Layout by HoneyHornet Studio,
Amanda Oaks, and Crallspace Creative

795 CR 1, Palm Harbor, FL 34683
www.thecrallspace.com

Together we took on the world,
but we couldn't conquer time.
I miss you Mom,
Sherri,
Ric.

Contents

M.A.	1
First Strike	4
Fifteen Minutes	16
Weather Or Not	20
Off And On	24
Mere Mortals	31
Life's A Picnic	37
Deja Vu	40
Old Family Recipe	44
The Girls	48
This is a Test - This is Only a Test	52
Five In Five	60
The Last High Low	64
Pity Party	67
Dragonslayers	71
No Matter What	79
Pet Peeves	83
Gaelic Gall	87
Hold Please	91
Bet On A Longshot	95
When Your Panty Hose Catch Fire	101
Waking Up Ma	106
Choose Your Poison	110
Dressing The Queen	114
The Incontinental Divide	118
King Kegel	121

God Save The Queen	125
Gray Matters	127
Use It Or Lose It	132
Don't Think	135
World Piece	140
Play Through The Pain	143
Pay Back Time	146
Sunday Morning	149
Run, Bambi. Run!	160
Give Way	166
Slow Starters	173
Ladies Home Companion	176
The Nursery	180
Stack Em Up	184
The Jungle	187
Emptying The Nest	190
Move The Fish	193
Happy Holidays	199
The Thought That Counts	200
Think Again	206
I'm The Mother. It's The Law	213
Plague! You're It!	219
Cashing A Reality Check	222
Buy One Hundred - Get One Free	227
Gramma Kiss	230
Move The Body	236
Lights Out At The A.L.	241

The Incontinental Divide

M.A.

I could have the body of a twenty five year old, but I'd have to buy him lots of drinks, leave the lights off, and make sure he didn't graduate with my kids.

I had a twenty five year old body a quarter century ago. Mine was a low mileage, low maintenance, curved and polished steel beauty. I could have parked in a garage to preserve my finish, but I didn't. I rolled down the windows, jacked up the music, dirtied the ashtray and drove my Classic '57 right into capital M, capital A: Middle Age.

In my twenties, 'MA' was a term of endearment. That first sweet, garbled "ma-ma" brought tears to my eyes.

Pressed for time in my thirties, "mama" became simply, "Ma!"

"Ma! We're goin' to Ryan's!"

"Ma! The dog peed on the VCR!"

The distress bleat of teenagers (and sheep) was an extended version of "Ma!" "Mmaaa! We're out of milk!"

"Mmaaa! Have you seen my shoes?"

Like any good shepherdess worthy of her flock (lambs, kids – same thing) my responses were predictable. "Do not call me, 'Mmaaa'. We are not sheep. We're not out of milk unless the barn's on fire." And

"Yes, I've seen your shoes. They're the size of a Cessna. I can see them in satellite photos of the house."

My response to the passage of time was less predictable. Sometime after my fortieth birthday party — the black armbands, pretend we're in mourning, denture cream in my coffee, party — I left the "Front." I walked away from the front line of my youth with a collection of war stories from the trenches, forty extra pounds in my pack and arms too short to read the print on the back of a Lotto ticket.

I wandered between youth and middle age, bipolar crazy. I discovered the joys of aging and laughed so hard I wet myself. I laughed until the thought of wetting myself made me cry. To regain some control, I paused to straighten the guest towels no one ever used. I paused to send my kids off to college and bury some dear friends who died before reaching middle age. I paused for another brush with cancer. I definitely paused when I was struck by lightning a second time. Laughing one minute, crying the next, I paused to primp the guest towels again because that's what crazy women do when we're not sure whom or what might stop by.

According to all the women's magazines, I am Middle Aged. If I'm in the middle, logic dictates there *was* a Front and there *will be* a Back part of life. I've never been good at directions, so I'm not sure at what point the Front ended or where the Middle began.

The exact location of the Back is confusing. My back has always been south of my front. Since I left the Front for the Middle, my Middle back is south of my original back from the Front, and I don't think it's coming back.

To help regain my bearings, I had a donkey tattooed to the back of my upper thigh. It turns out that's where my ass is going anyway. Like my favorite book from childhood where a burro is the hero of the story, when I leave the Middle for the Back, my trusty ass will lead me on. Until that, "Brighty of the Grand Canyon" moment, I resolve to enjoy being MA.

I used to be cocky about wrinkles and gray hair — before I had either. Bring 'em on! Uh-huh. I'll wear them like a badge of honor! Sure. I've earned them! Blah. Blah. Blah. My Middle Ages could be fun. Maybe.

Screw it! I'd Botox, liposuck, duct tape, staple, dye, stitch and spackle every sign of aging to the back of my big head if I could. I'd buy a good wig or have some Texas Cheerleader Big Hair, teased and combed over the lump. Then I'd host a beauty pageant for all of the over-forty-no-longer-law (of gravity)-abiding-parts-missing-mastectomy-mamas like myself, enjoying the second coming of bell-bottoms.

Topped with a misshapen crown, carrying an over-polished hood ornament scepter, Ms. Middle Aged would sashay down the runway to the plastic surgery hall of fame. Don't kid yourself, honey. Priorities change.

In fact, everything changes, except the need to enjoy the moment. Now, when I pick up the latest issue of Cosmo and warning sirens scream *MA woman! Too old for* Cosmo*!* I'll buy it anyway because I can. According to Cosmo, persons in my age bracket have more expendable cash than the waif-like twenty-somethings they feature, so I can afford to waste my money on a women's magazine for which I am too old.

I'll enjoy the moment that full-frontal hysterectomy scar below my rounded belly grins up at me in the mirror like some bearded circus freak. *Ha ha! You're MA!* I'll grin right back. No tears. Ha ha, I'm MA! I'll be the happiest damned middle-aged woman on the planet! Happiest damned middle-aged woman on…the happiest… damn…*I'm a middle aged woman.* A middle-aged woman?!

Damn.

I might have to rethink this no tears thing.

Ma-ma?

First Strike

Electrocution may be a spectator sport for the morbidly curious, but it wasn't much fun to be the spectacle during my first lightning strike. I was twelve, barefoot, in the rain, at the carnival. My pockets bulged with coins stolen from my mother's purse. Technically, I didn't *steal* her money. I asked permission as she slept, knowing she would say yes because — if she was napping — she said yes to everything we asked.

"Can I get a tattoo, Mom?"

"Yes."

"Can Vickie dye her hair green for St. Patrick's Day?"

"Yes."

"Can Steve drive us in your car to the grocery so we can buy cigarettes with your only full book of S&H Green Stamps and this permission slip with your forged signature on it?"

"Yes, but…" *Uh-oh! She might be waking up!* "…Put gas in the car."

"We'll siphon some from the neighbor's car, okay, Mom?"

"Okay. Yes."

'Sleep Question' was a childhood survival technique I practiced, but never perfected.

Yes, it was an evil thing to do to a single parent mom who worked all hours at three jobs struggling to feed and clothe and house her children, then come home to cook and clean until she dropped. But Mom could take care of herself. She learned to sleep standing up — to confuse me. I learned to use Sleep Question with caution because the procedure was never as wicked as the fury I'd endure when Mom opened her eyes.

Since my siblings weren't home the day of the carnival to help me with Sleep Question, when I saw my mother napping, I also saw an opportunity to circumvent authority and poverty on my own. Permission to hang out at the carnival and harass the toothless Rock O' Planes guy was previously denied. Cash for the carnival would not be available unless I captured a leprechaun with a pot of gold to give my mother to pay the bills.

Without any mythical cash that day, I turned my selective hearing on, and then whispered my carefully phrased inquiry. "Mom, can I have some money to go to the carnival?"

"Yes."

Two questions, one answer! I did a quiet happy dance across the room to my mother's coin purse, emptied the jinglies into my pockets and ran off to the park.

⚡

Squeals and voices of every timbre mingled with the heavy scent of diesel fuel and fried dough. Torn canopies flapped in the summer breeze. From a crooked speaker nailed to the cotton candy stand the Archies sang, "Sugar Sugar," as we danced in line in the sticky grass.

Kelly giggled, "You get a corn dog and we'll split it."

"What, are you mental?" I said. "It's a wiener on a stick."

"Yeah. How we gonna split it?" Dana chimed in.

"Chris takes a bite, then me, then you."

"No."

"Yuck."

End of discussion. We skipped away with a cone of cotton candy to share. Imitating the teenage girls we so desperately wanted to be, flaunting silky hair, emerging breasts and smooth skin, we paraded around the midway, giggling. Dana walked with her arms folded protectively across her chest. Kelly's face bore dirty smudges of unknown origin and I had cotton candy stuck in my hair — but we tried. We answered the call of a transistor radio near the Tilt-O-Whirl when it beckoned. Twirling until we were dizzy, we screamed our throats raw. Ride to ride we laughed and plunged, spinning upside down long enough to break a Rock-O-Plane endurance record. My friends were pale and nauseous and my hair was a tangled blonde fright wig, defying gravity.

Dana swatted my head. "Nice afro. You need a comb." We bounced around the exit gate, laughing.

"Nice face," I said. "You guys need make-up. No, wait. You need spray paint."

Kelly punched me in the shoulder. Tickling and tittering we raced over to the row of games.

Lobbing darts at under-inflated balloons, we amassed a collection of cheap loot.

"Why does prize every time have to be the *same* prize every time?" Dana lamented our stash while Kelly and I played with it.

"There's only one a' these." Kelly stuck a jumbo clown comb into a snarl on the back of my head and then annoyed Dana with the click, clack of a cricket shaped noisemaker.

"Stop it." Dana protested.

Kelly wiped droplets from her cheek. "God Dana, say it, don't spray it!"

Dana hissed, "I didn't spit."

While my friends bickered, I leaned back to let heavy drops splatter my skin.

"Nobody's spitting. It's raining, you mentals!"

I flicked water on my pals, snatched our jewelry prizes from the booth and jumped out into the shower. Kelly joined me for a howling, arms waving rain dance. When Dana worked up the courage to step

The Incontinental Divide

into the rain, a downpour pelted her as the sky clouded over and the thunderheads rolled in. Lights stopped flickering and the rides shut down. Canopies were drawn. When lightning cracked from the clouds above, we squealed and splashed and ran for cover under the trees near the beer tent.

Breathless and dripping we huddled together laughing. "Where's your comb?" Kelly asked.

"I dunno. In a puddle? Wasn't mine anyway." I donned a plastic necklace. "This is mine."

"You're not gonna wear that, are you?" Dana asked.

"Yeah. Why not?"

"Cuz it's plastic."

"So? Twiggy wears plastic."

Twiggy was the only super-model we'd ever heard of. Her name lent authority and finality to my argument so I didn't have to explain to my friends why, wearing carnival jewelry outside the carnival could bring me a carnival of punishment.

Our tomboy Kelly wasn't interested in high fashion. She squatted in the mud between us, intent on peeling wet cellophane from the soggy half pack of Old Golds she'd pulled from the waistband of her shorts.

"Wanna smoke?"

"Whose are those?" Dana asked.

"Mine."

"Where'd you get'em?" I asked.

"I had 'em."

I had them, was child code for, *don't ask, don't tell*. So we didn't. I didn't voice my relief when Kelly extracted one squashy cigarette after another and Dana didn't mention gratitude for wet matches. We didn't speak of smoking because we didn't know how to smoke. Despite Kelly's best efforts, we wouldn't be learning today.

"Get up, Kel. You look like a caveman tryin to start a fire," I said.

7

"Shut up."

"No. She looks like that gorilla at the Milwaukee zoo. What's his name?"

"Shut up, Dana."

"You shut up. Sampson! You look like that Sampson ape tryin to pull apart burlap."

"Takes one to know one," Kelly snapped.

I intervened before banter came to blows. "Listen. Listen!" Creedence Clearwater blared from the loudspeaker behind us. I sang aloud and held an invisible microphone to Dana's chin. We laughed, jumbled the lyrics together and howled until Kelly abandoned her task to the mud, to join us for the chorus. *"There's a bad moon on the rise!"* We screeched loud, proud, and off key until the dark clouds rolled away from the park. The rain let up. The rides started moving again.

The sun peeked in and out of the clouds as I hopped up and down, giddy with excitement. I was third in line, barefoot in the wet grass, to ride the sleek silver Scrambler. I wanted to be on the outside of the cart where the squishing action took place. My friends scooted across the torn vinyl to take their seats on the spongy wet cushion.

Dana yelped, "Ick! My butt's wet!"

I teased, "Did you pee your pants?"

"Let's crush her," Kelly said.

"With what? Your wet diapers?"

Giggling as I grabbed the metal bar, I heard the deep belly grumble of what I thought was distant thunder. I felt an odd tremor, placed my bare foot on the wet metal step and pop! The carnival, my world went black and silent.

Static crackled. There was leprechaun gibberish. *Ní, teidhir abhaile riú. Ní hea, ní!* Lights flickered. A transistor radio played, "crimson and clover over and over, crimson and clover…"

My eyelids fluttered. I blinked.

The Incontinental Divide

A greasy, green-toothed carney flashed before my eyes. He spoke but I... "Hey kid, can you hear me?" ...could only make out bits and... "Get her off the metal fence!" ...pieces of what he said. I couldn't breathe. I couldn't... "No! Don't touch her! Little girl, are you all right?" ...speak. The taste... "Oh, Christ, she's bleedin'!" ...of cooked hair and copper pennies filled my... "Someone call her parents!" ...mouth. I drooled. My tongue was burnt. The fillings in my teeth... "Call her Dad!" ...felt soft. My heart raced. "She doesn't have a phone." The plastic necklace... "She doesn't have a Dad." ...was melted to my shirt. "Call an ambulance! Hey kid, can you hear me? Should we get a doctor?"

I couldn't feel my hands or feet as every muscle in my body seized and cramped into tight knots. I tried to speak. I choked. The acrid stench of sulphur and rot hung in a cloud of diesel exhaust and burnt sugar ozone. I spit and mumbled. My chest was tight. I wanted to lie down on the cool wet grass, but I was half-seated, leaning against a fence, thrown fifteen feet from the Scrambler.

I didn't know whether the ride was struck by lightning or I was struck by lightning or some electrical short caused by rain on bare metal zapped me. Breathless, blind, deaf, and confused, I could sit there and die from the injuries caused by electrocution or I could have my injuries treated then die by Irish Temper when my mother found out I'd been at the carnival.

I managed to sit up and babble, "no docthors." I'd rather spend the rest of my life traveling with the carnival freak show billed as 'The Bad Girl Welded To The Crowd Control Fence' than have Mom learn of my disobedient, criminal activity. If some Good Samaritan served up my fried head on a platter, lined with yet another doctor bill she couldn't pay, I would be praying for death – swift and clean. Her silent disappointment would take my life too slowly.

"Thake me home," I whispered.

Despite protests from the adults in the crowd, my friends helped me stand, then carried and dragged me out of the park. No more laughter for us. I mumbled and drooled.

My friends chattered:

"What did she say?"

"She said she does too have a dad."

"How can you understand her?"

"She sounds like my dad when he's drunk."

"Yeah, she does, doesn't she? What did she say now?"

"She wants us to call him."

"Call who?"

"Her dad."

"She doesn't have a phone. Do you know where her dad is?"

"No, but she does. Chris can call him. Can't you, Chris?"

I tried to nod. My head flopped up and down.

"See? She said yes. She'll be okay. Let her use the pay phone in Rexall."

On a good day, my friends and I would stop at the Rexall Drugstore soda fountain, slurp down a cherry fizz, giggle into the phone calling boys who said they liked us, read all of the greeting cards to get our daily dose of literature, and then skip home. There would be no cherry fizz or literature today.

Kelly propped me up near the pay phone as I fumbled in my pocket for a dime.

"What's she saying?" Dana asked.

"She needs a dime. Look at her money!"

The coins in my pocket were melted together in a warm ball.

"Cool! Can I have that? I'll buy it from you. That's groovy."

I offered the odd hunk of metal to Dana and mumbled, "Fow a dine."

"What?"

"A dime. She wants a dime."

Dana held the receiver to my ear and I drooled into the mouthpiece. Ill or injured, he'd never paid any attention to me before but, "Paze Dah, cong pih me uh. I doh few guh." persuaded my father to answer my plea. I was surprised a ten-cent conversation was all that was necessary to convince the man that I was sick and needed his help.

Dad agreed to meet me at my house, in a few hours, if my mother wasn't home, unless something came up. He always gave himself an 'out.' Dad often left my siblings and me sitting dressed up and sparkled, staring out the picture window, waiting for him to whisk us away. We waited hours. We waited days. We waited years until sad reality lowered our expectations. By the age of twelve, I expected my father wouldn't show up as planned. When or if he did, I was pleasantly surprised.

Pausing to let me vomit in the neighbors' hedges, my friends pushed, pulled, dragged and carried me the rest of the way home. When I was semi-standing on the front porch they made plans to desert me.

"But, what if her mom's home?"

"The car's gone. She's not home," Kelly said.

Dana panicked. "But what if her dad comes and we're still here? I'm going."

"We can't just leave her on the porch. Chris? Open the door."

"Ith nah lahghd."

"What did she say?"

"It's not locked."

My friends opened the door, offered hasty good-byes and shoved me across the threshold.

"Hetho?" My speech was garbled but my thoughts were clear. "Mah?"

Please don't be home. Please don't be home, please? "Mah?" My mother was at work. *Yes!* Unfortunately, my usual happy dance was not an option.

In a daze, I towel dried my thick hair and peeled off my wet clothes. Even with my circuits fried I had the presence of mind to hide my plastic coated shirt under the garbage in the bin. Leaning against the wall for support, I struggled to dress myself in jeans and a sweatshirt. I pulled wool socks over my cold feet and ice blue hands. Appropriately decked out for skiing in the Arctic on that sticky summer afternoon, I settled on the sofa to wait for my dad. The breeze blowing through the open window chilled me. My heart beat at an odd pace as I wrapped myself in an afghan. I was so weary, so cold. My heavy eyelids fluttered as I passed out on the couch.

⚡

"Hey, Chris, wake up. Chrissy? Wake..." My father stroked and patted the top of my head. As I opened my eyes, I defensively swatted my sock covered hands across the top of my mane. The roots of my hair tingled, too sensitive to touch.

"Ooh, sorry. Sorry. I didn't mean to scare you," he said.

I blinked hard trying to focus. *Man's here - doesn't live here.* Thick glasses magnified his eyes. *Man's too close to my face.* Curly hair made his head appear gigantic. I popped my eyes open to stare blankly at my father. "Hi."

"Wow. Don't feel good, huh? You look awful. Yeah. You look like hell. Let's go."

Going would require movement and speech. I wasn't prepared for either. "I gotha white a node do thell her where Ine ath."

"What did you say? What the hell is wrong with your tongue?"

"I bid id."

He laughed. "Jesus Chrissy, you sound like a retard! Better take them puppets off your hands so you can write your note. Let's go. I'll be in the car."

Yeah, I bit it. Wanna see? I stuck my fat tongue out and watched him go. He was always leaving. *They are not puppets. Okay? They are socks and nice to see you too, Dad.*

Because she knew I seldom saw my father and I prided myself on *not* getting sick, the note I scribbled would never pass muster with my mother. "Got sick at Dana's. Spending the night at Dad's. XXOO Chris."

My father blasted the car horn. Before the carnival, I'd survived every childhood scrape; illness, burn and bike crash with maximum efficiency and minimal scarring. When I *was* sick, I wouldn't acknowledge it. Since my friends were sworn to secrecy, I could pretend the cotton candy deposit I made in the neighbor's bushes never happened, but I couldn't pretend I was fine. I wasn't. My normally impeccable handwriting, now scrawled across the paper would certainly betray me. I was too tired to care. For disobedience and stealing five dollars, if my mother could come up with a worse punishment than being struck by lightning — more power to her. When Dad blew the horn again I left the note on the table and wobbled out the door.

Unlike home, Dad's house had electricity. I could take a hot bath without first going outside to boil water. I could read after dark or watch television. If my pounding headache would end, the whooshing sound in my ears would cease and I could focus my eyes, I could almost enjoy my first sleepover at Dad's bachelor pad.

My father and I were virtual strangers. He didn't know how to take care of a sick kid and we quickly ran out of commonalties to chat about. Forty-five minutes into our visit, when I couldn't enunciate or sit upright, my father went out. He announced he might pick up dinner, 'chicken soup or something' to make me feel better, as the door closed behind him.

Okay, Dad. Nice visiting with you too. I tried to sit quietly and wait for his return, but a wave of nausea propelled me to the bathroom. As I bent over the toilet and my long tresses swept someone else's organic matter on the outside of the bowl, a new kind of nausea rushed me to the sink. This wasn't exactly the giggle-play-Monopoly-eat popcorn-sleep-over I'd fantasized most of my life.

After rinsing the porcelain I rinsed my hair then wandered back to the empty living room. I tried to nap on the sofa, but my rapid heartbeat allowed no rest. Hours later, my father returned with a take-out box of cold chicken and fries. He was disappointed I couldn't eat. I was disappointed I'd disappointed him — again. I was a bright, beautiful, talented, tenacious disappointment, ghostly invisible to my own father. He didn't know me. He didn't see me. There was no other explanation in my twelve-year-old world. Too dehydrated for tears, I must have been a sorry-looking disappointment. My lower lip quivered when he kissed my forehead and left the house again.

I spent the night alone on my father's sofa, wishing I'd stayed home. At home, my mother would be upset enough to kill me but she would pace herself. If she didn't have to work, she would not leave me burned, bruised and alone. Mom would stroke my hair and speak softly to soothe and comfort me. She would hold my body gently to her chest until I fell asleep. My mother would wait until I felt better, and then kill me.

Alone in the dingy apartment, I was too frightened of my own body to relax, too exhausted not to. My heart was a fluttering bird trapped in my aching chest. My teeth hurt. My lips cracked. My skin was tight and dry. My senses all malfunctioned so I tried to shut them down by closing my eyes. I drifted off to sleep, and then fell into a petrifying nightmare. I dreamt or — I died.

Floating on my back under dark water. Can't breathe. Get to the surface. Pounding in my chest. Too dark, too – there's a light up above. Hurry. Can't open my eyes. "No. Ní hea! Don't come home." *Almost there.* "Don't come home girl, no." *Closer. Move to the light, so warm, so bright, the beautiful light. I'll be safe.* "No! Don't come home girl!" *I sink into darkness. Scream into the abyss, in pain and terror. Someone shouts,* "Ní hea, teidhir abhaile riú! Ní, ní hea!"

My eyes popped open.

I didn't blink. I was afraid to close my eyes lest the dark part of the dream return and pull me into the netherworld. The utter blackness horrified me. I opened my eyes wide, hoping to find the warmth and light from the surface of my dream, but the only light in the room was the flickering television screen showing *Brigadoon*.

As Cid Charise and Gene Kelly danced across the hills and heather I listened for the Gaelic voices of my dream. I heard none. I strained to hear the leprechaun whispers but they'd vanished. Onscreen, the people of mythical Brigadoon were already home singing, *"What a day this has been. What a rare mood I'm in."*

I draped one of my father's soiled shirts across my back and shuffled into the kitchen for a drink of water. I downed a full glass then another before putting my face under the faucet to soothe my parched lips and skin. The stabbing pain in my chest was gone. My heartbeat was steady. I sipped a third glass of water, dribbling from the corner of my mouth as I wandered back to the living room. My tongue was still swollen and I ached all over but I felt strangely energized. Any minute my hair might stand on end. *'What a day this has been. What a rare mood I'm in.'*

The Incontinental Divide

⚡

Had I known that rare mood would be the norm for the rest of my life, I might have paid attention. I didn't. Twelve-year-olds have other priorities.

Frightened by the absolute darkness there, I wanted to forget my dream. I didn't know the white light and the warnings of my Irish ancestors were part of a near death experience. I didn't know the leprechaun voices would continue to sound off whether I was asleep or awake. During times of stress or during precognitive dreams, I would hear the Celtic whispers.

I likened my dream to other homecomings where a loving parent met me at the door and urged me back outside to play. I wasn't unwelcome. It just wasn't time to go home.

At twelve, I didn't know a lightning strike was a monumental thing. I couldn't predict the effects of an electrocution on my body or mind. Cancer, mental illness and the addictions I would develop chasing a high I'd never catch, were adult troubles still so far away.

I had no idea my father and I would always be strangers. I didn't know my mother would work our way out of poverty, marry a good man, have more children and give us a comfortable life away from the gnawing hunger that could make a little girl lie and steal for a thrill ride. A day after being struck by lightning, I told my mother I fell and bit my tongue. I got on with the business of being twelve.

Fifteen Minutes

The fact that I have the National Lightning Safety Institute's number on speed dial is merely a precaution. My body's energy system is a little off, that's all. My theory is: the jolt I experienced as a kid altered my physiology enough to make me sensitive to small electrical discharges other people don't feel.

Decades after the first lightning strike, my hair still feels like it might stand on end. Lights short out. Appliances act up. Computers fry. Microwaves fritz, and for decades, I lived in a house that was struck by lightning more than twenty times.

I used to take my relationship with electricity for granted. I knew if there was static in the area, it would find me and say hello, but I didn't know other people considered my everyday encounters with electricity, extraordinary.

When I ventured to a local electronics store in search of computer repairs, I touched the door and received a painful shock. I touched the door again – *Zap!* I grabbed the handle again. *Zap!* Again. *Zap!* I paused to let the static dissipate then opened the door. The baffled men watching from behind the counter greeted me in unison, "Did you get a shock?"

"Yes. I always do."

"Standing on cement?"

"Yes."

"Touching a glass door?"

"Yah. Happens all the time." I stepped up to the counter.

"Oh my God! Did you see that?" One man pointed at the computer on the front desk. The other man glanced between the monitors displayed on the shelves, and me.

"Look at this! Look!" He blinked and pointed — at every flickering, frozen screen in the store.

Oops.

A local paper ran a story about my strange electrical encounters. Newspapers across the Midwest picked it up, and regional television crews came to my home for sound bytes and snippets of my 'Electric Lady' stories. I, naive Princess, was amused.

I was fascinated by the stands and cords and lights and tripods and cables and furniture moving TV crew members shuffling papers, reciting lines, adjusting microphones and...

"Three..." The air was charged with excitement.

"Two..." Cameras rolling, the banter began, "So, tell us about your first electrical..."

I smelled the smoke a split second before the hairs rose on the back of my neck. Pop! Smoke streamed under the Reflectasol. The bright lights flickered. The sound of a cap gun banged as the lights went out.

Maybe no one will notice me – On air, cameras rolling, on TV, in the dark. Oops.

USA Today printed a tiny blurb and I was struck again, not by lightning but by a storm of national publicity. The average little life I thought I had, was really a Marvel Comic.

From New York to Vegas, Pow! Pittsburgh, Chicago, L.A., Bam! Radio stations called for interviews. They played music from the Twilight Zone.

"Have you read, The X-Files?" David Brenner asked, "Are you having a current affair?" Boom!

Letterman wanted something shocking. "A 'Stupid Human' trick, perhaps? Have your people call my people."

The Tonight Show wondered, "Can you control it? Like the new movie, *Powder?* Have your people call my people." Zap! Crack! Buzz!

The clock started ticking on my, "fifteen minutes of fame." I enjoyed the odd perks like when I got pulled over for a burnt out taillight and the cop was amused by the static shock he received when I handed him my license and registration. I was shocked he was amused. I was shocked he recognized me from TV. When he laughed and told me not to worry about the taillight I drove off in the dark. In shock. Okey dokey Smokey!

I accepted the odd pitfalls when people blamed or credited me for every electrical malfunction and battery operated malfeasance in the city. Streetlight burnt out? My fault. I drove under it. Office coffee maker died? I had a cup of coffee that morning. I killed Mr. Coffee. Slow elevator? I must have drained the power out of the building when I pushed the button, because according to some reports, I was an energy-sucking vampire.

The whole country thought I was weird, and I thought the hype was crazy. Fifteen minutes of fame is a long time if you don't have people to call people. If you have a new puppy piddling on the floor while you describe the true meaning of heartburn to some disc jockey a thousand miles away; if you have kids who need to get to school but they missed the bus while you were on the phone and the battery in your car is dead but you can't call for help because you can't get off the phone; if you have a husband who is perpetually ticked off that his phone keeps ringing and you keep answering to thank well-wishers for the support you didn't know you needed and to tell drunks and potheads, "No, I *don't* wanna catch a buzz." Fifteen minutes is a long time.

I fantasized about the joys of sticking a paper clip in a light socket when the crackpot strangers called. Those who wanted to fly me to Pennsylvania so electro-physiologists at some university could study me called first.

The people who wanted me exorcised to protect me from the devil, called *and* wrote.

The Incontinental Divide

Bubbas who wanted me to marry their sons *couldn't* write, "Yur purdy. Ma boys, thays real big an strawng."

Some people called collect.

"*Why* did you accept charges, Ric?"

"How was I supposed to know? I thought it was a relative, one of your uncles or something. You've got a big family, Chris."

"I know I have a big family, but not in prison! I don't have family in prison! Don't accept collect calls! From prisoners! In prison!"

When I stopped accepting calls from inmates and future stalkers, they wrote.

"Dear Christina, I saw your picture, your face on TV. You light up my life." They sent explicit drawings and notes, *"I got your lightning rod right here, baby!"* They sent long rambling essays and poetry laden with sexual innuendo *"...We are soul mates...you are my salvation... I cherish you adore you understand you... Sublime flower of femininity... precious petals spread... wet inner dew... enter your garden... sip your wild flower... penetrate you so, so..."*

So, stop already, wouldja? Stop the clock on my fifteen minutes of fame. The storm of publicity expired and I was grateful. Time passed. Seasons changed. I am grateful for my *normal* life where there are no reporters to remind me I'm a little, off.

Weather Or Not

Wisconsin Winter weather is brutal but it's easy to predict. You don't need a degree from a Highfalutin School of Meteorology to report that it's gray, it's cold and it's snowing. It's winter in Wisconsin. That's all one needs to know.

Oh sure, minor diversion can be found: standing outside a market next to a six foot high snow bank; depressed and ornery because I haven't seen the sun for months; wind chill factor thirty-six degrees below zero; breath crystallizing and dropping to the ground the second it leaves my lungs; snotsicle hanging from my nose; eyes frozen shut, when some cheesehead asks, "So, whadaya thinka ar weather here, eh?"

I punch him in the head, and his ear snaps off. "I think it's cold, it's gray and it's snowing, dumb ass." It's winter in Wisconsin. It's depressing. It's predictable.

If I could hibernate like a bear through winter, I would. I'd begin preparations in autumn, gathering twigs and berries to stash under my bed. I'd buy jumbo bags of chocolate and taffy to 'put away' for Halloween. When I've put away my horde of candy by eating it, I could lumber out of my den to purchase more. November could be devoted to growing hair and longer fingernails. Gorging myself on breads and cakes and cookies over the holidays would give me the sustaining layer of body fat I would need for a long winter sleep. On New Year's Day, I'd stake out my spot on the couch. With one hairy leg thrown over the armrest, the other leg dangling over the sofa's edge, I'd lie on my back and scratch my belly with my long nails. I'd yawn and stretch, waiting for hibernation to commence. I'd sleep for a long...

I'd have to get up to pee.

Middle-aged women have to pee.

A lot.

I'm an MA woman. I can't hibernate like a bear.

Without respite from thunderstorms or mental illness, the short days of winter in Wisconsin are long on tears. I try to fight depression with exercise or meditation. I've even strapped a full spectrum light to my head hoping the UV rays will fortify my bipolar brain. They don't. When freak lightning strikes during February-blizzards knock out the power, I'm left snowed in, lights out, brooding then bobbing around the house, looking like a deranged coal miner. Throughout the long winter I entertain myself, crafting decorations from the twigs and berries I find under my bed.

I scrape pornographic drawings and "S.O.S." in the frost on the windows.

I sleep. I eat. I cry.

I make long lists of clever ways to off myself. I write short lists of the people I hope will discover my body. If I dislike someone enough to write their name on the short list, I wouldn't trust them with my corpse so I can't kill myself. I wait.

I wait for a mood swing.

On manic days, I turn my suicide lists into epic poems or a great American novel. I scrub and Shop-Vac every room in the house. I rearrange the furniture; finish the oil painting I started last Fall, shovel the sidewalk, and then bake four dozen cookies and a turkey in case I'm hungry by afternoon. I build a snow fort, curl my hair, paint my nails, sing and dance, rearrange the rearranged furniture and then — I crash.

I sleep. I eat. I cry.

I wait for a mood swing.

By March, my mind is a punch-drunk boxer, bloodied, reeling and bouncing off the ropes. In my head, the crowd cheers. I duck and weave. In my head, the crowd boos. I stagger and stumble. I try to hold on until the bell rings. To make it to the next round, I have to hold on.

I have to hold on until spring.

Like me, Spring in Wisconsin is also bipolar. Manic-depressive weather for the manic-depressive woman. It takes a few days for the snow and ice to thaw. During those few days, Mother Nature's mood swings a few hundred times.

On the first day of Spring, rain melts snow into gray-cream slush, exposing brown, dead grass and mud. It's brown. It's slushy. It's raining. It's not exactly pleasant.

On the second day of Spring: rain melts slush to black-brown mess, to re-freeze when the temperature drops overnight, to plug up the culverts, to flood my yard with mucky run-off at dawn. It's brown. It's mucky. It's flooded but it's amazing how quickly things change. One minute my neighbor's lawn gnome is floating down the road. The next minute, the rain stops. The sun shines brightly and the whole world turns green. *This* is pleasant.

I pack my miner's helmet away for the season, and then dress for dining out. I chuckle when I drive past the gnome standing on his head in the squishy, green grass. I park blocks from my destination to stroll on a lovely spring evening to my restaurant of choice.

I stop chuckling when I realize I've locked my keys in the car just as Mother Nature's mood swings. A raindrop splats atop my head. Another drop falls and another, until I'm caught in a downpour outside the restaurant. Wearing new suede stilettos, I slosh through a puddle the width of the Mississippi. My dry-clean-only jacket bleeds color through my blouse as my bra cups fill with water, and my breasts float near my chin. Mascara streams. Waterlogged panty hose slide down around my ankles.

My thick hair drips wet and heavy, pulling my head back at such an angle I almost miss seeing the one-eared cheesehead in the Green Bay Packers raincoat, trip in the muddy pot hole and impale himself on his own umbrella. It's funny until he recognizes me from the police lineup in February and screams, "So, whadaya thinka ar weather here, eh?"

I think it's wet and dry. It's frozen and thawed. It's warm and cool and changing. I think it's Spring in Wisconsin, dumb ass. It's bipolar.

Christina Crall-Reed

Off And On

Because my body's electrical system is a little off, summer is the big *on* season for me. I am on guard, on point, on my toes and on the lookout for the next summer storm that might strike me dead.

I don't need the Weather Channel. I forecast the weather myself. They don't need me either but The Playboy Channel or Comedy Central could use my special weather forecasting services because I *feel* the weather. I can sense a thunderstorm brewing hours and miles away. I've learned to gauge the severity of an approaching storm by the muscle contracting, prickly-skin-sensations of my own body. My forecasts are not always accurate as to exact location or duration of a storm but hey, I'm a woman not Doppler radar.

Early in our marriage, I learned to prepare for each approaching storm. Our home was in the middle of a wide-open prairie. Exposed and vulnerable, inclement weather had no choice but to find us. After a decade of practice I knew what to do.

When the first weather rumpus of the summer blew east across Wisconsin, my hands and feet began to tingle. I closed the windows. I lit candles.

Compelled to plug any hole, seal every crack and cover every

The Incontinental Divide

switch plate so sparks didn't shoot out during the impending storm, I rummaged through the junk drawer searching for the plastic outlet plugs gone MIA over the winter. The purpose of the junk drawer was to house perfectly usable stuff that had no apparent purpose: The expired coupons, I tossed. Two colored balls, I left free to roll around the drawer. A broken back scratcher, I used. A half-wrapped cough drop, I ate. But I found no outlet covers. I closed the drawer, and then climbed the stairs to check on my children.

My boys didn't have my pre-storm senses but we shared a wicked sense of humor. During my storm preparation ritual, if they couldn't ignore me without guilt, my sons teased me without mercy.

"Guys, do you have any extra outlet plugs up here?"

Tethered to a video game box, Kelby and Bailey sat at the edge of the bed, grunting at the screen. Eyes fixed on the television, only their hands twitched and jerked as they maneuvered duel joysticks.

"Guys. Outlet plugs, you have any?"

No response. I would or could be many things for my children, but invisible in my own home, was not one of them. I hopped the video wires and plopped between the boys on the edge of the bed. Wedged between them like a fat lady's thong, I forced my sons to give me their undivided attention.

"Hi guys. My name is The Mom. When The Mom speaks the kids are supposed to listen."

"You smell like menthol," Bailey said.

"You smell like rotting tweenagers, wasting away playing Nintendo."

"We are."

"Why don't you go do something productive?" I suggested.

"Like what?"

With a storm brewing, my usual 'go outside to play' response wasn't an option. "I don't know. Go find a cure for cancer or something."

Kelby smirked, "You told us no more experiments."

"I told you no more explosives. Building a bomb with toilet bowl cleaner was clever, not productive."

"You didn't come up here to punish us again, did you?" Kelby asked.

"No. I can't find the outlet plugs."

"Aren't all plugs outlet plugs, Mom? What other kind of plugs are there?"

"Yes. No. Smarty. There are nose plugs, ear plugs... but I need those little plastic covers."

"For your nose?"

"Boy, you're full of it today. I need 'em for the outlets."

"Why, Mom?"

"Yeah. Why, Mom?"

They were baiting me. I bit. "Storm's coming." Two words, thrown out like thick, juicy slabs of meat for my smarmy little cubs to pounce on.

Chuckling, Kelby leaned back on his elbows as Bailey threw himself flat on his back, laughing. They jabbered and giggled together, spouting idle threats of imaginary danger.

"Storm's coming Bailey. We better call the President. Tell him it's raining – somewhere!"

"We should hide in the closet!"

"Auntie Em! Auntie Em!"

"Hey, call the newspaper Kelby! Tell em it's gonna rain - someday."

Too late to consider birth control, I smiled and stood to take my leave. "You guys are nuts. And in about half an hour when the storm hits, you'll be sorry you made fun of me."

Kelby pursed his lips, kiss-kissing the air. "No, we love making fun of our little electric Mommy. Our little Mommy loves us. We tease her, then she makes us lunch."

"Yeah, we're hungry, little Mommy." Bailey feigned an angelic smile. "If you feed us we'll be nice."

"I doubt that. If I feed you, you'll stay to bug me or come back for more, like stray cats."

"You didn't feed us this morning and we're still here."

"Where was I this morning?"

"In the bathroom." Bailey giggled, "We peed outside."

"I told you to stop doing that. It kills the grass."

Kelby deadpanned, "But starvation kills children. You should feed us."

"I fed you last month."

"We came back for more. Meow."

I was halfway down the stairs when my chest muscles tightened and goose bumps rose on my arms. This was not a heart attack related to the stress of raising the tomcats I left meowing and howling upstairs, but an oncoming storm. I felt a subtle change in air pressure as the energy surrounding me swirled and danced. The storm was moving quickly. Over my shoulder, I hollered, "You've got about fifteen minutes before you have to unplug that game!"

"You said half an hour."

"I said Kevin Costner was your real father, but that was wishful thinking too!"

"We're hungry!"

"I know. I know. Lunch, I'm on it."

Lunch was on me. In a rush to slap sandwiches together while checking the nonperishable food and bottled water supply, I smeared mayonnaise on the front of my shirt, spilled half a gallon of milk, and littered the kitchen with potato chips when I popped the bag open.

Cleaning the mess while crawling around on all fours, I took the opportunity to check the 'millionaire' surge protectors on the appliances I couldn't unplug. The expensive surge protectors were supposed to make me rich because they came with a "connected equipment warranty." Ten, twenty, even a hundred thousand dollars in insurance coverage promised that my connected equipment would not be damaged by a power surge! *Ha!* I thought I'd make a fortune.

I didn't make a cent. The damned surge protectors worked exactly as their packaging claimed. I was still poor and my ten-year-old appliances were humming along after numerous lightning strikes. The surge protectors were ready for the upcoming storm. I was not.

I checked the flashlight batteries, helped the dog hide in the

27

bathtub then unplugged the phones and lamps. I put lunch on the table and turned my attention back to the unprotected outlets.

During previous storms I'd experimented with various materials to cover the outlets. Modeling clay was greasy. Play-Doh dried and crumbled into the sockets. Cellophane tape wouldn't stick and duct tape was so sticky it stripped the paint from the wall around the outlet. Whatever melted, broke or blew up wasn't repeated but I needed *something* – soon. My body hair stood at attention. My heartbeat quickened. Two living room outlets were unprotected and I was running out of time.

I yelled upstairs, "Hey, guys, you got any Silly Putty?"

"You said you were making lunch!"

"I am. I did."

"With Silly Putty?"

"No. I..."

"We want real food!"

"Don't get snippy. Lunch is on the table!"

The boys clamored down the stairs, apologizing as they ran.

"Sorry Mom."

"Yeah, sorry. We thought you cut out pictures of food and put 'em on paper plates again."

"Once. I did that one time." I heard the distant rumble of thunder.

The boys giggled nervously. "Hey Mom, a storm might be coming."

"Oh really? I hadn't noticed." Gray clouds rolled past the kitchen windows. The room grew dark. "Silly Putty, do you know where it is?"

"You were the last one to play with it, Mom. Where'd you leave it?" Kelby asked.

I was the last one to play with most of the toys in the house. *Where'd I leave the...* "Junk drawer!"

The colored balls rolling around the junk drawer were two plastic eggs containing Silly Putty. I cracked open the eggs, extracted the putty, ran to the living room and stretched the transferred images from the Sunday comics over the outlet.

Once my storm preparations were complete, I sat.

I waited.

I sat and I waited. Did you know the odds of winning a gabillion dollar lottery equal the odds of being struck by lightning in one's own living room? The sunlight disappeared behind black, rolling clouds. The wind picked up as the temperature dropped. My muscles contracted and my hair stood on end. I sat motionless on the sofa waiting for my Powerball Jackpot.

"Mom, can we eat lunch in there with you?"

"Of course, but you won't be able to watch TV. The power will probably..."

Lightning flashed. The lights flickered and snapped. The room went gray and still until the front door flew open and Ric burst into the room.

"Wow! That was a boomer!" Dripping and breathless, he re-enacted his quarter mile trip down the road from the barn to our house. "It hit right in front of the truck. I ducked on the seat and had to swerve down in the ditch! Holy shit! Almost drove into Mc Nutt's pond. Storm came outta nowhere!"

"Mom knew it was coming." Bailey said.

"Oh, yeah?" Ric peeled off his wet jacket and dropped it on the hearth near the woodstove.

Between mouthfuls Kelby muttered, "She started freakin out about an hour ago."

"I wasn't freakin out."

"But this time she was on time."

"Don't talk with your mouth full." I said.

"It's okay, little Mommy. We'd love you even if you were off." Kelby swallowed.

Ric teased, "She's always been a little off. When I first met her she wasn't this weird, though." He leaned over and kissed my forehead.

I smiled up at him. "And when I met your father he was so shy he wouldn't speak. I kinda miss that guy."

We giggled and munched on sandwiches as we nestled on the couch to wait for the storm to pass. As long as I was with my family and we were safe from the outside world, I was content to be a little weird, a little different, a little — off.

Mere Mortals

Storms are beyond mere mortal control. I'm a mere mortal so, I've slept, unprepared and unaware like a rock in a cave, through storms that rattled the rafters with lightning strikes that blew phones off the walls and melted the splashboard below the kitchen cupboards.

I'm not 'Electric Wonder Woman' but I do respect the super-hero protective instincts I earned at my first electrocution. Usually. I acknowledge the heart racing-body chemistry producing-hair on the back of my neck standing, feelings I experience before a storm by making my preparations. Then I ride the storm out on the couch.

But when I quell my fears and suppress my instincts, there is usually unusual trouble.

The last time there was *trouble*, I felt that storm coming hours before it did. I made my preparations. I sat it out on the couch. The howling wind rattled the windows. Rain pounded the siding and thunder rolled.

I didn't mind sitting motionless for an hour. I didn't care if I never moved again. In the throes of a depression only death or Prozac could fix, I was forty-something, awake and dressed. It was all that I could manage.

Early in the week, my friend Clarie was diagnosed with cancer. Our friend Anne lay in a coma in an L.A. hospital following a devastating car crash. Her injuries were extensive and Clarie's prognosis was bleak. My friends were in big trouble and I was powerless to help them. In case I wasn't sad enough, my husband was drinking, the mortgage on the farm was late, and my teenagers were getting high in their room. I couldn't remember a day without tears.

The constant pain of ceaseless cramps from my never-ending menses made me ill and lethargic. I'd felt weariness in my bones, for days, for weeks, for months, suspecting the cancer that plagued me in my twenties had returned to demonize me again. I didn't have the energy to put cancer back on *my* to-do list, so I streamlined my agenda: Feel better and ride the storm out on the couch.

When the rain stopped, I wandered around the kitchen. I made a cup of tea. I peeked out the window just as the sun peeked out from behind a cloud. *Suh-weet!* Maybe a little fresh air and sunshine could bring me out of my funk. As I turned on the television the weatherman issued an 'all clear' bulletin. My storm sense told me the weatherman was wrong but I ignored my instincts. I hollered upstairs, "Hey, Bailey? Wanna' go fishin?"

Stupid question. *Wanna jump Russell Crowe, Chris? Do ya? Huh? Do ya?*

My son took the steps two at a time, had the poles rigged, bait ready and car engine running before I pulled my boots on. I knew the storm lingered out there. Soon, we'd be out there, too.

You can see for miles across the open prairies where we live. We parked the car by my mother-in-law's house and walked down the muddy lane, a half-mile to the pond. The exercise eased my cramps but did nothing to suppress the skin tingling sensations I always felt before a storm. I scanned the sky and fields for signs of trouble but saw none. The sun was shining on a colorful landscape made deep and rich looking by the recent downpour. *We're going to have fun fishing, damn it!* I banished my thoughts of doom and gloom.

I spent the next hour laughing, joking, and fishing with my son. Bailey caught a blue gill on his first cast while I picked weeds and algae from my hook. He relived his favorite pond story about the day

The Incontinental Divide

the eight-pound bass jumped in his boat. "That was awesome! Do you remember that, Mom?"

"You mean, the day you came peeling in on your bike, screaming and jumping up and down, looking for a net to carry the gigantic fish that just jumped in your boat? That day?"

"Yeah, that was aweso..."

"Sorry, B. I don't remember. Why don't you tell me about it," I teased. We giggled as Bailey turned his attention to another fish on his line.

"Two to zip in favor of the young, handsome guy. Why *dooo* you bother, Mom?"

"I come here for the breathtaking scenery."

The pond was nestled in a little valley near the woods, surrounded by corn and hay fields. Once you'd crossed the fields and walked down hill — there you were. At the pond there was no scenery. There was, The Pond. You had to walk back up the hill for scenery.

"I knew there was a reason. It's obviously not to catch fish." Bailey laughed as I flailed and struggled. I had somehow managed to entangle myself in fishing line and snag my jacket with the hook.

"You know, I married your Dad just for this pond, so I could..." Distracted by the fishing line, I gyrated, trying to grab the hook in the middle of my back. "I come here whenever I..." I paused mid-sentence to rotate in semicircles, flapping and swinging my arms. "I wanted to..."

"Need some help there, Babe Winkelman?"

"No, I'll get it, if I can just..." I slipped my jacket off, dropped it to the ground and stood triumphantly untangled. "Tah-Da!! I do *too* come here to fish."

"To *catch* fish, Mom. The point is to *catch* fish."

Truthfully, most of my fond pond memories involved no fish, but two randy teenagers, music, some sort of mood altering substance, a parked car, and steamy windows. Not exactly the kind of stories I'd share with my child on a Hallmark card afternoon.

I pulled the hook from the fabric and draped my jacket over my shoulders when I felt an all too familiar chill. "You catch em. I'll pretend."

"Works for me." Bailey reeled in a crappie, too small to keep. "Here's *your* fish, Mom."

The sun ducked briefly behind a passing cloud and I knew, instantly, our Hallmark card afternoon was over. "I think we better go, B."

"Okay. Just a few more casts."

"No, Bailey." My body hair began to rise and tingle. "We need to go now."

"Really? Now?"

The same instincts I ignored earlier squeezed my chest, warning me to get my child out of harm's way.

"Yes. Now." Quickly I gathered our gear and turned to walk up the hill. Bailey followed without question. He knew all about my internal storm radar. He knew I *knew*.

I walked as swiftly as I could: ill, overweight, out of shape, wearing mud laden combat boots, carrying two aluminum fishing poles and a five gallon pail, with two dying fish and a pack of cigarettes in it — trying not to panic.

"I think we better run, Bailey." I knew if I could see the storm, even miles away, when I reached the top of the hill, it would be too close for safety. We would be caught out in the open field.

"What? Whadja say, Mom?"

"I said run! Get to the car!"

I crested the hill a few steps ahead of my son. Across the prairie, menacing thunderheads broiled and churned, black and crimson like a furious bruise rolling over the horizon. Too close. Too soon. It headed straight for us.

"Run, Bailey!"

"What?"

"Run! I said RUN!

"Why?" Bailey topped the hill and took off running.

He quickly passed me as I trotted across the muddy furrows. I tried to run but my boots gathered mud and weight with every step. My belly cramped as my lungs tightened. *If I stop...*

Bailey got halfway to the car before he turned back to me, "Come on, Mom! I'll help you!" He ran a few paces in my direction.

His beautiful life passed before my eyes.

With a self-loathing anger for endangering my child, furious strength made me scream, "Don't wait for me! Don't you dare! I – SAID - RUN!"

He hesitated, "Mom?" saw the look on my face, turned and ran.

Cornhusks and chaff swirled across the field in the cool wind. I tried to keep running, keep going. *Don't stop. Bailey's almost there.* My leg muscles clenched as I ran, as I stumbled. *He's fast and strong. He'll make it to the car. He'll make it!* The dark sky growled and boomed as the rain stabbed and smacked my skin. Lightning sliced from the clouds above my in-law's house. *Run! You have to run!* As my stomach muscles seized and cramped, doubling me over in pain, I couldn't run any farther.

In a flash, everything I knew about getting caught out in the open during a thunderstorm came into play. Lay low. Grab your ankles. Stick your butt into the air to give the lightning an escape orifice. I was already bent over in position to grab my ankles — and kiss my own sweet ass good-bye.

Lightning struck the ground, boiling across the uneven surface of the plowed field. I could smell the sulfur and ozone. I absorbed the shock, the tremors, chest tightening, my blood burned.

On fire... ground's burning. I'm cold. I'm... Red car... Don't run me over... I'm here...

The passenger door flew open and Bailey screamed, "Mom! Get up! Get in the car!" He plucked my convulsing body from the muddy earth and sped across the hay field without stopping to close the door.

Bailey dragged me from the car and pushed me through the front door of our home. Breathless, we stumbled into the entryway as the full force of the storm hit our Little House on the Prairie, with an Armageddon of lightning, wind and rain. Tree branches bent and snapped. Windows rattled. Doors slammed. No power. Lightning hit the roof. The antenna exploded. Glass shattered. The house shuddered and moaned.

I lay motionless on the floor. My heart beat the erratic 'after the carnival' rhythm of my youth. Bailey stood above me, dripping rainwater.

"Mom? Can you hear me?"

I opened my eyes but couldn't speak.

"Mom?" My son knelt to gently touch my cheek. "Mom? We made it. We're home."

⚡

Some of us need strong reminders of our own mortality. I was middle aged when I finally got the message – life is finite. Mere mortals can wait for the perfect conditions and the perfect time to be perfectly happy, but I could wait no longer. I had to find a way to weather my own storms. If I threw my head back and opened my mouth to catch raindrops on my tongue, maybe I'd remember the joys of a good downpour. I couldn't hide from every thundercloud. I didn't want to. I wanted to relearn to play in the rain.

Life's A Picnic

With the occasional lightning strike, bug bite, sunshine, laughter, and food poisoning, no doubt about it, life's a picnic. If you want to go to that picnic you've gotta' bring a dish to pass.

An MA woman should learn to make a dump cake or brownies – something simple, because age messes up our personal fruit salad. Leave any dish out in the sun long enough (1957 - this morning) and *something's* going to spoil. Gravity sucks and tugs and pulls and stretches that old family recipe mercilessly, leaving bananas hanging where our melons used to be. Some of us are pear shaped and no longer cherry. Our plump, juicy grapes are now raisins. If our skin looks smooth and creamy, like fruit salad dressing, it could be. Or it could be some car wax compound mistaken for wrinkle remover, because we can't see without wearing the bifocals we can't wear while smearing goop on our faces. Deal with it.

Rather than hide indoors on a beautiful July afternoon and miss the opportunity to watch Aunt Ruthie argue with Uncle Mike about who threw away whose dentures (the ones wrapped in a napkin) next to the plastic dinnerware Aunt Patsy was collecting, to wash for reuse at the next family reunion, I take my messed-up-fruit-salad-MA-self, outdoors.

I won't waste my daylight hours worrying about how big my butt looks in those coral Capri's. It looks huge. I'll forget about the bunion showing through my pretty sandals because pretty shoes gave me the bunion in the first place. I paint my toenails and go barefoot. If you're an MA woman who doesn't like her own body, you should. Someone at the picnic will love your dish to pass, and they're out there waiting to see what you bring to the table. Your fruit salad might be messed up but if you *believe* it's sweet and tasty made with that old family recipe, everyone else at life's picnic will believe it too.

If your bosom, ample or otherwise, has obeyed the law of gravity and moved below the Mason-Dixon line for an extended vacation, take your Southern Belles to visit our friend Vicky.

Any would-be MA Queen should make it a point to discover all of Victoria's Secrets. Vicky's stores are wonderlands full of engineering miracles in every shape, size, texture and color imaginable. There are pads and fillers for the flat of heart. There are bands and stoppers for the full of heart and there are lifts and separators for the faint of heart. They have garments that can hike 'the girls' back up to the neighborhood they grew up in and still be comfortable enough to *wear* outside the kindly lit dressing room.

A V.S. bra could probably help you move to a new house. You could purchase the largest "convertible bra" in store, then fill one cup with your books, cleaning supplies, furniture and family photos. The other cup could hold your valuables: the 'good' china (used once a year) the spices that came with the rack you received as a wedding gift (I've kept mine although I have no idea what dish calls for 'whole' caraway or 'rubbed' anything, because spices cost a gabillion dollars a pound) and the 'good' scissors (razor sharp, honed and polished to a blinding sheen - kept locked in the safe so spouse doesn't cut pizza with them like he did with the last pair of good scissors) Before your cups runneth over, you can hook up the convertible bra, adjust the straps, then relax while Vicky moves you to that new, three bedroom brick ranch up the block.

Even if you don't feel like moving you can treat yourself to at least one well fit pair of black lace panties that won't run up your backside causing that uncomfortable, loosen-your-wedgie-one-legged-side-step, every few paces. Wearing something lovely, close to your skin feels good at any age. The neighbors may wonder, "Why's *she* so happy with that Peter Frampton, *Do you, you, feel like we do?* music blaring and crackling from the reel to reel, glass of Boone's Farm Strawberry Hill (yes, they still sell it) in one hand and a weed whacker in the other?" We may be MA but the whole world doesn't have to know we're wearing our silkies under our sweat pants while edging the lawn. Vicky will keep our secret.

Be cautious climbing the afore mentioned Strawberry Hill after forty because gravity can get you at any age. At twenty-five, gravity (and tequila and six double screwdrivers) could take hold during a wedding reception, and suck me right down to the floor. Waving and crawling leeward on all fours I'd yell, "Hola Padre!" as I spotted the parish priest. I'd giggle as I crawled past the happy couple, "Hey the bride's not wearing any underwear!" I'd pause briefly under the trees, but wake the next morning, in someone else's bathroom, wearing only my shredded pantyhose.

Obey the laws of gravity and kill enough brain cells in your twenties and the only gray matter remaining to dedicate to social drinking will be a dozen sensible cells chiming, "You're getting sleeeepy." A thirteenth cell, (a wicked little rebel whose mantra is a lie) will taunt the MA woman. *Keep drinking. You're having F-U-N. You're having F-U-N. You're having F-U...* You're having a prep session to knee walk out of church tomorrow. Gravity sucks.

At the Front, I could wake up hung over (or not) - pee, take a quick shower, brush my teeth, throw on some clothes and I was good to go. My picnic basket was packed and ready.

Waking up MA, morning rituals are a bit more complicated. Following that old family recipe is not an exact science, but there is method to the MA madness.

Deja Vu

Each morning, I spend at least ten minutes thanking God I'm awake. The sun came up, no stray voltage found its way into my dreams, and I'm breathing. Thank God. Any day I wake up and draw breath, not electrocuted, is a good day. I scramble to the bathroom and the door isn't locked - Thank you, God! Empty the bladder. Go to the sink to wash my hands and take that first peek at my MA self in the mirror — Oh Gawd!

My mother stares back at me.

I think, *God, help me. Okay. Calm down. Thank God for genetics. Mom's a good-looking woman. Always has been. I can do this. But how did* She *get here?*

She started showing up at the Front when I was raising my children. My mother's face and mannerisms and quirks and habits were sneaking into my house while I slept. Long before I had any children I promised myself I'd be a faster, younger, stronger, smarter, *different* kind of parent. But I wasn't. I was her.

Like Her, when I was angry, I couldn't eat my young. It wasn't civilized. I couldn't kill them. It wasn't legal. I didn't *really* want them dead. I loved them. They were my children, flesh and blood. So I sold mine to the circus, knowing full well they'd be returned to me when the ringmaster discovered they'd eaten all of the cotton candy, shaved the bearded lady and wouldn't behave in the little clown car. I *wanted* to be a different kind of parent, but I was Her.

Okay, my mother never sold me to a circus or rented me out for cheap labor, although the thought must have crossed her mind. Often.

No property exchanges took place, but I could tell that Mom was over the top, mad, crazy, angry whenever she addressed me by my full name. While misbehaving, if I failed to respond to the list of names she called out trying to get my attention; Vickie! (my sister), Steve! (my brother), Patsy!, Ruth!, Cathy!, Mary!, Barb! (Mom's younger sisters), or if she was really pissed, Calvin! (my biological father), my mother would use the name on my birth certificate in a threatening manner.

"VickieCathyMarySteveRuthPatsyBarbCalvin! Christina! Marie! Do. You. Want. A. Spanking?"

"Do I *want* a spanking? No. No, thank you."

"I'll spank you!"

"No you won't. If you were going to hit me you would have already done it."

"Oh."

All mothers are mentally exhausted after reciting their list of names, because they ask dumb questions after. The, list of names-dumb question-parenting technique, is a natural phenomenon created by the Almighty to protect children caught in potentially dangerous situations.

Violence must be swift, hard, unexpected and — violent. The mere threat of violence is not effective. A violent mother does not ask directions from, nor seek permission to, cause bodily harm to a gifted child. The little buggers will deny your request every time. Mine did.

God knew I was angry when my children, flesh and blood, returned from the circus, took the wiring from my stereo, the big square battery from my emergency spotlight, two desk lamps and a new box of steel wool pads to their tree fort to make their own electricity like Bill Nye The Science Guy. God knew I was angry so HE started my list for me as Her words popped out of my mouth.

"God!RicVickieSteve Bailey! And! Kelby! Reed! Do. You. Want. A. Spanking?"

"No. No, thank you." Deja Vu. I should have sold them to the gypsies.

Of course, fathers have their own version of the, List of Names / Dumb Question, parenting technique. My father had a Take Action-Stupid Statement procedure.

When I was a six-year-old angel, I always washed my hands before dinner. One night, I left the plug in the sink and the water running, knowing full well that, after the evening meal, my father would bring the evening paper to the bathroom for a little R&R. It seemed like a grand idea. *Won't it be funny? tee-hee.*

Wasn't it funny, tee-hee, when he started a list, like my mother's list, only with cuss words instead of names? "Goddamn! What the hell? Little sons-o-bitches! Where is she that goddamn little — Christina! Marie!"

Wasn't it funny, tee-hee, when he sloshed from the flooded bathroom, grabbed me by the arm, swung me around and smacked me so hard on the backside that my fillings rattled? I stood there sobbing, thinking, *that wasn't what I had in mind.* I knew what was coming.

"Stop crying or I'll give you something to cry about!"

Take Action-Stupid Statement. Parents are funny. Tee-Fricken-Hee.

It's crowded in my bathroom in the morning. She's there in <u>my</u> mirror, with her organized lists and questions and Kleenex in her pocket. I haven't seen my biological father in years but he's there too. My kids are there as young boys splashing water, as nearly grown men leaving whiskers in the sink. My dog's there, drinking Vanish from the toilet. I'm there in my husband's pajama top, with Kleenex tucked in my sleeve, in case my grown children stop by for a spit polish like in times past.

"Kelby! Reed! I told you not to get dirty."

"I didn't get dirty. It got me."

I licked my thumb and rubbed it across a streak of dirt on my child's face.

"Stop that."

"What? Hold still."

"Stop. If I spit on you, you'd spank me."

"Uh, yes I would, but you're dirty."

"Spit isn't clean."

"Oh." I pulled a tissue from my purse and let my son wet it, to wipe his own face. His own saliva was acceptable, just as mine was, years ago. Deja Vu.

I spend the next ten minutes bringing my old self back to life. Start the coffee. Let the dog out. Turn on the hot water. Get 'The Others' out of the bathroom. For the next half hour I quietly thank my mother for teaching me skills traditionally reserved for the men of her generation, like plumbing, engineering, mechanics and how to spackle dry wall. I thank my mother for not coddling me, for making me tough and smart and courageous and resilient because I'll need to draw upon all of these strengths to get naked in front of a full-length mirror.

Old Family Recipe

The pipes make a clunk, clunk racket as the tepid water barely trickles from the shower head. I bang on the spigot with a bottle of shampoo until a blast of water sprays my face. (Plumbing.) Fixed it.

The water doesn't drain from the tub. Close the drain. Open the drain - nothing. No action. Close the drain. Open the drain - nothing. As I walk to the front hall closet to fetch a wire coat hanger I pull the tissue from my sleeve to wipe my face. Back in the bathroom where the water rises in the tub because I forgot to turn off the shower, I extract a soapy, slimy, small mammal-like, hairball from the drain with the bent hanger. *Yuck!* I thank my mother for not coddling me - for making me tough. (Plumbing. Engineering, and Mechanics) Fixed.

I unfasten the lone button to let the oversized men's shirt I'm wearing drop to the floor. I have to look. I can't help it. I smell the milk when I already know it's sour. I can't help it.

"Hi Mom."

Okay, it's not my mom, but my variation of that old family recipe. I have to look. From bottom to top and head to toe I have to check it all out. Maybe my body changed while I slept. It could happen. Happens all the time in America. Well, once... It happened once.

The Incontinental Divide

I went to bed five foot two, forty pounds overweight, thinking, *I need to do something about this fat and this, and oh, that doesn't look good either, maybe Jenny Craig or Sugar Busters or something like the, "All Broccoli / All Day / Fart and Burp the Fat Away" diet. Or exercise, I could start jogging but then my butt would bounce up and hit me in the back and I'd get frightened that I was being assaulted on the road by myself so I'd have to run home and find some comfort food and nah, just go to bed. Things will be better in the morning.*

Invasion of the Body Snatchers.

Things weren't better. Things were worse. Things were catastrophically, undeniably, horrifyingly worse. I went to bed, chubby. I woke up and heard on the morning news that the surgeon general had revised the standard recommended weight and height guidelines for all Americans. *They can't do that! This is America for God sake! Can they do that?*

Apparently, they can.

According to the Surgeon General, I woke up, five foot two, 'knock down a wall 'cause I won't fit through the doorway, then use a crane to load my behemoth bulk onto a flat bed and haul my gigantic body off to the morgue,' obese! The news was devastating. I could barely choke down that last Krispy Kreme. It was even more difficult to pick the little flecks of frosting out of the box and lick my fingers, my hands were shaking so.

Four years later and forty pounds lighter, for the most part, I like what I see in the mirror: My feet are cute. Even after bunion surgery, still cute. My toes are like little round candies with nails painted happy pink. You could pop 'em in your mouth and eat 'em up.

My legs are still lovely. No, my legs are gorgeous. Shapely and well proportioned. My goodness! Nice gams!

I turn so I can see some of my backside. There's my ass and my other ass, that kicking donkey I had tattooed to the outside back of my upper thigh. My biological ass was drooping to my thighs so I created a rendezvous spot. I thought it would be a hoot to ask people if they wanted to see my ass and then show them a cute, little, colorful ass, near My ass. I slap my hands over my butt cheeks and lift. Release. They fall. Lift. Release. They fall. The definition of insanity is doing the same thing over and over again, expecting different results. Lift. Release. They fall. Lift. Release. My donkey is still kicking. I'll have to work on that.

Around front, the shortncurlies are all trimmed and coifed. Bikini wax? Yes, I actually pay someone to rip the hair from my Bermuda Triangle. It's not exactly a do-it-yourself project. Not that I'll ever wear a bikini again, but I won't have planes and ships getting lost in the underbrush either.

Inside, the baby's things are gone but the playpen is still there so I don't mind the hip to hip hysterectomy, bladder surgery scar on the outside. That's my, 'save my life scar.' That's the get rid of the cancer and the tumors, put my bladder (which was pushed around *by* the tumors) back into place, scar. That's my, 'no more periods, no more PMS, no more crazy hormonal mood swings, no more obsessive compulsive organizing all the irons (clothes iron, curling irons, waffle iron, cast iron pans) in the house when I have PMS', scar.

No more head spinning 360 degrees, *'I love you honey... What do you mean you used the cast iron pan to cook dinner in? My cast iron pan? The one I just washed!? The cast iron pan from the box labeled, "IRONS"? I don't care that you made dinner! So, you fed our kids, la dee freakin' dah. It belongs with the other irons! I! Had! Them! Organized! Linda Blair, spitting pea soup, oh, you washed it? You put it back in the "IRONS" box? I love you, honey. Did you get enough to eat, boys?'*

No more periods that last for weeks. No more eating a nearly raw pot roast by myself while making throaty, animal growling, protect-my-food-because-I-need-the-iron-in-this-red-meat-to-survive-because-I'm-bleeding-to-death noises, then poking my fork in his direction when my child asks, "Can I have a bite?"

No more crying at the dentist when the hygienist says my son has nice teeth. No more crying during Mountain Dew commercials. No more crying because I'm crying and I can't stop crying so I cry.

No more.

My, 'hysterectomy-save my life scar' is also my, 'sex doesn't hurt and I don't have to worry about birth control' scar. It's my *'I feel so good I can think about sex'* scar.

I feel so good I can think about *having* sex. I feel so good I can have sex. Sex feels so good that I feel so good I could have sex again. Not solo this time. I have a husband and he likes sex. Sex is good. I feel so good. He feels so good. I feel so good that we feel so good about sex that feels so good that we have sex again. We feel so good about feeling so good about good sex that I don't even mind when he asks me if I'm high. He says he can't keep up. He says, "Are you on something?" I feel so good I could be on something. I could be on top and it will feel good.

I felt bad when my forty six year old husband had a heart attack, but now he feels better and I feel good.

Maybe a cold shower this morning...or sex...or...nah. I check out the bat wing action on the underside of my upper arms. I flex my biceps and turn only my torso Mr. Universe style. I hold my breath until - phew! My stomach looks pretty good today. Not quite flat. Not quite bloated. When I flex my biceps, my breasts move back up to the starting gate.

My breasts: big, beautiful, round, firm breasts. When they were young I didn't know what to do with them. By the time I knew what to do, I was busy doing something else. Now, I've got the time and the knowledge, but the breasts are gone. 'The girls' got tired of waiting around for me to get ready so they moved down south. Now, they're waiting for me to run out of hot water. I hope they'll still be in the neighborhood when I get out of the shower.

The Girls

Sure enough! There they are: Big Boob and Little Boob; The Boss and the Apprentice; My Knockers; Rack; Headlights; Jugs – whatever. My Girls are my D-cups-before-Cancer-a-cup-and-a-half-after Breasts.

The girls are looking good today. *Not too bad. Not too...* Okay, they'll never be firm and high like mountains in the sky, but I'm getting used to that.

When I found a lump in my breast one February, I called my doctor. He couldn't see me until June, so I made the appointment. MA women are patient. I was patient only because I had a mammogram scheduled for the next week. Before I hung up I told them I had a lump in my breast. They suggested I schedule a mammogram. *Thank you. Why didn't I think of that?*

I'd been having mammograms for years. The girls were problematic even when I was a teen. They required close supervision lest they sneak out at night, after the bra went in the hamper, to meet up with those trouble-making cysts down the street.

I knew the mammogram drill. I prepared by closing the refrigerator door on my naked breast. I squeezed the vacuum seal until I counted to ten or passed out. I don't remember which came first.

The Incontinental Divide

Hold your breath.

Until March. "March Madness" meant basketball for spouse, mammogram for me. Life's fair. Almost. Okay, no it isn't.

He got to sit around in his shorts, eating pizza, remote in one hand, cold beverage in the other, shouting, cheering, cussing at strangers who couldn't hear him and wouldn't respond if they could because they were 'working' at playing a game, so he could watch March Madness, then NBA Action, on the big screen TV.

I got to stand around topless, breast on a cold slab of plastic, hand wrapped in a death grip around a bar on a big screen torture device, cussing at a stranger who'd seen more tits than a Wisconsin dairy farmer, so her expression didn't change when she flattened my breast like a pancake. "Hold your breath."

How the hell can I NOT hold my breath? My boob's in a vise!

"Now the other side."

I made a mental note to buy maple syrup on the way home.

I waited for the results. I checked my breast. I checked the mail for the familiar, 'Good Time! - Your Boobs Are Fine - Wishin' You Were Here!' post card.

I was used to waiting but the lump was growing so I checked the mailbox again. I checked my breast again. I checked the mail. Checked my breast, mail, breast, mail, breast, day after day, I checked the mail. I checked my breast, picked up the phone and called the clinic.

After telling my life story to the switchboard operator, she said, "I'll connect you. Hold please."

'On Hold' is a universe parallel to our own with infomercials one can't avoid and music we can't bear to listen to.

"Thank you for holding. How can I help you?"

When I'd told my life story to the doctor's receptionist, she said, "Your date of birth, please?" I knew what was coming. "I'll look up your record. Hold please."

I caught the tail end of the 'Healthy Heart Month' activities calendar as the <u>Evita</u> soundtrack began. "Don't cryfor me Ar gen tina. The truthis I ne ver…"

49

"Ms. Reed? Thank you for holding. I'll connect you to Dr. Martin's nurse."

"But."

"Hold please."

"Don't cryfor me Ar gen tina. The truthis..." What did that comedian say? What better time to force you to listen to an infomercial about the benefits of colorectal screening than when you're sitting around with your thumb up your ass waiting for a human to come back on the line?

"Hello, Ms. Reed. This is Dr. Martin's nurse. I understand you have some questions regarding your mammogram results?"

"Yes. Hello. I um, ah, I..." When I'd told my life story to my doctor's nurse, she said...

I started swearing. In Spanish. And singing in Span-Glish. "Come mierde. Tu madre con. Hell-eewwe. Hello Jell-O! Me llamo Cristina. Hola? Anyone out there? Don't cryfor me Ar gen tina. The truthis I ne ver, liked you. No may goose tow oo stead. Key arrow oo stead dead. You are a poopy head. I bet you wet your..."

"Hello?"

"Hello. Hi. I was singing. Sorry."

"Yes. Well. Christina, normally, results of any health screenings contra-indicating areas of concern are mailed directly to our patients. It is my understanding you did not receive such notification. Correct?"

"Yes. Correct."

"And the lump is still there? Which breast is it?"

"Yes and right. The lump is much bigger than it was."

"I see. Well. Doctor would like to discuss the results of your mammogram with you. No cause for alarm. But, Doctor would like to see you as soon as you can schedule it."

"When?"

"Today? Or—no cause for alarm—Tomorrow, or as soon as your schedule allows."

I felt the smoke entering the orifice my thumb just vacated. She may as well have started singing to me. *We'll cryfor you soon Chris ti na.*

The Incontinental Divide

The truth is we lost your re cords. We did not contact you. Your next of kin will sue.

So, they messed up my mammogram. So? So, they made me wait three months to talk to my doctor about the dime-sized lump in my breast. So? So, the lump grew to the radius of a golf ball. So? So, I was already wearing the "Been There, Done That, Cancer Sucks" T-shirt I got years before. So? So, I planned to Be There, Do That, because Recurrent Cancer Really Sucks. So I took them up on their offer to take the girls to the doctor in the morning. So we didn't die.

Christina Crall-Reed

This is a Test - This is Only a Test

⚡

Everyone who was too busy to see me was busier than ever, holding my hand and kissing my backside to cover their own. In the morning I had a needle biopsy. *Aspiration* sounds like a word for something wonderful. It isn't.

Aspiration is a big needle stuck in your breast to draw out fluid. Aspiration sucks. Been there, done that, couldn't wear the T-shirt as I lay there topless. The girls knew the drill:

Long needle in your breast lump, aspiration, fluid = cyst/harmless.

Or:

Long needle in your breast lump, aspiration, no fluid = tumor/trouble.

I lay there breathless, staring at the ceiling. Doctor Martin inserted a long needle into the lump in my breast; *aspiration* – no fluid. From a different angle he tried again; *aspiration* – no fluid. I lay there breathless, staring at the wall. He pushed the needle in a third time; *aspiration* – no fluid. *Aspiration* – no fluid. I lay there breathless, staring at my doctor. He stood there breathless staring at the empty vial. The girls were in trouble. *Aspiration* sucked.

By mid morning I had an ultrasound. The ultrasound was a pleasant diversion in the middle of my nervous breakdown. Under dim lights, there was lubricant and massage while I watched NASA videos on a little TV by my head. I had a million questions for the technician.

"That's the inside of my breast?"

"Uh huh."

"Looks like moon rocks. Like the surface of the moon."

"Uh huh."

"You're bouncing sound waves off the moon rocks?" I looked at the ceiling, then back at the screen. "So you're mapping it out? Drawing a map of my breast? On the chart?"

"Uh huh."

"So, this massage wand is like a mouse for a computer? It moves the cursor on the screen then you click on a spot to highlight it?"

"Uh huh."

I looked at the ceiling then back at the screen. "Is it bad? How's it look?"

"All finished."

Nice chatting with you.

By lunch time, the already thick Patient: **REED, CHRISTINA M.** file was as fat as a New York phone book. I was tired, and I passed hungry in the hall about an hour before. Next on the agenda was lab work: height; weight; take my blood pressure; check my temperature — "Do you have any allergies?" *Yes.* Scribble, scribble; draw blood and urine. I knew the drill.

With my plastic cup they handed me a packaged towelette and gave me detailed instructions as to how I should go about using it. *Duh, thankya' ma'am. I ain't never seed one ah these here fancy warshcloths before.* If I got into trouble I could always modify the hand washing instructions posted on the walls. Climbing up on that sink could prove challenging, but I figured out 'Bidet in a Bag' all by myself, like a big girl.

When I broke the seal on my "toxic biohazard" sticker sealed specimen jar I imagined a swat team in HAZ MAT radiation suits would run in, red lights flashing, sirens blaring, OOOEEHN! OOOEEHN! Security Breach!

I positioned myself on the toilet. I couldn't merely sit and pee. There was protocol and planning involved. I had work to do and I took my job seriously. So seriously that I couldn't pee.

I sat. I reminisced. Fond memories of childhood illness flooded my mind.

If I was contagious, (mumps, chicken pox, measles,) the doctor came to me. Way back at the Front, doctors made house calls. Check-ups were different. If I required medical attention unrelated to a childhood plague of the day, I went to the doctor's office, bearing gifts. My mom kept a stash of empty jars and bottles with tight lids so I could take a urine specimen to the doctor with me. I was lucky if she had a small bottle in her collection, mortified when she handed me a Hellman's Mayonnaise jar.

"Can't we just say I'm contagious?"

"No. Pee." She gave me an, 'I-mean-it' look and shoved the jar at me.

"But."

"Pee!"

I couldn't. I checked out the posters and the little cupboard door on the wall. It reminded me of Senor Wences' box from the Ed Sullivan show. I opened it. "Sawright? Sawright." I closed it. The cupboard door resembled a door in a confessional. Why not? I opened the door.

"Forgive me, Father, for I have sinned. It's been twenty years since my last, first and only confession, being a Protestant and all, with an ectopic pregnancy that had to be terminated because it was growing outside my womb and it was never going to live and I was going to die so you called the bishop to make sure it was okay with him that I abort a pregnancy that was killing me and he said it was okay by him and blessed the baby that never got to be a baby and blessed my husband the good Catholic who took me, a heathen, to the church in the first place and blessed me so I didn't die. I said four Hail Marys without conviction and, from that moment on, I talked to the Big Guy myself and skipped the middle man. Sawright? Sawright."

I was thirsty. I turned on the faucet for inspiration. Cupping my free hand under the spray to give myself a drink, I managed only to

The Incontinental Divide

wet my lips, dribble water down my arm, on my shirt and on the floor. What I really needed was a group of beer drinking buddies.

Two buddies, two Bud Lights and a funny story, that's all I would need. The first beer, I'd drink. Ha-Ha share the fun. Open the second Bud, bring the bottle to my lips and think, *maybe I have to pee.* Another swallow, laugh, and I would definitely have to pee. I'd be drinking beer and I'd have to pee, but I wouldn't want to because once I peed if I was drinking beer – that was It. That's All She Wrote. That's all I'd get to do for the rest of the night – pee.

"Did you hear the one about the old guy and the parrot?"

"Hold that, I have to pee." I'd go to the bathroom and pee forever. I'd tuck things back in, pull myself back together, wash my hands and check my make-up before returning to our table.

"...and the old guy says, I thought you were my son!" Everyone but me would crack up. I'd probably laugh too if I'd heard any of the story. I'd probably laugh if I didn't already have to pee again.

Houston, we have lift off!

I screwed the lid on my toxic biohazard specimen jar and placed it in the cupboard. As I turned to wash my hands before pulling up my pants, the cupboard door opened from the other side. A guy in a radiation suit was staring through the wall at my naked butt.

Embarrassed beyond reason, my imagination took over: *"Security Breach! Subject failed to close the door!"* OOOEEHN! Red lights flashing, sirens blaring OOOEEHN! OOOEEHN! *"Put your hands above your head and back away from the confessional!"*

"But."

"Subject's uncooperative! Back away from the confessional!"

"But I have to pull my pants up!"

"Subject's moving!" In my imagination, I got hit in the neck with a tranquilizer dart. Red lights flashing, sirens blaring OOOEEHN! OOOEEHN! Just before I passed out, I wet myself from fright. Figures. *"Subject's down! We have urine!"*

In case I wasn't already so tired, hungry, dehydrated and exhausted that I could drop, they needed to draw a few gallons of my blood. No mere pin prick in the finger would suffice. They needed blood. Lots of it. Somewhere in the hospital, they were filling a pond with all of my bodily fluids.

I took a seat in a chair with a pull down tray. I fastened my seat belt. I prepared for take-off, wondering what the in-flight film would be. A phlebotomy student speaking broken English attempted to introduce herself as she wrapped a rubber strap so tightly around my upper arm, it made my forehead bulge.

"Too tight?"

"Yes. It's too tight." The soundtrack of the movie didn't match the action. I saw her lips moving but heard only poorly dubbed dialogue.

"Sorry."

It was going to be a bumpy flight. She tapped the crook of my arm in search of a suitable vein. She shook her head, grabbed my other wrist, examined the crook of that arm and nodded.

"Do over here."

I had a pounding headache. I was grumpy and impatient. My stomach rumbled in protest, but I didn't say a word as the young, movie extra moved the rubber strap to my other arm.

"Better."

Not better for me, as she jammed the needle into my arm and missed the target completely.

"Ouch!"

"Poke."

"No. That's a stab. That hurt."

"Sorry. Do over."

I nodded in agreement. Sure. Do over. Every phlebotomy student has to learn somewhere. Tiny beads of sweat formed on my upper lip and forehead.

"Poke." The second time she hit her mark but drew no blood. She wiggled the needle around in my arm, which began to swell and bruise. "Sorry."

I felt cold and clammy but offered no protest. Every phlebotomy student whose nametag also bears the name of the technical college she is attending has to practice on someone. I needed food and water. I was lightheaded.

"Do over." She pointed at my right arm.

I wiped the sweat from my brow before bending my bruised, swollen, bleeding arm to squeeze a gauze bandage in place.

"Arm up."

I was queasy and seeing auras. The student tightened the rubber strap around my right arm as I raised it above my head, and then she growled at me for doing it wrong. "No right arm! Left arm up!"

I was confused, but I knew every phlebotomy student whose nametag bore the name of the technical college she was attending and indicated she was a second year student at that college had to practice on someone. I hoped it was a two-year program — as I fainted.

I opened my eyes when she handed me two Fig Newtons and a tiny cup of juice. "Break-fast important meal."

The nametag of the *new* nurse who examined the back of my right hand indicated she was a woman of substance; credentialed, student supervisor, head Dracula of all the blood sucking nurses. *All right! The boss is going to draw my blood!* She swiftly tied the rubber hose around my arm and poked the tender skin on the back of my hand with the needle. No blood.

"Ouch."

From a different angle she poked the tender skin on the back of my hand with the needle.

"Ouch."

The student stepped forward. "You see. I told you no good."

The Boss looked like my mother.

When I was a child, acting up in public, my mother could silence and fold me into a fetal position with just one look. THE Look. The, *Oh my God-sorry-I'm sorry Mom-don't-look-at-me*-Look.

The Boss *looked* like my mother — at the student.

As my blood began to flow, the soon-to-be-unemployed-before-being-hired phlebotomy student rolled herself into a tight ball in a dark corner of the lab mumbling, "Sorry. Am sorry."

It was a good thing I downed that apple juice shooter and filled up on Fig Newtons because Boss filled three vials before withdrawing the needle.

"Done?"

"Just about."

"More blood?!"

"No. Bandage." Rip, zip and leave a tip! Boss patched me up with speed and efficiency. "Elevate, please."

"Which one?"

"Both."

I put both arms into the air. Happy to be done, I waited. *Please return tray tables to their locked and upright position.* Glad my brother Steve wasn't there to tickle me, I waited.

With my arms in the air, all bruised and beat up, I was defenseless. Steve would have a riot torturing and tickling me when I was defenseless. If I sat around much longer, Steve would have the opportunity to clear his work schedule, hop on a plane from Raleigh, fly to Chicago, rent a car, drive to Wisconsin, check into a hotel, have the concierge locate me, drive to the hospital, take the elevator to the third floor, walk into the lab, tickle me and laugh because his tough, big sister who spent countless childhood hours tickling and torturing him, was defenseless. I waited. *Please remain seated until the aircraft comes to a complete stop and the Captain has turned off the fasten seat belt sign.* I waited until Boss Nurse gave me permission to put my arms down.

It was late afternoon when Dr. Martin's nurse popped her head around the corner to remind me of the surgical consultation I would be having the next day. She handed me a card imprinted with a name I couldn't pronounce.

"He's an excellent surgeon — one of our best — so he's very busy, but he'll see you right away. Dr. Martin made arrangements. I've written the appointment on the card."

"Thanks." I turned the card over and attempted to read the name.

"Dr. A. SscanIbuyavowelPatSajak?? MD.
Surgery - Oncology."

Bold, black letters spelled out a name I couldn't pronounce and an agenda I couldn't avoid. Today was a test. *This was only a test. If this had been an actual emergency, I would have been instructed where to tune in my area for news and local information. Right?* I left the hospital with the Emergency Broadcast System alert, beep-beep-beeping in my head.

Five In Five

⚡

I drove from the hospital to our farm in search of my husband and a hug. When Ric walked around the corner of the shed, covered with silage and sweat, and told me he was too busy to talk, I wasn't surprised. The last time my emotions were this raw, I turned to my husband for comfort but found none.

⚡

Back at the Front, after cervical cancer destroyed my chances of having more children, I lost my way. My purpose in life was uncertain as I stumbled into addiction.

Using cocaine, amphetamines, diet pills, whatever substance might get me close to that first buzz I felt after lightning struck me as a child, I set out on a new quest.

I would hurry up. If I moved quickly enough through my day, I could get on with my *real* life. The life where I would be happy was a handful of pills and a few hands-on chores ahead. Some people knew I was chasing a high I would never catch, but I wasn't one of those people. *I* knew I was a barren, bipolar wife and mom, nothing

The Incontinental Divide

special or noteworthy – yet. Convinced I was preparing myself for a life of significance, I tried to be fast and first. Certain the future would be better than the present my *preparations* lasted until the age of thirty-two.

With four hours of sleep in seventy-two hours; forty-eight hits of speed in my one-hundred-nine-pound body and a sincere desire to keep taking more until all of my chores were complete, the numbers added up to overdose.

My heart threatened to explode in my chest. I worried my tongue in tight circles around the roof of my mouth. Ric and I didn't speak. Jaw clenched, my lips were stretched too tightly for conversation. He drove me to the hospital then abandoned me to the care of strangers. When the double doors to the emergency room closed, I surrendered my identity. I was no longer a wife or mother. I wasn't an artist or friend or neighbor. I was no one's daughter or sister or even a woman in trouble. I was an overdose. And if I died on that gurney, people wouldn't remember how I lived, but they would talk about how I died.

In the ER, I prayed I'd give them nothing to talk about. The room buzzed with noise and activity I didn't fully comprehend. Terms like tachycardia and arrhythmia were bandied about, but I didn't pay attention until they wheeled a crash cart next to my gurney. I recognized the defibrillator paddles from television doctor shows and I panicked. No one was going to electrocute me again! I quickly shifted focus to deep breathing. If I could slow my heartbeat, the doctors wouldn't have to work to keep my heart beating.

"What did you take?"

"Ephedrine. No, White Cross. Both."

"How much?"

"I don't know. A lot."

"When was the last time?"

"A few hours ago."

"How many did you take a few hours ago?"

"Five. Seven. I'm not sure."

"Before that?"

"Twenty or thirty."

"Are you having pain? Chest pain? Arm? Jaw?"

"No. Just tight. My heartbeat's too fast."

"Yeah. We're going to start an EKG. See what's going on."

"Where's Ric? My husband."

"We need to talk to you right now. Is it common for you to use twenty or thirty hits at a time?"

"Yes. No. Not all at once. Over days, two or three days. Can Ric come in here?"

"You'll see him in a bit. I have to ask if you were trying to kill yourself."

"No. No! I was going to paint the bathroom after I did the laundry. I was trying... I was..."

I was an overdose.

After hours of prodding and testing and waiting, I was an addict taking her first steps toward recovery. I peeled away remnants of the goo used to anchor the EKG wires to my chest, and buttoned my blouse. I thanked the attending staff for their compassion. Grateful I had a present *and* a future, I left the hospital clutching papers to rehab.

My soul lay bare and exposed to the elements as I walked next to my husband across the dark, deserted, parking lot. We were the only creatures moving at four in the morning

"It's chilly."

"Yah." Ric placed his hand on the small of my back and hurried me across the lot.

I drew in a long jagged breath. "Wait, Hon. Stop. Can I have a hug?"

"Why?"

"What do you mean, why? I *need* a hug."

"No. Someone might see me."

"What?"

"Someone might see us. No."

Five words, five seconds — my epiphany was brief and hideous.

Five words, five seconds — such a small thing, no.

Exhausted but hopeful that I was alive for good reason, I'd left the hospital in the company of the man I'd pledged my life to. I thought I left the hospital with my husband. Five words and five seconds later, I was utterly alone. I wouldn't scream. I couldn't cry and I didn't understand how I'd become the pill-popping maid my husband could fuck, but wouldn't comfort.

We drove home in silence. Until I was wrapped in an afghan, curled into myself in the corner of the sofa, I did not cry. At home I unraveled, rocked, wailed, alone. I sobbed until my swollen eyes closed.

My days of 'hurry up' were over, not because drugs were killing me, but because drugs made me vulnerable. I couldn't let myself be that open to pain again. Decades later, I'm still trying not to stumble back into addiction. Five words in five seconds told me there's no one to catch me if I fall.

Christina Crall-Reed

The Last High Low

⚡

Everything I knew about drug rehabilitation I'd learned from movies. I didn't know what to expect in the real world. *Maybe counseling is supposed to be like this. She's probably heard this before. Maybe I'm not doing this right.* At my first session, I learned rehab was boring - not for me, but the counselor couldn't keep her eyes open.

Her heavy eyelids drooped as she nodded, "Uh huh. Yes, uh huh, go on."

I chattered nervously while her chin inched closer to her chest. *Maybe she's reading her notes. Maybe I'm supposed to lie down on this couch so she can see me. Her pen's not moving.* As I stared at the bald spot atop the counselor's head, my thoughts wandered from getting my life together, to getting the woman's attention by poking her in the ear with a stick.

This is counseling? She needs a nap. Maybe she's not a real counselor. She's young to be losing her hair. Maybe Narcolepsy makes your hair fall out. I'm wasting my time. Maybe she's high. Maybe she should do a line of coke before she counsels me.

"Uh huh..." She nodded off.

I left counseling in search of drug substitutes. Food, sex, movies, power cleaning the house — whatever I could toss into the black hole amphetamines used to cover, I tried. In a year's time I'd gained seventy pounds, forgiven my husband enough to wear him out, and I'd earned platinum status at Blockbuster. While cleaning a space that wasn't dirty, I discovered a crumpled baggie of seeds, some yellowed E-Z Widers, and a stale joint, tucked into an old shoebox at the back of my closet.

Suh-weet! My old 'Chemo' stash! I certainly didn't need the appetite stimulation this pot provided after chemotherapy, but...

Pot wouldn't kill me. Pot made me laugh. Just this once. A little toke could take the edge off my day. Just one hit. One little toke.

A little toke made my old sofa comfortable; made Cheetos sufficient for an afternoon meal; made television (which I watched with the sound off while my favorite music played from my stereo) interesting and funny. Since I was high, I concluded that the remote control was the single most amazing invention. My cheesy orange fingers were beautiful and the contestants on Family Feud cracked me up. I spoke to the television and giggled uncontrollably.

"HaHa look at these guys! They look like chickens! Their heads are bobbing all over, back and forth, up and down. What's wrong with these people? They don't even look at the camera, up and down, round and round! Like birds! HaHa. They don't even look at each other!"

Still laughing after the commercial break, I licked my fingers one by one, then turned down the stereo. I turned up the volume on the TV in time to hear Richard Dawson congratulate the family on screen. He said, "I think it's wonderful that you all traveled here to be with us. And you came all the way across the country together? That's quite a feat. All visually impaired? You're all legally blind, is that right? Well, you're winners regardless of how you do here today. Let's play The Feud!"

Let's play the, Huh? I stopped giggling. *They're blind? Nooo!* I went pot head mental and burst into tears. Whaaa! "They're not chickens. They're blind! Those poor people! Whaaa! What a loser I am! I don't have anything better to do with my life than make fun of blind people on Family Feud!"

To be treated like a decent human being, I suppose you have to be one. I felt indecent as I rolled into a fetal position on the couch and cried my irrational self to sleep. When I woke from my long nap, I brushed my teeth, washed all traces of junk food from my hands and then scanned the yellow pages for a psychiatrist. The blind game show contestants story was an easy one to share at my first twelve–step meeting. Funny or not, being high was lower than I wanted to go.

Pity Party

My most recent hospital report card was ugly. I'd failed every test. Getting high wasn't an option, and comfort from my emotionally stunted spouse was unavailable. After three months of waiting and worrying about recurrent cancer, I stood at my kitchen counter wondering if *this* might be the appropriate time to feel sorry for myself.

A good pity party needs a sad agenda, a short guest list and some comfort food. I had a soda, a cardboard sandwich purchased from the hospital vending machine and a dog to keep me company. My sad agenda was to think about my sad agenda. All set up for a pity party, I offered the food to my only guest.

"Want a treat, Bud-D?" He sniffed my hand and quickly turned his attention to an itch on his rump. If the dog, who ate everything, (his food, my food, rocks, Jehovah's Witnesses, my in-laws, neighbors out jogging, friends who called my house while parked in my driveway, too frightened to get out of their cars because my dog would eat them) wouldn't eat the sandwich, it was inedible. I threw my no-comfort food into the trash and tried not to think about the hospital.

I took a swig of soda then belched like a redneck at an all-you-can-eat buffet. I was a mess. I looked like hell. I had no manners. I felt sorry for myself, but the dog loved me anyway. Years after I overdosed and our marriage frayed at the edges, I got a pet instead of a divorce. My dog lived in the moment, which forced me to do the same. Bud-D was always happy to see me, didn't care about my flaws and he never once betrayed my trust while crossing a hospital parking lot.

"Wanna' go outside Bud-D? Bud-D, wanna go outside?"

Stupid question. *Do you want Kevin Costner to kiss the back of your neck, Chris? Do ya, huh? Do ya? Wanna lick Denzel Washington? Wanna climb Liam Neeson? Do ya? Do ya, huh?* Asked and answered as one hundred plus pounds of hair and raw muscle leapt around me like a dinosaur on crank. I grabbed the phone then straightened the knick-knacks toppled by the happy-dog-earthquake, before we headed outside.

Ric wouldn't be home for hours and our sons wouldn't be home at all. Bailey was at a friend's house. Kelby lived in Florida. If I called them, I'd scare them. If I worried them, they'd offer to come home. If they came home, we'd sit around, upset and frightened, playing board games to pass the time, waiting for results I didn't have, for tests that weren't complete. They'd let me win at Monopoly but I'd cry. *Don't call.*

"Get the ball Bud-D." His ears perked up and he tilted his head. "Get the ball." I repeated every command and pointed in the direction I wanted him to go.

Playing with the dog was akin to speaking to my husband. "Your wallet's in the cupboard, Ric." My spouse would tilt his head. "In the cupboard." He'd have a wide-eyed, blank stare. "The cupboard right in front of you." I'd point. "Right in front of you."

The dog dropped a small rock at my feet. "Not a rock Bud-D, get the ball." I pointed. "Get the ball." He stared at me. He looked at the rock. He looked at me. Rock. Me. Rock. He tilted his head and poised to sprint. I picked up the rock. "Get it!"

Bud-D was at the edge of the lawn when the rock plopped twenty yards behind him in the gravel driveway. I threw like the girl I was, but the dog loved me anyway.

I checked the phone messages as my dog deposited his muddy, spit-wet stone on the steps. Kelby called to say hello. Bailey called to

The Incontinental Divide

confirm his whereabouts. I saved my sons' messages so I could listen to their voices later, but I didn't call them back. *I'll cry. Don't cry.* The message from Throndsen Lettering told me the T-shirts I designed for the family reunion were ready and last message was my mom asking, "Are the T-shirts ready?"

I could return Mom's phone call as long as I kept my emotions in check. I could do almost anything but break down in tears – because my mother didn't cry. Once, in my forty plus years when her good conscience forced her to betray a troubled friend, I saw her cry. She wept like a child. She sobbed while I wept, watching her crumble, too young to help her, frozen in fear. When she saw my face she dried her eyes. No apologies, no excuses, no more tears. She never cried again, at least not in front of me.

The dog rolled around in the grass, legs in the air, rock under his back. As I placed the phone on the steps, he abandoned his plaything and trotted over to investigate. He didn't run at me. He didn't dare. During playtime, the dog knew not to run full speed in my direction. He knew, when his head met master's head at full speed, it made master unhappy. Master didn't like the whiplash and concussion she got. He didn't like being neutered and castrated after master recovered. He'll never run full speed at me again.

Bud-D and I had an understanding, akin to my relationship with my spouse: Both of us got food, water, play time, rest, loyalty and companionship. Neither of us peed on the furniture. He would kill for me, die for me, and protect me from all peril. I would not let him. He wouldn't play rough with me and I wouldn't have him put to sleep. The same was true for Ric and me.

"Go get a stick Bud-D. Get a stick." I pointed in the general direction of the elm trees as I walked to the mailbox at the end of the long drive. The dog trotted off.

I sat on the front steps, thumbing through the mail. There was a bill, bill, junk mail, a torn, soiled envelope bearing a US Postal Service sticker explaining the damaged condition of the letter, more junk mail, a party invitation... *That letter was post-marked three months ago.* ...junk mail, bill... *The return address was MHS Cancer Center.*

The dog pulled a log from the woodpile then dropped it at my feet with a thud. "No, Bud-D. No log. A stick. I can't throw that big thing. I can't…"

Just like that, I cried.

I cried in fear and I cried for pity. I cried because I beat cancer once, because I didn't know if I could do it again. I cried for mercy. I cried for what I didn't know. I cried for all I remembered. I cried for my friend Clarie, because cancer beat her. I cried because I held her as she drew her last breath; because she wasn't there to hold me; because I wouldn't see her again; because I might see her soon. I cried for my children because they loved me and needed me. I cried because I loved them but they weren't home, to hug or hold me. I cried because my husband wouldn't hold me, wouldn't hug me. I cried because he could, but he wouldn't so I cried. I sobbed myself breathless. I wept like I did as a child. I cried myself hollow. Aloud, alone, I cried.

Bud-D stopped gnawing the log, tilted his head and trotted over to me. He licked my hand and pushed the mail out of the way with his massive head. I drew a jagged breath as he laid his ears back. One hundred sixteen viscous pounds of teeth, hair and raw muscle sat motionless. As gentle as a bunny he laid his head in my lap. I buried my face in his fur and I sobbed.

After deflating the balloons from my pity party, I put the mail on the kitchen counter, blew my nose and returned to the front steps to drag the log back to the woodpile. The dog followed me, whining. I restacked the wood as Bud-D tried to snatch the log. "Drop it! Leave!" He obeyed, but whined again. "Quiet!" He was silent. "Bud-D, come." Ears down, tail tucked, he followed me across the yard. I scratched his head as we walked. "Good boy, Bud-D. Good boy."

A dog wants what he wants when he wants it. A master gives what *she* wants when she wants to give it. When my pity party ended, I wanted to be master of something. I needed to regain control. If my world continued to spin off axis, at least I could master a dog.

Dragonslayers

When you need to vanquish a beast like cancer, call a doctor first. Then venture into the woods and find your dragon slayers. Support may not always come from a spouse, but the forests are full of friend and family warriors, who are armed, dangerous and ready to fight, the moment they hear your battle cry. Dragon slayers watch your back or kick your backside, depending on the battle requirements. Best friends and good parents do both.

After my pity party, I called my friend Sherri, first. She was a dark haired Amazon, and I was a Miss Clairoled midget. So we looked dopey standing side-by-side, but that's what we did best. We'd been standing together, standing up for each other or standing on each other's toes since we were kids. Since her big sister Clarie introduced us as children, we'd shared heartbreak and smiles like the family we were. On her deathbed, Clarie asked us to take care of each other so we tried to do just that.

"Hello Sunshine! Whadja find out?"

I gave Sherri the lowdown on my low, down day. We laughed about the phlebotomy student, and the lab tech who saw my butt. I glossed over the needle biopsy then made bad jokes about ultra sound, lumpy boobs and hospital waiting rooms.

"Okay, Lumpy, did you talk to the boys n' Ric?"

"No I'll tell 'em after I go tomorrow. I wanna know what's going on before I call."

"Whadid Ric say?"

"He's not home yet."

"So? He's right up the road."

"I know. I stopped at the farm on my way home, but I couldn't find him. When I did he said he was busy."

"I'm gonna' smack that boy."

"We'll talk when he comes home. We'll do lunch or I'll have my people call his people."

"I'm your people. I'll call him. Then I'll smack him."

"No smacking. We can't both be in the hospital at the same time. Who'd feed Bud-D?"

"Cujo? Not me. When's your mom coming?"

"This weekend."

"After the reunion, is she gonna stay for your surgery?"

"I doubt it."

"You didn't tell her, did you?"

"No."

"Again? You didn't tell her, *again*? Christina Marie, shame on you."

"I didn't tell her yet. I will."

I didn't tell my mother the first time I had cancer. She was busy. I was nuts. Post partum depression made me crazy.

Back in 1982, reality and the thoughts sliding and crashing around my mind didn't meet. I had a new baby to care for, a toddler to play with, a busy husband and a huge circle of family and friends I *could* turn to when depression threatened to suck me into an abyss. But I turned to no one. I confided in no one. I appeared to be an average, recently pregnant woman, so I pretended I was.

The day after Bailey was born, I had surgery to freeze, cauterize, sculpt and rearrange my plumbing, which rid my body of cervical cancer. Radiation wasn't necessary. My hair didn't all fall out. Chemo made me sick but no one had to know I was totally off my bead.

I had a baby I couldn't nurse, a toddler who stroked the back of my head while I vomited, a husband who denied my illness and an emotional disconnection from the rest of the world. I was an average, recently pregnant, whacko with cancer. Convinced I was alone in the universe, I made sure I was. It was a strange time of separation, especially for my mother and me.

⚡

A year after treatment, I visited my family's home in Canada. I had no mental illness, no cancer, no husband or kids with me, and no responsibility to do anything other than enjoy myself – so I did. It was easy to relax in Cinderella's castle.

Atop a cliff overlooking Lake Ontario, the house was far removed from the scarcity of my youth and light years away from the privation of my mother's childhood. This house was not a shack or warehouse with blankets hung as walls to contain my mother and her thirteen hungry siblings. No overwrought woman scrubbed and screamed and rag-picked through her days in this house. No lice and rats chewed on the babies. No drunken man terrorized and molested children here. My mother earned an adult haven by surviving the destitution of her youth.

My step dad earned his creature comforts as president of a Fortune 500 company. But when Vern came home from work, I didn't see the money or the power.

I didn't greet the boss who drove the fancy car and wore expensive suits. I saw the *father* who put his life in my hands, during my first driving lessons. I saw the *Dad* who screened our dates while standing in the garage, sharpening a Bowie knife, casually questioning our young suitors – "What time will you be bringing my daughter home? Where will you be going with my daughter? What will you be doing with my daughter?" All while honing the knifeblade to a blinding sheen.

An only child of modest background, he married into our loud, lively clan already sixty members strong, then stepped into the role of parenting three teenagers and a toddler – without flinching. He made us a stronger family by choice, not by blood. Vern was a brave dragonslayer.

My parents deserved every luxury in their home. I enjoyed the amenities with them. We had morning coffee on the deck, days boating or shopping or sight-seeing around the bay, and then evening cocktails as the sun set over the water. We walked the terraced gardens together and strolled the lakeshore to skip stones and bitch and count our blessings.

I played 'Star Wars' with my little brother, Mat.

"Luke, I am your Father." I said.

"You're not supposed to say that. You're not Darth Vader."

"Who am I, again?"

"Princess Leia."

"The one with the Cinnabuns on her head?"

"They're braids!"

"Whatever. They look like pastry."

"Have you *really* never seen Star Wars, Chris?"

"Nope. But I'm sure you'll keep telling me about it." When Mat opened his mouth to begin another fanatic Star Wars litany, I interrupted. "Let's go eat. I'm kind of hungry for *cinnamon rolls*."

"They're braids!"

Whatever.

My baby sister Liana had toys that made me even hungrier.

I held each bubble headed figurine under my nose to take a whiff. "Who's this one? She smells good."

"Orange Blossom. They're named for their smells."

"Who's this? Coffee Table? She smells like furniture polish."

"Almond Tea. I don't really like that one either."

"Do they taste like they smell?"

Liana blushed. "I don't know. Only babies put toys in their mouths."

"You've never tasted them?"

The Incontinental Divide

"No. I'm not a baby."

"Oh. Sorry." I'd insulted her.

"Did you used to lick your Barbie dolls, Chris?"

"No, but if they smelled like dessert I would have."

"Mom wants you."

"What? No she doesn't."

"Yes. She's calling you." Liana furrowed her brow as she snatched Mint Tulip from my hand. Afraid her twenty six year old sister was going to tongue her collection of miniature Strawberry Shortcake figurines, Liana tucked her toys back into their 'Berry Happy Home.' She squeezed her tiny fingers around my wrist and ushered me from her bedroom.

I stood in the hallway, staring at the closed door. *Sheesh! I'm an adult, a wife, a mother. I'm not going to lick those little plastic toys just to satisfy some childish curiosity. I'm a grown woman! I'm not going to put toys in my mouth, like a baby – At least not while you're watching. I'll sneak in tonight when you're asleep.*

Mom was in her sewing room working on a quilt. Straight pins sticking out of the corner of her mouth, both hands guiding a fabric square under the machine needle, she didn't take her eyes off her project as she spoke. "What's up?"

"I've been banished."

"Were you naughty?"

"Of course. I insulted Princess Leia, then I ticked off Princess Liana. She thought I was going to eat her toys."

"Were you?"

"I wasn't going to leave tooth marks."

Mom pulled the pins from her mouth and stabbed them into a wristband cushion. "Tooth marks would definitely make her mad. She's a bit of a spitfire. Reminds me of one of her sisters." She rolled her eyes in my direction.

"You must mean Vickie 'cause Chris is all calm and relaxed. She's on vacation somewhere in Canada."

"I think Chris is bored or she wouldn't be watching her mother sew."

It was comforting to watch Mom make something happen without a fight. The shy little woman working the treadle of her sewing machine was the same hellcat I'd watched hurdle a bar, baseball bat in hand to go after a drunken man twice her size because he wouldn't stop bad-mouthing her family. In the 1960's, she'd stormed City Hall demanding fair housing for divorced women and their children. She'd fought off potential date-rapists, battled sexual harassment, taken on the PTA, school boards, teachers, doctors, lawyers – if she *had* to fight, she didn't back down. She protected her children and kept us in line with her mighty spirit, much love and a good dose of fear. Mom was a quiet spitfire. I was never bored watching her.

"I like watching other people work." I said.

"You could watch a movie."

"With popcorn?"

"Not on the sofa."

"You're no fun."

"I'm The Mom. No fun, is part of my job description."

On my way through the kitchen I snatched two cookies. From somewhere deep in the house I heard, "Not on the sofa!"

How does she do that?

After perusing the collection of John Wayne movies, children's videos, dramas and love stories, I chose a film I knew nothing about. You can't go wrong with Jack Nicholson. Debra Winger had a cool voice and I loved Shirley MacLaine. She reminded me of my mother.

I figured out the buttons and controls on the fancy, new Beta Max video player, all by myself, like a big girl. I popped in the film, brushed cookie crumbs off the sofa and an hour into the film had an all encompassing, out-of-the-blue and into-the-black, breakdown.

Terms of Endearment pulled me off a ledge I didn't know I was standing on. Cancer was the farthest thing from my mind until it was the only thing on my mind. When Shirley MacLaine screamed for Debra Winger's pain medication, I lost control of my senses. No restraint, I bawled and sobbed, using every Kleenex in the house except the one in my mother's pocket. I paced and rocked and cried – not just for their pain, but my own. Shirley MacLaine wasn't like my mother, she *was* my mother on screen. But, I wasn't Debra Winger.

The Incontinental Divide

For a year, I'd shut my mother out denying her the chance to fight for me.

An hour after the film ended, I remained teary-eyed and breathless. When Mom questioned my overreaction to the movie, I couldn't explain. I couldn't defend myself or my crazy actions, a year after my crazy cancer actions, which made my crazy reactions to a film seem even crazier. I didn't tell her a year ago. I surely couldn't tell her now. The first time I had cancer, I left my dragon slayers in the dark.

⚡

"Are you gonna call her?" Sherri's voice barged into my thoughts. "No. Wait. You *are* gonna call her."

"Yes, boss. I'll call her."

"Promise?"

"Yes. Nag. I'll call."

"You're lucky I'm a nag. Somebody needs to keep you in line, Lumpy."

I wanted to stick to the original plan to call my mother in the morning because I was afraid to deliver bad news. My mother had this, Irish Temper-Mother Lion-combo plate, personality, when it came to her children. Mom could be kind and fierce, viscous and vulnerable, all at the same time. Whenever we put ourselves in peril, the Irish temper preceded the unconditional love. If someone else puts her cubs in harm's way, that person would do well to get out of Her way — or die. No excuses, no apologies, no tears, no kidding. Hurt her children? You're dead.

Illness was different. There wouldn't be anyone for her to kill. If I called her with bad news, without a dragon for her to slay, I'd get the combination platter temperament:

Joan Crawford's, *Mommy Dearest* with June Cleaver's, *It'll be all right, Beaver.*

If I called her, she'd get angry and confused first, calm down and sort it out later. She'd probably tell me to be selfish and take care of myself. Then she'd give me cruel reminders that I was a selfish child.

After I overdosed, I called my mother for advice about my troubled marriage. She paused mid-sentence, to ask Vern, her third husband, to turn down the volume on the TV before reminding me that marriage is, 'Til death do us part.' I know she loves me as deeply as she wounds me, but it's the injury I feel first and remember longest.

That afternoon, I couldn't defend myself. I needed the unconditional love. That night, I changed my plan. I dialed my mother's number then crossed my fingers like a wishful child.

"Hello, Mom?"

"What's wrong?" *Mother Lion.* I relaxed as the warmth of her voice cocooned me. If cancer was coming for me again, it would not find me alone this time.

I'd called my fiercest dragon slayer out of the woods.

No Matter What

⚡

I was definitely tuckered out by the time Ric got home.
"Jeez-us! You look rough."
No hello. No, *How was your day?* No, *Why do you look like you just got run over by a semi?* My husband began his nightly diatribe: the farm, money, the weather, his brother, the hired man, money, the farm… Every night, he vented his anger and frustration with the life he chose. He ranted and raved about things I didn't control so I tuned him out until he finished reliving the bad parts of his day. The gentle, funny man I married sometimes followed the tired, frustrated one home, but not often. That night, I had no tolerance for the good farmer / bad farmer drama, so I interrupted his harangue with one of my own.

"Well, thank you for the compliment Ric and welcome home. I'm so happy to see you too. And how was *your* day, Chris? Oh, pretty normal, all except for the might have breast cancer part. Thanks for askin. What's for dinner? Well, I'll just see what the cook prepared for us. Oh, *Cancer.* Are you scared, Chris? Yes. Scared shitless. Thanks for askin."

"Oh my God, honey I'm sorry. I'm - What did they say? What did - what - how do you know?"

"I don't know anything for sure. I have a surgical consult tomorrow."

At least I wouldn't have to replace the roll of toilet paper in the bathroom. Both of us were scared shitless. "But you're not sure? They're not sure?"

"This lump is huge, that's for sure. The biopsy was awful."

"But we don't know it's can… You don't know for sure. We shouldn't get all worked up if we don't know what's going on."

True to form, he wouldn't say the word. If he said it, it might be real. I was in no mood for customary illusions. "But what if it is cancer?"

"Then you'll handle what comes when it comes. You're strong. You can do it."

"I don't wanna' be strong. I don't wanna be sick!"

"But if you are, you'll deal with it." In the communication game he was normally the king of denial to my queen of confrontation. That night, his was a voice of reason in the midst of what could have been my hysteria. Normally, that would piss me off.

"What am I gonna do? What am…"

"You're gonna have dinner with me. Then we're gonna sit and watch TV or something. Then we'll get some sleep and in the morning things might be a little better."

"How?"

"Okay, different. You'll get some rest and sort out some of the things running through your head."

His, was the voice of reason again. It confused me.

We ate dinner and watched television together. I had no idea what I ate or what program was on TV but we were together - almost - with an issue the size of a John Deere tractor parked between us on the couch.

Ric wasn't a cuddly guy, but he knew his way around farm machinery. "Come 'ere." He extended his arm so I could nestle beneath it. I scooted across the couch and snuggled up next to him as he wrapped his arm protectively around me. I seized the opportunity to lay my head against his chest. I could hear his heart beating. I tried a different angle to get comfortable, but his round belly was in the way. I laid my head on his stomach and he laughed. "What are you squirming around for?"

"Just tryin' to get comfy."

He laughed again and my head bounced up and down. When my head bounced then rolled downhill, we cracked up. He laughed as I laughed, which popped my head up and down to make me laugh some more. Then he laughed at my head bouncing. The two of us couldn't stop giggling so my head bobbed and jumped like popcorn on a trampoline, until the dog barked to be let outside. Ric opened the door then returned to me on the sofa. He stood in front of me staring, silent. He stared long enough to make me uncomfortable.

"What?"

"My God, you're beautiful."

"Thank you."

"You look so little. So lost."

"Not lost. Just tired."

The span from mourning to morning was too vast to cover alone. Ric had no words to ease us along so he offered what comfort he knew. He bent to cradle me in his arms. He kissed me tenderly, gently at first. There was no uncertainty of illness, no fear in his kiss as his lips slid to my throat. *I can't be sick.* My body responded to the familiar warmth, the old sensations renewed. I shivered. *I can't be ill.* Our bodies were designed for nothing beyond the room. I closed my eyes. *Nothing beyond the feeling.* His lips brushed my shoulder. *No pain. No cancer. Touch.*

We made love like it was the first time, like it was the only time, like it was the last time. I cried because it might be.

⚡

"Let's get some sleep." He kissed my forehead and eyelids. "Chris, you know I love you. No matter what, I'll always love you."

I tried to smile. "I'll be up in a bit." I got a drink of water, let the dog in, and glanced at the letter on the counter. I was like the letter

- damaged, unopened, full of bad news already heard. I turned off the lights. *Ric's loved me since high school. No doubt, he loves me. It's the 'no matter what' I fear.*

Pet Peeves

No matter what, the sun came up in the morning.
Thank you, God.
No matter what I looked like in the mirror.

Oh Gawd! I saw a strung out junkie; mascara under my swollen eyes, pale skin, bruised, bandaged, track marks on my arms and hands, hair sticking up in all directions. I sniffled and giggled at myself in the mirror. "Hey man, you got any stuff? I need it. Just one hit." I wiped my nose with the back of my trembling hand. "Yeah, I'll get ya the money. Just gimme somethin'. Just one hit, man."

"Who are you talking to in there?" My husband opened the bathroom door and walked in. "Jeez-us! I hope you feel better than you look."

"For better or worse, darlin'. Whadda' ya think? Wanna' marry her again?" I pointed at myself in the mirror.

"Ah, no. But thanks for askin'. What time do we go today?"

"We?"

"Yeah. Unless you don't want me to go?"

"No. I want you to go. I just didn't think you would. Aren't you chopping hay today?"

"It'll be there when I get back. I wanna' go, if you'll lay out some clothes for me."

The man is neither helpless, nor colorblind, but he dresses like he is. If I want to be seen in public with him, I have to choose his outfit. On my Top Ten list of pet peeves, dressing a grown man ranks number four.

Number Three: Grown man loses his wallet. Every few months I endure a door slamming, drawer pulling, teeth grinding, man swearing, dog hiding, cushion lifting, laundry throwing, cancel the credit cards, hissy fit.

Calmly, I try to answer his questions, "Yes. I looked under the cushions. No. I didn't move it anywhere. Yes. I'm sure I looked under the cushions."

The irritating sounds of PMS, (Pissy Man Screaming) fill the house. "If this place wasn't such a fucking mess I might be able to find something around here, but no, I have to do everything, work every day... You didn't wash it did you? Cancel the credit cards!"

His lost wallet is always my responsibility because, evidently, I don't fold his work shirts the way his mother did or sort the recyclable plastics from the papers correctly? Quietly, I go about my business. Half an hour after I call the bank to cancel the credit cards he finds his wallet in the pocket of the jeans he wore that morning. His head spins 360 degrees.

"What? What's wrong with you? Why so quiet? You didn't cancel my credit cards did you? You should have waited, honey."

Then I get PMS. (Please Makehim Shutup)

Pet Peeve Number Two: Grown man can't put dirty laundry *in* the laundry hamper. His dirty clothes lay on the floor. His dirty clothes lay in front of the laundry hamper. His dirty clothes lay on top of the hamper, beside the hamper and behind the hamper but they seldom see the INside of the laundry hamper.

I get tired of picking his dirty clothes off the floor so I leave the lid up to show him the target. I get tired of complaining about dirty clothes on the floor so I buy a bigger target, bigger hamper. He gets tired of me complaining about his dirty clothes on the floor so he tosses the occasional stinky sock in the hamper.

The Incontinental Divide

I grow weary of nagging. I get tired of picking and sorting, washing and drying, folding, pressing and carrying his clean clothes upstairs. I am so tired when I open the dresser drawers that I <u>just can't take</u> that final step. So, I stack his clean laundry on top of his dresser. I stack clean laundry in front of the dresser, beside and behind the dresser. I think, *I'll not put his clean clothes away until he buys a bigger dresser or leaves the drawers open so I can better see the target.* Logically, dirty clothes that never see the inside of the hamper don't need to see the inside of the drawers just because they're clean. His jeans don't care and his tidy whities don't know why they're tidy. I am perversely satisfied doing housework.

My Number One Pet Peeve has much to do with satisfaction and nothing to do with logic: Grown man should never, e v e r use his grown woman's toothbrush! Don't. Ever.

It is logically satisfying when a grown man's mouth meets a grown woman's mouth and lips and tongue and various body parts. It is logically satisfying when a man and woman kiss and nibble and lick and swap spit and have shut-up and swallow sex. But, if my toothbrush is not clean and dry when I go to use it, logic jumps out a window. My satisfaction will come with his bloodshed. Don't do it. Don't go there. Don't use my toothbrush – ever.

"What time did you say?"

"Eleven."

"Be there by eleven or here by eleven?"

"There by eleven. Be here by ten."

"It'll be close. You'll have to lay clothes out for me."

I rolled my eyes and smiled. "I will. Now, go away. I have to take a shower."

"Ooohh yeah, need help washin' your back?" He kissed my neck.

Considering the sweet, wet possibilities, I shivered. No. I'll be late. *All that lather, it could be worth it.* No. *To be...* "No. Go away. You'll make us late. Shoo. Shoo."

"You're no fun." Smiling, Ric stepped over to the sink.

I teased, "I'll be fun later."

He grabbed my toothbrush.

We arrived at the hospital precisely at eleven. At eleven fifteen a nurse informed us that the doctor would be delayed. At eleven forty five the nurse informed us it would be a few more minutes. At eleven fifty my husband reminded me that we could have had sex. He glanced slyly at me from behind a month old copy of Sports Illustrated. "I knew we had time."

"You were too busy brushing your teeth."

"Whatever!? I didn't use your toothbrush. I only touched it, accidentally." He grinned and bounced his eyebrows up and down. "You could have cleaned em for me."

My husband loves to see me squirm, in bed and out. In the waiting room, he was relentless. He leaned over and whispered in my ear. I nodded at the eavesdropping receptionist. Like a ventriloquist, I spoke to my spouse without moving my lips or clenched teeth. "Stop it." I fidgeted in my chair. He whispered again. I rolled my eyes. "I mean it. Stop it." I smiled at the receptionist as goose bumps covered my body. If I didn't consult with the surgeon soon I'd be consulting a lawyer about charges of public indecency. I hoped Ric wouldn't actually do the things he whispered to me — in public. At twelve fifteen a nurse wearing surgical scrubs opened the door to the inner sanctum.

"Christina Reed?"

I rose. The first part of my 'consultation' would be yet another breast exam. I smiled at my husband. "Read your magazine and behave."

"I can't be - hayve. I don't even know what a hayve is. We didn't have any hayves on the farm. Must be somethin' you city kids had." He winked at me as I disappeared into the surgeon's chambers.

Gaelic Gall

⚡

Dr. A. SscanIbuyavowel stared at the clock on the wall as he sprinkled fishy smelling flakes into a large aquarium below his extensive collection of diplomas and certificates. The arrogance of the man galled me immediately.

GALL: to vex or irritate; bother; provoke; annoy; to injure the skin by friction; to chafe; to run wearing heels, so your thighs rub together 'til your pantyhose catch fire: GALL

He meticulously washed his hands before acknowledging my presence in the room. "Hello, Constance, is it? I'm Doctor A. Ssimmuchsmarterthanyou."

"Christina." I extended my hand, which he didn't touch.

"Yes. Well, I understand there is a lump in your breast troubling you?"

No. Tight shoes are troubling. An empty toilet paper roll in a public washroom is troubling. The lump in my breast is terrifying. "Yes."

He pointed. "First door on the right. Everything off from the waist up. There's a gown. I'll be there momentarily."

Sit, Constance. Get the stick, Constance. I was a well trained dog. Because he came so highly recommended, I *would* exit the room I just entered, enter an adjacent cubicle, strip, cover my half naked self with an ugly robe, then wait for Dr. A. Ssnotimeforpleasantries to honor me with his presence. I would wait for the gifted surgeon.

I waited fifteen minutes.

I toyed with the bulb on the blood pressure sphygnometer.

I checked my teeth in the mirror above the sink.

I parted the blinds and watched traffic flow in the parking lot.

I considered building a shelter of tongue depressors and cotton swabs when Dr. A. Ssmytimeisvaluableyoursdoesntmeansquat entered the cubicle. "So, Carol, which breast are we looking at?" He began to prod my left breast.

"Christina. It's my right breast."

"Yes. Well." He poked, squeezed and prodded my tender breast like a butcher rolling a rump roast. His fingers pressed so deeply into my tissue that I anticipated some psychic surgery hocus pocus where he'd pull his hand away and produce a bloody mass of something.

"Troubling..."

No shit, Sherlock. He was pushing deep enough to rescue those seven trapped miners. He stopped torturing me only long enough to draw arrows and circles and lines on a diagram in my patient file.

"Troubling."

Teeth clenched, I grimaced. "Can you stop doing that and stop saying troubling?"

"Beg your pardon?"

"Nothing."

"Yes. Well, get dressed and I'll explain the surgery."

No, "Do you have any questions?" He would speak. No, "We'll discuss your options." I would listen.

I heard the far off whispers of my Celtic ancestors. "Tis woeful da way hay spakes tah hare." The music of the march began - the music that stirred my blood. I heard the pipes. He *would speak*. The rhythm of the drums. *I* would *listen.*

He wiped his hands on his scrubs like he'd handled tainted meat.

As he left the cubicle he nodded and pointed in the direction he'd walk, in case I'd forgotten his office was next door.

I always hear the ancient whispers just before I lose my temper. "Sure n' hays causin' Herself graif." The pipes were calling me to battle — the distant thunder, drumming, rhythm building, louder, faster, closer. *But.*

"Hays avil."

But.

"Hay shud shoot has mooth. Hay shud…"

But we need the man's skills. I forced Herself to silence the drums. The pipes quieted as the fierce Celtic warriors in me stood down.

"Can I get my husband? He's in the waiting room."

"Of course you *can.*"

He sounded like an English teacher. "Can I get a drink of water?" "I don't know, *can* you?" "*May* I get a drink of water?" "Yes, you may." *What a dick.*

I wondered if my husband heard the music of the march.

Dr. A. Ssyourwifethinksimapatronizingprick introduced himself to my spouse and shook his hand. The 'men folk' made small talk while I watched and listened, in awe.

"I was telling Kelly about the procedure."

"Who's Kelly?"

"Your wife. Mrs. Reed." He looked at the name on my chart for the first time then apologized to my husband. "I'm so sorry. I meant, Christina."

Foolish, selfish little woman I was, I thought surgery on my breast was about — me. I spoke before the drumming in my head resumed. "Tell me about the surgery itself. You're not going to do a mastectomy." It was a statement, not a question.

"Am I going to perform a mastectomy? No. Not initially."

"I didn't ask about a performance." The pipes called. The drums beat. "Tell me about a lumpectomy."

My husband heard the music of the march. He'd seen that look on my face before. For a quarter century he'd seen that look — just before

I sliced off some man's testicles with my sword. He called it my 'Phyllis look', my mother's name. He interjected to save the doctor's life.

"She, we, would like to know, exactly what *are* you planning to do?"

"Yes. Well." The doctor proceeded to describe the entire surgical procedure. From A to Z, anesthesia to zwieback, he gave us all of the gory, bloody details.

When he described slicing my breast tissue like a loaf of toasted bread around a roll of sausage it was my turn to interject on my husband's behalf. Ric was pale and perspiring. I'd seen that look before. For a quarter century I'd seen that look, just before he lost his lunch.

I can't play Gross Out with my husband. It's too easy to make him gag. At home, at work, in public, on the shuttle bus between Epcot Center and the Magic Kingdom when some kid picks his nose then brings his boogie laden finger up to his mouth, Hubby will hurl. It's not even sporting to tell him something off color. He'll throw up and I'll win the Gross Out game every time.

My chartreuse colored husband leaned against the large aquarium. I understood all I needed to understand about the surgery, for the moment. Before my stricken spouse and I could leave the doctor's office I needed one last thing. I wanted one small but essential thing, a simple declaration from the surgeon:

"Do you, Dr., (state your name, which I cannot pronounce, here) solemnly swear to cut the lump, the whole lump and nothing but the lump so help you, God?"

"I so swear."

Consultation was over. Breast cancer likely. I scheduled surgery.

The Incontinental Divide

Hold Please

⚡

I would be having Outpatient Surgery. IN: with my cow slippers, lumpy boob and fuzzy robe. OUT: with my bandaged boob, cold can of Sprite and a bendy straw. I chose Outpatient Surgery because Dr. A Sshebetterbeasgoodasheiscocky solemnly swore to cut the lump, the whole lump and nothing but the lump, so help him, God.

They took my blood pressure and checked my temperature, "Do you have any allergies?"

"Yes."

Scribble, scribble. Next, they gave me an injection of something to help me relax.

Occasionally, I suffered the mental retardation which followed a night of trying to coax a worm from a bottle of tequila, but I hadn't used recreational drugs for years. After the painful episodes in my life when I overdosed and almost died, I stopped getting high. I didn't take drugs unless they were prescribed for serious illness or surgery - like today.

I relaxed to let the drugs kick in. The blurred vision, distorted sounds and the feel of cotton-mouth, were as familiar to this recovered addict as an old bath robe.

Relax. *There's Doctor Martin come to say good bye. I love that doctor. There's the nice nurse to wheel my gurney down the hall.* Relax. *Those ceiling lights are too bright. There's Dr. A. Sspleasedontbutcherme walking in ahead of me. I don't love that doctor. There's my husband, looking stressed.* Relax. Ric kissed me and let go of my hand. *He never kisses me in public. I love him anyway. He must be upset about something. Wonder what?* Relax and...

Hold, please.

I floated in and out of consciousness. Between Kevin Costner's <u>Waterworld</u> and a solid place where someone called my name, I drifted. In my imagination, I swam beneath the handsome actor. *"Mrs. Reed are you awake? Mrs. Reed?"* In my head, some comedian was onstage delivering her routine. *"So? Kevin Costner had webbed feet. Big deal. He's so hot. I'd do him anyway and not look at his feet."* I thought I was giggling. I shivered.

"Mrs. Reed? Are you awake?"

"I'm cold." I opened my eyes.

"Mrs. Reed? Mrs. Reed, you're in recovery. The surgery went well. We're just giving you a little something for the pain." I felt the I.V. tube attached to the back of my hand move, but I felt no pain. "Biopsy was good. They didn't find any more cancer."

She has a lovely voice but that's not my name. "Don't call me Mrs. Reed, please. My name is Christina Marie." I closed my eyes and dozed off, concerned for some weird reason, that Kevin Costner would know I was married.

A heavenly warmth spread over me, blanketing my entire body. *Wake up! It's the heavenly warmth! I'm dying again! Stay away from the white light!*

My eyes popped open and I looked frantically around the room.

"There you are, Christina. You nodded off again." The nurse angel with the lovely voice tucked a heated blanket around me. "Is that better?"

"Yes. Thank you." I struggled to keep my eyes open. "My breast?"

"The initial biopsy was good. That's good news right?"

"Is my breast gone?"

The Incontinental Divide

"You should heal nicely. Doctor will talk to you about the surgery a bit later."

Hospital policy: put you on hold - blow smoke up your ass.

"Is my breast gone?"

"You still have two breasts. Let's get you back to your room."

Back in my cubicle they gave me nourishment and the remote control to a television positioned so high up on the wall I couldn't look at the screen without injuring my neck. I suspected that was how the hospital got repeat business. *We amputated your limbs but, oh, does your neck hurt? You should see a doctor.*

I wanted to see my doctor but he was nowhere to be found.

The nurse took my blood pressure and temperature. I dozed off while spouse channel surfed. Dr. Martin stopped by to check on me. The anesthesiologist stopped by to check on me. Ric called our significant others with a progress report. The nurse took my blood pressure and temperature again, (probably just for shits and giggles because she was as bored as we were), while we waited. We couldn't leave until Dr. A Ssimbusysellingyourtitontheblackmarket, dismissed me. I waited hours, with an ice pack and drain occupying the bra cup my breast used to fill. The third ice pack was melted by the time Dr. A Ssyourenotimportantanymore, spoke to me.

He told me everything the nurses already told me, wrote out prescriptions for pain medication and antibiotics and handed them to the nurse. When the surgeon walked away, the nurse whipped open the curtain on my cubicle and called out his name. "Excuse me, Doctor? She's allergic to this medication."

"Excuse *me*, nurse." He grabbed the prescription and my patient file, scribbled something and stormed off. "Make her appointment for follow up!"

Embarrassed and contrite, the nurse turned to face me. "Little mix up, there. Sorry."

"Don't apologize." I was drugged, heavily medicated, relaxed and feeling no pain but I was fully aware that nurse just saved my life. "Thank you."

I left the hospital in a wheelchair. Groggy, uncomfortable and anxious to go home, I clutched my follow up instructions and amended prescriptions. Once seated in the car, Ric slid the shoulder harness behind my back, careful not to touch my chest with the strap. He buckled and tucked me in for the ride.

"After the pharmacy Ric, will you stop at Blockbuster to rent a movie?"

"Aww, jeez-us I hate pickin' out videos for you. All those chick flicks. They'll think I'm gay. I don't suppose you could come in there with me?"

My heavy eyelids fluttered as I laid my head on the seat back. "Suppose not." I briefly opened my eyes. "Honey, you should get some counseling. Maybe talk to someone about your issues with your sexual orientation." I grinned. "I'm sure there's a video."

"Oh, aren't you funny? Woman, if you weren't wounded I'd show you my issues. Whadda ya want me to get?"

"Kevin Costner movies."

"Movies? More than one?"

"Sure. Get 'em all. I have issues." I smiled. I needed to close my eyes.

"What else do ya want? Subtitles? Porno? Musicals?" He smiled back at me.

"Yeah! Brigadoon!"

"Bring a what?"

"Brigadoon. It's a musical."

"Aww, jeez-us! I was hopin' you'd say yes to porn." He rolled his eyes, shook his head and disappeared into the store.

I spoke to myself before nodding off. "They don't have blue movies at Blockbuster, Ric. I already checked."

Bet On A Longshot

If I was a gambler, playing the odds, I wouldn't bet on me. My life has too many variables. Even the slow, quiet days can change in an instant, from nothing going on, to life flailing out of control.

At home, Bailey had the sofa in front of the big TV decked out like a hospital bed. There were childproof gates in the doorways so my dog couldn't come in to injure me with affection. My big, mean Bud-D was afraid of plastic laundry baskets and baby gates. My son stood in front of me expectantly.

"So, are you okay, Mom?"

"Yes honey. No more cancer." His look of relief was so profound my eyes welled up with tears along with his.

"Can I hug you?"

"You'd better."

"I don't wanna hurt you."

"It would only hurt if you didn't hug me, B."

Ric emptied two Blockbuster bags on the kitchen counter then set my medication, a drink and one of my favorite candy bars on the coffee table in the living room. He fluffed the pillows while Bailey smoothed the sheets.

"Need anything else before I go to the farm?"

"No, thanks. I think I'm set. What are you grinning about?"

"I'm just glad you're okay."

"Me too. What time is it anyway?"

"Late. I gotta go milk the cows or they'll need boob jobs too. They'll explode." His grin disappeared. "Oh, sorry. That wasn't funny. I'm sorry."

For the first time in my life, I felt oddly out of place in my own home. I was pleasantly surprised my men were trying to take care of me, but I wasn't really sick. I was ecstatic I didn't have breast cancer. I didn't know what I *did* have, but apparently it wasn't going to eliminate what was left of my breast or kill me that night. So, there I was, on the couch with little to do but sit on the couch.

"Boob *is* a funny word, Ric and I didn't have my sense of humor removed – just a lump." I smiled, trying to reassure him. "Boob job is *way* funnier than mastectomy."

"Yah." He stroked my cheek with the back of his calloused hand. "Get some rest."

The men were nurturing the nurturer. It was a weird situation for me.

Bailey hovered around the living room, long after Ric left for work "Can I get you anything else, Mom?"

"No, thanks honey. Oh, wait. How about a movie? Would you put a video in for me?"

"That's all?"

"Well, yeah. I'm not dyin, B. I'm just gonna lay here and be lazy for tonight. Tomorrow I might just lay here and be lazy too but I'll put my own movies in then."

"Which one?"

"Brigadoon."

"Aww, jeezus." He sounded like his father.

"Hey Mom, since you're not goin anywhere, can I use your car?"

"What's wrong with yours?"

"No gas."

The Incontinental Divide

"Okay. I'm just going to Brigadoon." I started singing lyrics from the musical. "What a day this has been. What a rare mood I'm in. Well, it's almost like bein' in love."

Bailey rolled his eyes, brought me a new ice pack, kissed my forehead and disappeared out the front door.

I called Kelby with my good news. "Dad already told me but that's great, Mom. I'm very happy for you and for us." Kelby delivered a monologue in baby babble, about his cute little Mommy having no more boo boos on her boobs then laughed at his own jokes before reminding me for the fifth time that he loved me - not that I was counting.

I cozied myself onto the sofa. The dog positioned himself between the couch and the coffee table, facing the front door so I couldn't leave my designated area without waking him first. For the next few days the dog would live with his head in my behind. Whenever I was sick, sad or injured my protective pet wouldn't leave my side.

My men had tucked me in, pledged their love and kissed me goodnight. My watchdog kept vigil. For the first time in months, I slept without the fear of cancer and death invading my dreams. Sleeping without them was glorious.

Ice-Pack-Bra-Kevin-Costner-Film-Festival-Day began at nine the next morning. Ric was in and out, checking on me. "Why are you cryin?" He said.

"Message In A Bottle."

"Oh."

Bailey was in and out, checking on me. "What are you laughin at?"

"Tin Cup."

"Oh."

I was in and out. Asleep - *Field of Dreams*. Awake - *Dances With Wolves*. The girls were accustomed to being unteathered and free to roam about the bed as I slept so resting while wearing a bra, an ice pack, and a surgical drain, was more than a little uncomfortable. My sleep was fitful until early evening when I finally allowed myself some pain medication. *Ahh, return to Waterworld.*

By day four I was ready for more than a sponge bath and movies. The dog rose when I did, attempting to shepherd me around the house. He walked one pace ahead, steering and bumping me with his rump and hips. He turned in front of me if he wanted me to turn, blocked my path if he wanted me to stop. "Knock it off and get outta my way." When I reprimanded him, he paused in front of me to pretend he was stretching. *Psych!*

I took a shower, careful not to get my incision wet, then banged my elbow when I tripped over the dog lying on the other side of the bathroom door. He gave me privacy during my shower but Bud-D knew I was wounded. As I putzed around the kitchen the dog followed me. I tried to empty the dishwasher. The dog ran into the back of my thighs.

"Jesus, dog. Move! You're not gonna miss anything." I tried to fold clean laundry. The dog brought me a dirty sock retrieved from in front of the hamper.

"No, Bud-D. Don't help." I returned the sock to the hamper, turned to fold more clothes and noticed the dog parading around the kitchen with the lid to the wicker hamper in his mouth.

"That's it. Stop helping me!" I hollered out the open window to Ric, in the garage. "Can he come outside with you? Give him some exercise. He's makin me nuts! Everywhere I turn he's got his nose up my butt."

"Are you makin' Chrissy nuts, Bud-D? Come on. Get out here."

I turned to open the door, but there was no need. The dog stood on his hind legs, smacked the handle with his huge front paw and shoved the door open with his head.

Ric threw a tiny stone from the driveway deep into the hay field. I watched as the dog disappeared chest high into the hay, emerged with the pebble in his mouth and trotted back to drop the rock at Ric's feet. *Amazing.* Even with bifocals perched atop my nose I wouldn't be able to find a stone the size of a toaster, in alfalfa that thick.

I carried a meager pile of folded laundry upstairs and stacked it on top of the dresser. My breast throbbed so I decide to rest. Pain medication, a fresh ice pack and the 'No Way Out' video would fix

The Incontinental Divide

me right up. Since I'd seen the movie three times before and already knew the 'way out,' I dozed off in the recliner.

I was startled awake by the terrifying sounds of my dog growling and barking in his most menacing tone and my husband screaming, "Chris! Come get him! Chris! Call Bud-D off!"

What are the odds? On a country road, miles from civilization, my loyal dog - extra vigilante because I was inside the house alone, recuperating from surgery - was loose following his exercise run, when two unknown vehicles containing strangers, parked at the end of our driveway.

The stranger from the second car left his vehicle. Walking toward the first car brought him step-by-step closer to the house where the dog's injured master slept. The stranger would take one more step, but go no further. Bud-D stood at attention. This stranger had a gun.

Ric screamed, "Get back in your car! Get in your car! Chris! Come Get Him!"

The sheriff's deputy ran for his vehicle. He dove in and frantically rolled up the open window as Bud-D leapt at the squad car to stand on his hind legs, front paws on the door frame, barking, growling, foaming at the mouth.

I burst out of the house, grabbed a stone and threw it at the dog to get his attention, while I screamed commands in *my* most menacing tone, "Stand Down! Bud-D stand DOWN!" The dog obeyed and turned to sniff the rock that smacked him in the rump. *What were the odds I'd have the physical strength to pull my dog away from the squad car? Odds were not good. Not good at all.* I grabbed his collar and pulled. He continued to bark and growl as I shouted, "Stand down! Bud-D, stand down! COME!" As I yanked him away from the roadside, my sutures popped, but I didn't dare let go.

My guard dog was ferociously determined to rid our territory of a gun-toting intruder. I was equally determined to pull my pet into the house before we both got shot.

The raised hair on his back relaxed only when I closed the front door. Inside, Bud-D paced nervously back and forth in front of me. I was safe but my husband was still outside with the stranger, with the gun. Bud-D didn't like it and I wasn't feeling warm and fuzzy about the situation myself.

Odds are the terrified woman in the first car will never forget this speeding ticket. Through the open window, I saw the speeder flip my husband off when the deputy gave her permission to drive away. The deputy wrote out a ticket and handed it to my husband. As I listened to the men discussing odds and chance and dog restraint and public safety on private property, I decided to become a professional gambler.

Odds are, the average person won't ever be struck by lightning or survive cancer, twice. So, the next time I think I have cancer, I'll forgo surgery, ice packs, the dog, and Kevin Costner films. I'll skip the hospital and go straight to the racetrack to bet my life savings on a long shot. I could make a fortune betting on long shots. Odds are no day in my lifetime will play out like this one again.

When Your Panty Hose Catch Fire

⚡

Most patients are reluctant to file malpractice suits against doctors they like. Most humans are forgiving. Even if our concerns are dismissed, our mammograms misread, the results misdirected and our health care systems disappoint us - we can forgive human error, because we make mistakes too. But, deny a fellow human being the basic respect and compassion we all deserve and life gets ugly. I get ugly.

A week after surgery I returned to the hospital to have my stitches removed. Grateful the mass wasn't cancerous, I was anxious to learn what went wrong so I could make it right. I hoped the official results and a plan of action would set the girls free.

Without a *hello* or *how are you?* Dr. A .Sswedontlikeeachotherletsgetthisoverwith peeled the bandage back and began poking my breast.

"Ouch."

"I've seen worse. You're lucky. There is some oozing. It's a nice incision but the sutures are broken here at the end. Have you been doing heavy lifting?"

Not with my breast. I couldn't explain the dog and the deputy so I shook my head. "Yes, you're lucky. This is nice work. Would you like to see?"

Before I could answer, he handed me a small mirror.

"We found the mass to be larger than anticipated. Larger than a golf ball. We…"

Unprepared for the mirrored image of what replaced my plump smooth breast, I felt tears well up. Dented and shruken, half my breast was gone. My voice caught in my throat. I whispered, "It's so much smaller than my left."

"We were concerned you would lose your breast."

I didn't lose my breast. You took my breast. "No, I'd notice right away if I put it down somewhere and it didn't get back up with the rest of me."

"Now, there's no need for sarcasm. We cut more tissue to be on the safe side but the initial biopsy was good. You were lucky. I've seen much worse. Should there be a recurrence in the same area we can reopen the incision."

We? Who's we? You and your ego? I had no perspective on the "lucky" angle in the mirror. My scar sliced nipple to underarm, like a caramel colored lollipop on a long red stick - spoiled candy no one would ever lick again. *He cut more than the lump, not only the lump so help him God, but I'm lucky?* I didn't feel lucky. I felt hideous. Bile rose in the back of my throat. *I'm gross. I'm disfigured. I'm lucky?* "If it's not cancer, what is it? Or what was it?"

"We're not certain. A mass. A cyst out of control. Let me reiterate, this is an acceptable outcome. Perfectly acceptable. It could have been much worse. You shouldn't be disappointed."

How would you know what I should be? I lay the mirror down as the music of the march began. The pipes called from a distance. The drums began to beat. *You don't even know my name.* Cancer was the enemy but an arrogant man, focused solely on his 'nice work' was suddenly all I could see. He didn't see *me* sitting there.

"Please stop saying that I'm lucky and just for the record, I don't want to know the horrors you've seen. You're an oncology surgeon, a cancer specialist, I'm sure you've seen worse. I haven't. I would like to know, if it isn't cancerous why did you have to cut out so much and why are you telling me that it might come back?"

"We think it's a form of fibrocystic breast disease, chronic and acute. The mass could return and would need to be removed so we can ascertain that it isn't cancerous."

"So I'll have to do this again and you'll remove more tissue!? From where? There isn't any extra." My 'cancer-free' joy ebbed away like low tide. "What about an implant or reconstruction?"

"Not likely."

"What's not likely, more surgery? Implants?"

"Without a cancer diagnosis, reconstruction would be purely cosmetic."

Of course it's cosmetic, you dolt! I'm not a wet nurse. I'm a forty four year old woman. I took a deep breath. "Let me get this straight. You took half my breast – without my consent and because the biopsy showed breast disease, but not cancer, I can't have my breast reconstructed?"

"Well, of course you *can*, but you would be responsible for the cost and it would be problematic. It's not necessary. You're not in any danger. I'm a good judge of what type of surgery you'd need."

"Excuse me? Excuse me! You don't know anything about me!"

Was this Karma in action? Because I'd kept to myself the first time I had cancer, it denied others the chance to choose a response on my behalf. Regardless of my noble intentions, I had no right to make those choices for other adults. This man had no right making choices for me.

"I felt a mastectomy was unnecessary but we removed a larger area than discussed, for my piece of mind."

"*Your* piece of mind?! You hollowed out my breast! Whadya, use an industrial melon baller? Look at me. I'm disfigured!" The pipes called me to battle. The distant thunder drummed.

"Now, calm down, Kirsten. You still have two acceptable breasts."

"My. Name. Is. Christina! And acceptable to whom?" The drums were pounding. My hand was on my sword. "Hay shud nah bay spakin dat weah tah Herself." I had to get out of there before I lopped off his head. Screw karma and fuck cancer! No one should feel unworthy of survival.

"Can I get dressed now?"

"Of course you *can*." He looked at my chart. "How tall are you? You're overweight for your height, which is probably fine. If you maintain this high level of body fat some tissue should fill in."

This high level? Not, A high level. "Stay fat and my boob will grow back. Is that it? My udder will fill up as long as I'm a cow!?"

"More like the lizards whose tails regenerate after amputation." He attempted a smile. "If you don't have any more questions..."

Oh, my God! Now he thinks he's clever! I was afraid to speak. *Lizard?* I was afraid the tears would start and never stop. "So where do I buy - how do I go about getting a prosthetic bra? Do I need a prescription so my insurance will pay for it?" He looked like I'd asked, 'How do I go about poisoning the rare tropical fish in your aquarium?'

"I thought you were a State case, welfare."

"What?"

"Your records indicate no insurance."

"No. I have excellent insurance, but what does that have to do with a bra?

He looked at the clock. "Your breasts are fine, just fine. You can buy a bra anywhere, Sears or wherever you people shop."

Full on frontal assault. White hot shame and anger coursed through my veins. The drums pounded, beat and banged. The pipes wailed. My ancestors shouted, "Hay shud nah bay spakin dat weah! Hays un avil focker! Hay shud nah bay spakin dat weah tah Herself! Hay shud nah bay spakin ah tall! Shoot dat avil focker's mooth!" The beat of the drums was deafening.

I didn't hear what he said next. In my head, swords clashed. Blade met flesh. Warriors screamed as the enemy bled but a lone voice whispered in the din of battle. "Hays nah warthy. Lat at goo."

In the midst of war and anger, humiliation, pain, I listened to that little voice and finally understood why my mother didn't cry. *He is not worthy of your tears. Let it go.*

I didn't know why he thought I was a fat, one titted, Po' White Trash, dismembered lizard, slinking off to buy undergarments in the Craftsman Tool aisle, but I did know he would not see me cry. I lay down my sword.

What I did next, whatever I said, only God and my ancestors

know. I remember he was alive, but as quiet as the dead. I left his office holding a bra prescription, holding a thin shred of dignity and holding my head high. With the grace of my mother I left his office holding back tears.

Galled beyond reason, I couldn't hear. I couldn't see. I couldn't sort my thoughts, but I did not cry in front of him. I ran. I made it (almost) to the elevators before my panty hose caught fire and the floodgates opened.

Sobbing, I drove to Family Dollar, parked the car and turned off the engine. The lot was nearly deserted. I wiped my eyes and blew my nose. Encased in stillness, I heard the far off whispers of my ancestors. "Why air ya hare, lass?"

I laid my forehead against the steering wheel. *I'll buy a set of steak knives as a thank you gift for the skilled surgeon. Scalpels, wherever I shop. See how he likes it.*

"Ya cannah make ham see."

Perfectly acceptable. It could have been much worse. Dollar store knives will be perfectly acceptable for Dr. A. Sshedoesntdeserveaname.

"Lat at goo."

I pulled the fabric away from my chest to stare down into my blouse. *This is an acceptable outcome?* One round and full, one smaller and bandaged, the girls were there, still a pair. Were they still me?

I ran my fingers across the top of my bra. *Maybe I'll feel better when it heals.* I stroked the underside of my breasts. *He was an asshole.* He didn't need to make me feel worse about feeling bad – but he did – and I let him. So, my panty hose caught fire. Anger happens. Tempers flare. I touched my breasts. *It could have been much worse.*

When I realized my anger gave him power over me, I had to let it go. When I realized my fears made me as angry as his arrogance did, I had to forgive us both. When I realized I was fondling myself in a public parking lot, I sat up and smiled.

I started the engine, put the car in gear and made a decision as I backed out of the lot. No one will make me feel less than deserving, again. If this is what I have to work with, then work it I will. I'll be the queen of my own life. I'll be an MA Queen.

And if my pantyhose catch fire again, so be it. Let 'em burn.

Christina Crall-Reed

Waking Up Ma

Now, I examine my breasts every morning. A recurrence of the cancer that wasn't cancer would have to cause a lump the size of a bowling ball for me to tell the difference between scar tissue and trouble, but I check it out anyway. I take a shower. I touch myself. *Oh, yeah.* Life is full of perks.

At twenty-five, cancer threatened my life and my unborn child. At forty-one, a lightning strike forced me to deal with a recurrent cancer I was trying to wish away. At forty-four a non-cancerous disease took half my breast, but gave me back the joyful soul I was born with.

Approaching fifty, I'm enjoying survivor's benefits *and* asymmetric breasts. My once, red and scary scar is barely noticeable. I stayed fat long enough for some tissue to fill in. My left side is still a 'D' cup and the right side is something else, but my breasts *are* acceptable. Maybe even, exceptional. Every morning, I greet the girls like my dog greets me after a brief trip to the store.

I'm so happy to see you! You came back! Scratch my head! Rub my belly! Happy! Happy! When (if) I think about what could have been, I don't fret about the physical condition of my breasts. I enjoy the thrill of seeing my body as is, because I'm still in it.

Satisfied my breasts are still there after my morning shower, I turn

The Incontinental Divide

my attention to my skin. This is the part of the MA ritual when I spread the moisturizer on with a trowel. I'm good at spackling and plastering. I've had a lot of practice.

Bipolar mental illness is a continuous up and down. Rough it up. Smooth it out. Apply makeup or mop the kitchen, manic depression lends itself to maintenance projects.

Back at the front, during a particularly long period of depression for me, my husband lost his temper. *Surprise!* When I couldn't stop crying, didn't do laundry or the dishes or leave my bed for days, he screamed that there was no such thing as mental illness. I should shake it off, pull myself up by my bootstraps, get some fresh air and make his dinner! He screamed about psychiatry, bullshit, psychology, crap, bipolar depressive disorder, excuses, and *me*. When he screamed at me for not doing enough around the house, and then called me lazy - my mentally ill mind snapped to attention. "Hay shud nah bay spakin dat way." I started planning my escape.

I tucked our children into bed. I waited for my husband to fall asleep. I put my plan into action by *doing stuff* around the house. By midnight, I'd torn up the carpeting with a pry bar, then thrown tools and flooring onto the front lawn. The carpet pad followed at 1:00. When I concluded that, underneath the wallpaper I'd stripped, the walls themselves were unacceptable, I decided to replaster.

With a tiny kitchen spatula and a vengeance, I replastered the living room. At 4:00 AM, my groggy spouse came downstairs to inquire about my 'crazy' activities.

"What are you doing, Chris? You're making a lot of noise. What's all the pounding?"

"I'm doing stuff around the house like a good little wife."

"Jesus, I didn't mean you should tear the house apart."

"Hmm. That's too bad. You should have been specific with your instructions."

"What the hell? Where's the recliner?"

"Outside. Excuse me, please."

"Chris, you don't have to do this. Come to bed."

"You're in my way."

"Honey, it's the middle of the night. This is crazy."

A crazy woman would have slapped him with the spatula. Technically, I wasn't nuts, but I was bone marrow angry. As my ancestors whispered to me, "Hay shud shut has mooth." I whispered to Ric, "There is no such thing as mental illness. You said so yourself. Now, leave me alone. I have work to do."

My ancestors and I, God, and my husband had a lively four-way conversation about *doing stuff*. We discussed verbal abuse, respect, mental illness, control, love and divorce, while inch by inch, I plastered. By sunrise we'd covered every sore spot but one.

"Why can't you just be happy?"

"For the same reason you can't just be a lamp, Ric. Our wiring is different. *My* wiring is different. If you don't understand bipolar, after all these years, then you probably never will. I wasn't born just to amuse you. I have a life that I need to live *my way*. If you can't handle it then get out of my way."

He did.

While replastering the living room, I stopped being the maid he could fuck and started being the woman he fell in love with years before. Inch by inch, day by day, I got stronger. I spackled. I reupholstered the furniture. I made an appointment with a psychiatrist. I painted. I refinished the woodwork. I plastered and replastered and plastered some more. I began taking antidepressants. It took me all summer to calm down and finish my project but I *did* stuff around the house. Our marriage was in big trouble but the living room looked great.

I remain bipolar, but <u>we</u> no longer suffer from mental illness. Now that I'm healthy, Ric is quiet. If it occurs to him, there might be an inequity in the work load around our home, he keeps his opinions to himself. He knows I'll *do stuff* about it.

I live in my re-modeled, bipolar world and I like it here. Until I don't. Then I do stuff about it too. A glimpse of myself in the mirror neither sends me on a manic tangent nor into a depressed state. My body, like the living room, has been rearranged, remodeled and plastered to suit my moods.

After my shower I pat myself dry with a big, fluffy towel then spackle the dry wall I call, skin. Back at the front, my skin could have played tug-o-war with a Stretch Armstrong doll and won. Here, in the middle, elasticity comes and goes so I spackle all the cracks and wrinkles. My skin is well worn, but the wrinkles are soft and sweet smelling. I have so many moles and freckles, my brother once connected the dots with an eyebrow pencil as I slept, outlining different constellations. My skin is damaged from cuts and scrapes, burns, the occasional lightning strike, smoking, growing up at the community pool without supervision, sun screen or sense, so moisturizing might be a waste of precious time. I do it anyway, just in case.

I do lots of things just in case. I get in the car, adjust the seat, check the lights, check the mirrors, check all of the gauges then fasten my seat belt — Safety first — before I light a cigarette. So, it doesn't make any sense. Just because I woke up MA doesn't mean I woke up smarter.

Choose Your Poison

We're supposed to get our cholesterol tested. Why? Does my cholesterol need an advance placement score so it can get into a better college? No. A Cholesterol check is one of the myriad things I am supposed to do now that I am middle aged. Because I'm MA, there are thousands of things I don't do. *Don't have to, don't want to, can't make me do anything. I am an MA Queen.* Besides, if I could abstain from food and drink, fasting for twelve hours as a cholesterol check requires, I probably wouldn't have high cholesterol in the first place.

At twenty something, I was anorexic. I didn't eat. I exercised. I weighed myself ten times a day and exercised some more. I believed if I was thin enough then everyone would love me and the universe would be mine. It wasn't. I weighed only ninety-eight pounds when I realized everyone wasn't supposed to love me and the universe belonged to other people.

At thirty something, I tried to fill the black hole in my soul with food. I formed close, personal relationships with Ben & Jerry, The Colonel, Long John Silver and all of the Wendys I met. By thirty-something, I was obese. I didn't love myself. I was hidden under

The Incontinental Divide

one hundred ninety eight pounds of fat and shame so the universe I wanted remained just out of reach.

If I had an epiphany about my body as I left the Front, I don't recall the exact time or date. My moment of Zen probably came as my friend Clarie, lay dying. As the two of us discussed the should-haves, could-haves, wants and needs that won't be met if I don't love myself enough to go meet them before I run out of time, I took a good look at myself. Clarie loved me and wished that I could see the person she saw in me. So, I tried. I keep trying.

Approaching fifty, I've learned to love life and it loves me back! The universe is mine — lumps, bumps, bulges and all. I don't know how much I weigh. I don't care. I still have some food issues, but not with how much to eat.

I try to eat right. (Low carb, less fat, high fiber, no sugar, fewer chemicals, more fruit, less red meat, more vegetables, low sodium, don't eat after 8:00 PM on Tuesdays, if there's a full moon and you're wearing tennis shoes, facing west, blah, blah, blah.) I could starve to death eating right. I've tried. It isn't right. It's right at my age that I should eat whatever I want. Right? I eat what I want when I'm hungry. I also eat what I want because I want it. I choose my poisons.

MA food issues are unique to my age. I strive for balance but reach for the Rolaids. I am well aware of the many foods I *should* avoid because they'll make me burp, give me gas, make me break out in hives, ruin my sleep, curl my toes, straighten my hair or somehow, void the warranty on my MA system.

But, I try to live in the moment. I don't buy green bananas because there's no guarantee I'll be around when they ripen. I buy yellow bananas to display in my matching yellow kitchen. If I live in the moment and actually eat a banana, I'll have vitamins, potassium, the pleasure of sweet, soft, fleshy fruit sliding down my throat - and indigestion for days. I know there are future negative consequences to living in the moment.

I try anyway. I drink regular coffee although it upsets my stomach. What's the point of starting the day drinking a bitter tasting hot liquid that stains your teeth and gives you bad breath if you can't get a caffeine rush? I make it a point to choose my poisons and enjoy my MA moments.

For breakfast, I might choose bananas, Froot Loops and bacon, then burp out a happy little tune to start my day. Even if I nuke that bacon long enough to change its molecular structure, indigestion will be mine, free of charge, no future obligation to do anything but excuse myself, when I belch.

The artificial flavorings in my beloved Froot Loops do a number on my MA system. (Yeah, it's weird.) I'd be better off stringing necklaces with some dental floss and the stale cereal from the bottom of the box than introducing all of those artificial fruity flavors to my digestive system. I eat them anyway. Enjoy the moment.

Midday I might want a snack. Occasionally I crave those candy bars packed with peanuts. But because I'm mildly allergic to peanuts, (which occasionally blister my lips, tongue, gums and throat, swell my eyes shut and close my airway) I live on the edge, and wait until Halloween to choose this poison. When I hear the knock at the door, "Trick-or-Treat!" I'll feel and fumble my way along the wall - drooling, slits for eyes, duck lips – and then answer the door, "What? It's my costume! What? Don't cry. Don't run away little boy. Want some candy?! I've got Snickers!"

If I eat red meat, the timing must be precise. New York Strip at night means the minute I take that first bite I'll hear the crowd cheer as the tuxedo clad announcer starts that rolling moan into the microphone, "aahhlllLLET'SGETREADYTORUMBLE!!!"

Spicy, hot peppers are my absolute favorite I-know-better-but-I-eat-it-anyway food. I go to Tony Paco's Restaurant in downtown Toledo, Ohio to eat a Hungarian style hot dog. The peppers aren't Hungarian, but demonic, evil, fiery, take-over-the-world-one-colon-at-a-time, creatures from another galaxy. I eat one hot dog. My nose runs, my eyes water, I sweat, I get the hiccups and I drink four pitchers of tap beer to wash away the burn. I enjoy the moment that, oohhh - hurts *so* good.

I had fun, right?

After feeding my MA self I know I am required to move the queen around the realm. I must exercise. I've tried exercise videos. It is discouraging that I don't look like any of the participants on screen, none of whom need an exercise routine in the first place. No one on the video is fat. No one is barefoot, sans makeup and bra, wearing an oversized, "I'm not a complete idiot. Some parts are missing." T-shirt, over a pair of tattered plaid boxer shorts. No one sweats. Everyone smiles (like they're having fun!?) What's up with that?

I *do* get plenty of exercise making preparations to watch an exercise video, however. I move heavy furniture out of the way and run back and forth between the kitchen and television for chips and diet soda.

In my living room one evening, my sister Vickie and I attempted to learn line dancing to work off some flab while acquiring new skills. Together, we learned the Achey Breaky Furniture. After a few bottles of wine, much giggling, a cracked lamp and a broken end table, we gave up. I'm not the cowboy hat, boot wearing type, anyway.

Unless, I'm having sex. I could learn *that* exercise routine in a heartbeat. Chaps and a lasso - *Oohh yeah, Ride Em` Cowgirl!*

"We suck at this, you know."

"Yeah but we look good tryin."

"Let's try something else."

"Let's try some more wine."

"Okay, then you can cut my hair."

If I did all of the things I'm supposed to do to live a long, healthy life, I wouldn't have any fun living it. I would never have discovered that the exercise bike is a great place to hang ironing, or if I pay my dentist big bucks, he'll craft special bleaching trays for my teeth which I can wear *any time*. I can bleach the stains caused by coffee drinking and smoking from my teeth *while* I smoke and drink coffee! Ain't life grand?

Dressing The Queen

⚡

I don't recall a day at the Front when I had to *concentrate* on getting dressed. If I was naked, I put clothes on. If I was uncomfortable, I played through the pain.

Here in the middle, grooming is time consuming. MA aches and pains are too numerous to avoid and covering an MA body in age appropriate, socially acceptable attire requires careful planning. Once my skin is spackled and my morning menu planned, I proceed to the next phase of 'Operation: Dress My MA Self.' The engineering, mechanics and physics involved in putting on underwear is spectacular.

Quality is paramount. I don't own ugly underwear. I won't wear cheap underwear. Thanks to Dr. A Ssnoname, my girls and both of my asses are Victoria's Secret's best customers. Even if I choose to wear a belted feed bag, (I might) fish bobber earrings, (I have) and garden clogs, (pick a color) my underwear is fantastic.

Getting dressed is hard work. Today's job requires a pink satin, matching bra and panties, uniform. I've cut the tags from my clothing as I always do - because I'm a freak. Fingernails on a blackboard don't bother me, but a label inside the collar of my blouse will put me over the edge. Clothing tags are like a car ride with my brother when we were kids. — "He's touchin me! Mom! He's touchin me!"

The Incontinental Divide

I'm not going to camp so I don't need a nametag in my underwear. I don't care which designer created my shorts. They're mine now. I paid for them. I read the cleaning, care and feeding instructions before I snipped out the tag. The size labels are gone. They don't mean anything, anyway. A size five in one store might be a zero (like the Emperor's New Clothes) in another. I know how to launder my clothing. I know what fits and what doesn't. I know I'd rather be naked but they frown upon *that* at the grocery store so I wear only what feels good, minus the labels.

To tether the girls I put the pink satin number on my back, hook it in front, twirl it around my ribs while leaning forward so the girls can swing freely as I line up the target cups. Left arm goes through the strap first. D precedes C in my bra alphabet because I need my right hand free to make any necessary Boss side (big boob) adjustments before I harness (little boob) the Apprentice. I wiggle-jiggle the girls into place as I stand upright to check my cleavage. A little cleavage is a beautiful thing. Too much and I'll choke to death. I *could* put the removable pad in the right cup to make my breasts symmetric - but I don't. I bend at the waist, pull the bra away from my chest ever so slightly, give the girls a split second of emancipation, tuck, push, wiggle, stand-up and Bra-llelujah! Move over nuclear energy, I've harnessed some real power!

If you are paying attention during MA morning rituals, then generic panty liners are fine. I never felt the need to purchase the more expensive, 'Breathable' panty liners. If you're breathing through a panty liner then you have larger issues than staying feminine fresh all day. If you are not paying attention when you place a panty liner, then, say, the phone rings, you pick up the receiver and pull up your panties at the same time – your conversation will be brief.

"HellOuch! Ouch! Ouch! Call back!"

If you can't breathe through the pain then you should consider purchasing the fancy *breathable* panty liners. With the money you save on a do-it-yourself-Brazilian wax job, you can afford them. *All* panty liners remind me to thank my mother for not coddling me - for making me tough.

I am too lazy to wear make up. I am too vain to *not* wear make up. I compromise. I wear mascara, lipstick and use an eyebrow pencil to fill in the blanks on my corresponding facial spaces. I wasn't invited to the Presidential Inaugural Ball and I haven't delivered a speech at the United Nations, won a Pulitzer or accepted an Academy Award in days, so most mornings, there is no special incentive to make me spend an extra fifteen minutes in front of a mirror camouflaging my skin.

Just as life is too uncertain to buy green bananas, life's too short to drink cheap wine. (Which, coincidentally, makes me burp.) Life's already wrought with pain so there is no reason to utilize the medieval torture device called an eyelash curler. Without highlighting my eyelids or enhancing the apples of my cheeks, I do housework, get the oil changed in the car, attend a meeting of the County Child Abuse Prevention Team, work an eight hour shift in a doctor's office, make dinner, walk the dog, write a page or two, and sleep soundly at night. Mary Kay might have a pink stroke but I manage to get happily through my day with little makeup and imbalanced skin tones.

Head to toe, I am a Queen so I wear what I want, when I want. I've been wearing stilettos since I was in pre-school. Just kidding. I didn't go to pre-school. One of the most comforting sounds of my childhood was the click of my mother's heels across the kitchen linoleum when she came home from work. I'd hear that *tap* and know the world was safe and warm. *Tap, tap, tap.* Dinner's on the way. *Tap, tap.* A hug is right behind.

Somewhere in the owner's manual for my MA self, there is a chapter about wearing sensible shoes, but I lost my book. The only shoes that make sense to me are the pretty ones that pinch and give me bunions and force an unnatural arch causing me to walk on my tip toes. High heels are a comfort, regardless of the pain they cause. Sure, I'm crippled after working (Monday, 9 to 5) in stilettos but didn't my legs look great? Oh, I *own* sensible shoes. I have the obligatory leather loafer flats, (gym teacher dress shoes) in my closet but I don't actually *wear* them unless I have to. (Tuesday, 9 to 5.).

I read somewhere that a person's feet and ears (or is it the nose?) keep growing over the course of one's lifetime. How unfair is that? I just break in that new pair of shoes and I have to buy new, bigger shoes! (Okay, I like that. I could never have too many shoes.) But, my ears and nose? Why can't my breasts and my ass keep growing? Well

The Incontinental Divide

into my 70's I could have a rack like Pamela Anderson's to hang the dry cleaning on and a big ole shelf butt to display a future collection of Hummels. If life was fair I could swing that rack and shake my bum around the room once a week, to dust.

Life's not fair. (Surprise!) The breasts, ass, feet, I can handle, but I'd have no chance of camouflaging a big honking nose or floppy Dumbo ears. I have to let nature take it's course and work with whatever I've got.

My gray hairs go wherever they damn well please; straight up in the air, sharp curve to the left. They're as thick as table legs and as surly as I was as a teenager.

I tear celebrity coif photos, no gray hairs in sight, from a magazine, to take to Great Clips. *Make me look like this.* When I get a twelve dollar haircut that looks pretty good, I tip the hairdresser one hundred percent. Even a twelve dollar haircut that looks like a twelve dollar haircut means I got my money's worth. My gray hairs don't care. They have their own agenda. I let them have their way.

I am clean and soft. I smell delicious. Bottom to top and head to toe, I am spackled and shined, tweezed, coifed, smoothed, tucked, dressed and accessorized. I let the dog in for another drink from the toilet. I pour myself a cup of coffee, put a Kleenex in my pocket and check Caller ID to see who phoned while I was pulling up my big girl panties. My dish to pass is ready for the picnic. The picnic probably started without me while I was trying to get ready, but that's the trade off — speed for substance. Youth for MA experience. Youth for MA... what is it that I have again? What's my MA prize? Is it a con, a rip-off, a cosmic joke? Nah. A girl's gotta do what a girl's gotta do to wear an MA crown.

Christina Crall-Reed

The Incontinental Divide

Life is plump with funny stories; funny haha, funny twisted, funny tragic, but laughing so hard I wet myself was a foreign concept at the Front. Humor and bladder control were not connected. My delightful stories took an ominous turn when I, Princess HaHa, left the Front and boarded the PP Express to middle age. I traveled across the Incontinental Divide.

Once upon a time in a supermarket checkout line not far from here, the beautiful Queen HaHa... (Yes. I *am* The Queen. No. I am *not* an aging Princess. Yes. I staged my *own* coronation. Yes. It *is* all about me. No. You *can't* have the remote. Yes. I straightened the guest towels *again*. No. Bitch, is *not* an insult. Yes. I *can* eat chocolate with Fritos. No. I *didn't* make you dinner. No. There *aren't* any Fritos left. Yes. I get *distracted, sidetracked, off on another tangent,* so!? Deal with it. *I am The Queen!*)

Once upon a time in a supermarket checkout line not far from here, the beautiful Queen HaHa laughed so hard at <u>The National Enquirer</u> headline, "Pee Wee Herman's Face On Mars!" that she wet herself. Drawing her cloak tightly around her mid section, the mortified Queen ran off, leaving behind a melting quart of blue moon ice cream; a friend's bewildered toddler still strapped in the cart and a

The Incontinental Divide

Malibu Barbie checkout clerk screaming, "Ma'am! Do you want your receipt? Madame! You forgot your…" Oh, and a glass slipper.

Back at the castle, the distressed Queen drew court and counsel near, "What to do? What to do?"

"Don't laugh," said the foreign minister.

"Put a cork in it," said the court jester.

"It's part of the aging process for some people," said the royal physician.

"Oh, shut up!" said the Queen. "This can't be right?!"

Laughing so hard I wet myself was the ultimate aging-body betrayal.

How humiliating was it? Very. Could I ever shop in that store again? Probably. Could I really die of embarrassment? Probably not.

I'd walked through fire to become an MA Queen. Could I let a leak in my big girl panties douse those flames? *Very, probably, no fricken way!*

It's not right that a beautiful MA Queen should be forever seated on a porcelain throne lest she giggle, sneeze or cough a bit too vigorously, and blow a gasket or water the lawn.

In the land of MA there are knights in shining armor to help us across the Incontinental Divide.

Sir Depends can come to the rescue. Anyone can wear those 'get back into life pads', just don't get back into the pool. (I stand near any available beach chair to observe and interact with the other MA and wee diaper clad folk.) I pay special attention to the Pampered toddler I earlier abandoned at the grocery store, hoping his mother will take pity on me because I can't go in the water. Perhaps she will think, I too am cute with my bulging bottom and my bowlegged cowboy my-thighs-will-never-touch-again, walk. Perhaps she will forgive me. Perhaps not. It depends.

Sir Takeapill is most efficient. Takeapill works. Should you choose to use the services of this good knight, take a second job or a second mortgage or a second to transfer all of the funds from your off shore accounts to pay the hefty price Takeapill commands. Do not attempt to garden or go singin' in the rain, because gotta go-gotta go right now-pharmaceuticals, will suck the moisture from the soil beneath your feet and dehydrate the clouds above your head to store *liquid* in each and every one of your internal organs until you bloat and float hours later into the bathroom. Prepare to remain seated for an extended period of time as it takes the better part of Spring planting season to drain your tank.

Sir Loin of Steak, also known as, the Earl of Exercises, A.K.A., the Lord of Lamaze and King of Kegel, is the champion of muscle control for every damsel in overactive bladder distress. Kegels (pelvic floor muscle exercises) can help slow the flow when you gotta' go. Kegel exercises were the cornerstone of the natural childbirth classes spouse and I attended in our twenties. Lessons learned at the Front are essential to happy life in the Middle. Without King Kegel, this princess would not be an MA Queen. Without King Kegel, I would have drowned while crossing the Incontinental Divide.

King Kegel

At Lamaze class in 1978, my 'Breathe Honey' coach and I lay around some pregnant stranger's living room floor on mats and blankets. With pillows tucked under my knees, between my breasts, beneath my head and squishing the fake ficus tree in the corner, we practiced muscle contraction / relaxation / breathing techniques. True, muscle contractions, panting and heavy breathing probably got me there in the first place but all the breathing I'd done naturally since I was born wasn't natural enough for natural childbirth. So, naturally, I took a panting / heavy breathing / Lamaze class.

Pregnant Stranger and the Chief Breathe Honey (Large and In Charge because they'd done this before) welcomed us, and five additional pregnant stranger classmates with pillows and 'Breathe Honeys,' into their home.

When everyone was comfortable (comfortable never happened until the end of the class when they brought out the snack tray and seven starving, round bellied women trampled their significant others to get at the last apple bran muffin. *"Look, I got the apple... Oh, am I standing on your throat? Just breathe, honey."*) Large and In Charge began a series of gentle chants to help everyone relax. "Breathe in, breathe out and again – in, out, breathe in, breathe out."

The pillow under my side pushed my enormous breasts into my windpipe. I was in trouble early on.

"Take a cleansing breath and everyone sit up."

Fifteen minutes later every Buddha in the bunch somehow managed to grunt and groan and roll into some type of seated position in preparation for Kegel exercises.

"Your vagina is an elevator. Gently contract those muscles and pull that elevator up to the first floor… doors open and relax… Contract a little tighter this time… squeeze… second floor… hold the elevator… tighter… and doors open…"

Hold the elevator my eye! Two months later, when my water broke, I shoved a disposable diaper into my panties to catch the overflow, but I didn't like the crinkley noise it made when I walked. So, I donned a pair of my husband's large, comfy, cotton briefs then stuffed them with all of my clean dishtowels. By the time (blizzard in Wisconsin time) I waddled through the snow and the hospital doors, wearing men's drawers, wet kitchen linens and open-toed sandals on my swollen feet, I was terrified to ride the elevator up to the Maternity Ward. I had never Kegeled above the third floor!

Breathe in breathe out and again, r e l a x…

"You're going to *prep* me? You're going to shave *what* with that disposable razor?" *I don't think I like you, nurse.*

Breathe in, breathe out, in and out and r e l a x…

"No, I don't want an enema." *you Licensed Practical Freak. I don't want a root canal right now either.* "I want drugs. I want…"

Breathe in. Breathe out. Breathe in. Breathe out and relax…

"I want morphine and heroin and whatever drugs you've got. No, this isn't a Lamaze delivery this is a *baby* delivery, my first squeeze a human from my loins experience and I don't want to breathe into that paper bag. I don't care if I hyperventilate!" *I want to be unconscious you Registered Nurse Ratchet, you.*

Breathe in. Breathe out. Breathe in. Breathe out and r e l a x…

"Seriously, Ric? You're asking *me* why the woman in the next room is screaming? My best guess is she's in *labor* and her elevator's stuck because she doesn't have a 'Breathe Honey' husband for a coach!" *Dope! If you ever touch me again I'll...*

Breathe in. Breathe out, and pant, pant, pant. Breathe in. Breathe out.

"What do you mean the doctor isn't here yet? What is this, the Twilight Zone?" Pant. Pant. Pant...

"There are doctors everywhere - it's a hospital!"

Breathe in. Breathe out and relax and...

"Can I *hold* it!?" *You Succubus! You, Top of your class, Soul-Sucker School of Nursing graduate!* "No! I won't wait for the doctor! I *AM* breathing, Honey! I'M BREATHING AND PUSHING!"

I lost the urge to pull her chin whisker out with my teeth when Nurse Succubus presented our slimy little, cottage cheese covered son to me.

"He's beautiful." I cooed.

My desire to have 'Breathe Honey' dismembered had nearly vanished when he said, "He looks like a boxer. He's all beat up."

"No, he's beautiful."

"Why's his head look pointed?"

"Push a ripe honeydew through a little PVC pipe, you'll see. He looks like his Daddy, yes he does."

"What's that ring around his mouth? Looks like a hickey."

"He's been sucking his thumb for months. That's so precious. He looks like a drunk put lipstick on him. He's beautiful though. Him's so precious, yes him is."

I was gone. Happily gone. I was Ga-Ga and head over heels in love with the toothless, bald, midget I'd just met. Gone, was the carefree girl. Gone was an eight hour sleep. Gone, was the firm young body. Gone, was total bladder control. Gone, was dry-clean-only clothing... *Whoa. Whoa! Back the cart up! What was that about bladder control? Both of us are going to be in diapers? Nurse? Oh, Florence Nightengale!?*

"When you're healed..."

"You mean when Dr. Start Without Me, stops bringing Med students and candy stripers and janitors into my room to check the recession of my impressive hemorrhoids?"

"When you're home you can do Kegels to…"

"You mean 'Elevator Up!' kegels? It's a two story house. Can't I just take the stairs?"

"Kegel exercises can help strengthen those PC muscles and give…"

"Politically Correct muscles?"

"If you're not going to listen."

"Sorry. I'm listening." *soul sucker.* "I always make bad jokes when I'm nervous. This new mother thing is kinda scary." *Soul sucking succubus.*

"As soon as you're feeling up to it and you have doctor's approval, start doing the same Kegel exercises you learned in Lamaze. Tightening and strengthening the muscles of your pelvic floor will improve bladder control *and* help your sex life."

The Jeopardy theme music was playing in my head, until I heard the word, "Sex."

The only thing worse than picturing this woman having sex, where all manner of whips, chains, black leather and hospital Jell-O cups would surely be involved, was to picture my Grandma Melva, who had birthed sixteen children; had breasts the size and shape of watermelons rolling down to her waist and a butt like a two cushion love seat, in a thong! *Eewwe.*

"You're looking a bit pale. You should rest for a while."

"No. I'm nauseous."

"Don't forget, Kegels, Control, and Sex."

Forget!? I'll need therapy. I'll have nightmares for the rest of my life. Eewwe and don't forget, Eewwe!

The nightmares ended when I discovered that Nurse Succubus knew two things. Not only can those exercises strengthen the PC (pee continuously) muscles but Kegels are a turn on!

God Save The Queen

The Kegel premise is simple: When doing pelvic floor exercises only the pelvic floor should move. Done properly, pelvic floor exercises can be done anywhere. The Kegel premise is only half true.

When you move any floor a whole lotta' things move with it. If I move the kitchen floor for instance, the refrigerator, stove, baseboards, kitchenette, cupboards, things in the cupboards I don't want my spouse to use to 'move the floor' with, (like the Irish linen tablecloth he'll wipe his hands on or the twenty dollar, Pampered Chef spatula he'll apply grout with) - *all* have to move. The steak knives I'll stab him with *definitely* have to move. Because, the do-it-yourself, move the floor project really means do it his way.

"No. Not like that. Do it like I did! No, over here. Hand me that thing. Help me. Could you just please get out of my way? The other thing! Will you make me a sandwich? You're in the way again."

Move a floor -- any floor, kitchen floor, pelvic floor — and prepare to move everything on it, around it, attached to it or near it.

The Kegel promise is more realistic than the premise: When doing pelvic floor exercises every nerve ending and muscle fiber in the pelvic floor moves. The Kegel Promise: *Oohh Yeah! Right there.* Done properly, pelvic floor exercises *can* be done anywhere.

In the privacy of your own home - on the couch, in the recliner, making dinner, in the shower, you can Kegel wherever, whenever you choose. You can ride that Kegel elevator to the top of your own Sears Tower if you want to. Whatever trips your trigger, gunslinger, it's your Okay Corral. Outside your home, however, you must use caution *and* discretion when contracting those muscles.

Where and when to Kegel are as important as how. 'Oohh Yeah! Right there' must factor geography into the equation. Kegels during your commute? Okay. It must be socially acceptable to slide off your seat on the subway. People do it all the time. Kegels at work? Also okay. While getting paid to work nine to five you can take your office chair for an enjoyable spin around the computer. Cool!

Drive and Kegel at the same time? - Not cool. Not okay. You can probably talk your way out of a speeding ticket with, "I was sneezing, officer. I have to pee, officer. I was singing along with the radio, *bad boys bad boys whatcha' gonna do?* officer." But squeeze those muscles together while driving from point 'A' to point *oh, oh yeah, oh oohoh!*, hop the curb and take out the mailbox on the neighbor's front porch, just once, and Loo-cee, you gah sum splainin' to do!

Even if you paste a demure, *Hello officer I'm someone's mother* smile, over your, *That was great for me how was it for you?* grin; even if you offer to replace the mailbox with one finer than your own, you can't talk your way out of a Kegel crash. Good night, brave knight, and God Save the Queen, I tried.

Gray Matters

Now that I've landed here in the middle, I sometimes think my memory is not as sharp as it used to be. If it's not, (this is one of the perks of being MA) I don't remember! I remember the really good times and the really bad ones and everything in between. The good, the bad and everything in between is called life. I remember life. Not always in chronological order, but I remember.

The day my youngest son came home from school nearly bursting with excitement trying to share some new found knowledge with me, I paid attention! Sons (boys, AKA men with training wheels) usually have to be prodded and poked and pinched and tortured until their little spirits break before they'll share news of their school day with you.

"Guess what I learned in school today," was angel-speak. It was a miracle!

Jumping up and down before me was the same child, my sweet baby, last of my lively, boisterous, beautiful brood, who announced on his first day of kindergarten years before, that I would not be giving him a ride to school in the family station wagon as planned. Unable to convince him that the black paint and wood paneled wagon was special, because no one else drove a wooden car, Bailey wanted his independence. "I'm riding the bus. I don't need you anymore."

Oh? OUCH. Just pull a strip of wood from the side of the car and stab it through my heart why don'tcha? OUCH! Ouch, ouch. "Okay. You're a big boy. You can ride the bus."

Okay. I was a big girl so I followed the bus. Okay. I staked out the school parking lot. I cried a little bit. Okay. I sobbed. Through my tears I watched him take those few little steps with his cute little back pack and his bright little tennis shoes, walking into the open arms of his new, *He loves her more than me,* teacher. But I got over it.

I got over it when Bailey, Mr. *I don't need you anymore,* Mr. *Are you stalking me again Mom? Sorry. I'm over it. Really.* When Bailey was prepared to tell me something he'd learned, without the usual post-school inquisition, I was prepared to listen.

In one breathless sentence he said, "Your brain is all gray and wrinkled and inside it all of the wrinkles have what you think and what you remember in them so every time you learn anything new or see something you never saw before and smell something or go someplace or hear a sound that's new your brain makes a new wrinkle and keeps the new stuff in it so every time you learn something new you get a new wrinkle in your brain!"

"Say what?"

"And men use the left side of their brains more and that's the logical side and women use the right but women can do both at the same time better because they have more connections between the two sides."

My gray matter throbbed. *Connections. Logical. Boy speak big words. Me no understand.*

"Mom?"

I'm not always the sharpest knife in the drawer but I was slowly beginning to grasp the magnitude of my son's news. He knew the secrets of the universe. He had the answer to THE Questions.

Why am I here and what's it all about?

Life Is About Getting Gray And Wrinkled!

No wonder my friend's barely old enough to speak, daughter

told her Grandma that Barney the dinosaur was gay. She must have overheard the, sexual orientation of The Tele Tubbies/Big Bird debate, between my sons, months before. Clever toddler stored the information in a new little wrinkle in her still wet gray matter then accessed and shared this information at the first inappropriate opportunity presented to her. Kids are awesome!

"Mom!!"

Occasionally, I leave the den headed for the kitchen intent on filling my coffee cup. I pause to dust off the TV screen with my sleeve, notice the cord to the vacuum is sticking out beneath the closet door, open the door to wrap the cord, spend the next half hour rearranging photo albums in the closet, run to answer the phone, trip over the vacuum cord I forgot to move, tell my girlfriend whom I just spoke to that morning that my knees hurt from falling on the hardwood floor, and the two of us talk about her daughter and my kids and men and the weather and food and sure, I have that recipe, so I go to the kitchen where I turn and circle back. I forgot my coffee mug in the den.

I do not, in fact, have Circling Disease as my husband always claims. Circling Disease is a hideous disorder (akin to 'Mad Cow' without all the publicity) where insane sheep and other livestock wander and rotate, twitching, one hoof planted in the dirt, aimlessly circling themselves until they die.

"Mom!!!"

It may appear to the casual observer, (my husband) that I am an insane ewe spinning my days away. I *may* have a little trouble focusing from time to time, (staying on task; remembering I'm an adult, etc.) but I'm not a diseased sheep. My mind is sound. Mostly.

I'm sharp enough to recall that the man who questions my sensibilities while I clean the house, is the same man who screams at the injustice of Pete Rose, not being 'indicted' into the Baseball Hall of Fame.

I know that the man sitting on the couch, questioning my sensibilities while I clean the house, is the same man who promised to perform the 'Hemlock' Maneuver on me if I were choking.

I am well aware that the man (whose outdoor property includes more than four hundred acres of farmland and woods; three stocked ponds; flora and fauna of every variety and species in the Midwest) on the couch, feet up, whining for a snack on a beautiful spring day while I clean around him, is *indoors* watching some camo-clad Bubba, ketch bigole' feesh, on the *Outdoor* channel.

He watches me work. He mentions circling. I leave the room, return with a tray, and he motions me aside. He can't see the TV. I spin around and hear, "Honey. Circling. Disease."

My overworked mind snaps. That's it! The man on the couch is about to have a close encounter of the white light kind. I'll *circle* him before I move in for the kill. I'll broadcast the hunt on the Outdoor channel. Yassirree, BillyJoeCletus. The man, the white light…

"Mmaaa! Are you listening?"

I make the connection between peace and prison. "Sorry, B. I was fantasizing. And don't call me Mmaaa."

"Did you know that before, about the brain wrinkles?"

"Actually B, I didn't. I did not know that."

"Ha! You just got a new wrinkle! You learned something new and got a new wrinkle! Mom's got a wrinkle."

"I knew it. Kids cause wrinkles. I knew it. I knew it!"

My MA memories are like the Christmas decorations individually blanketed in bubble wrap in the Rubbermaid container on the top shelf of the garage storage cabinet. The stuff is there, I just can't 'have at it' right this second.

I try to remember a classmate's last name. I knew his name a moment ago. I try to recall. I listen for echoes of old conversations rolling around in my head. I know what he looked like during the Bicentennial fireworks display at that park… by that place… with the things… I was there with that one guy… You know… and cousin what's her face… I try. I reach. I fumble in the dark then surrender.

So, *Life Is About Getting Gray And Wrinkled*. Why not? That's as good an answer as any, to life's big, 'What's it all about' question. Life is about constantly expanding my gray matter. Gray hair might just be the outward indication that the gray matter from my brain is expanding to explore new territory. So, if I'm alive, I'll wrinkle. If I think about life, I'll wrinkle. If I think about wrinkling, I'll wrinkle my

The Incontinental Divide

wrinkles. I finally get my ducks in a row then lose the map to the duck pond? That's life too. Since worry causes gray hair and wrinkles, I'm not going to worry about lining up ducks. Who needs organized ducks anyway? MA memory loss is merely a storage problem. The memory is there, I simply need to access it.

Months of middle age life will pass. I'll someday take the step ladder to the cabinet in the garage, climb up to the top shelf, pull at the corner of the Rubbermaid containing those Christmas ornaments, it will slip, hit me in the forehead and — Oh yeah! My classmate's last name was Elliott! Because I'm MA I don't have to stress about remembering every detail. I've still got it somewhere. In some wrinkle.

Use It Or Lose It

⚡

Twenty somethings might be saving themselves for that special someone or that special something they haven't found yet. Not me. I'm not savin' nothin' for no one! At fifty-ish I want the whole Christmas Club spent by the Fourth of July, in case there's a sexpiration date printed somewhere on my label. Sex is like the Medical Flex Spending account I have set up at work. I put my money in - if I need dentures or stronger bifocals - just in case. Now, whatever is in my account is mine for a limited time. Before the end of the year, I have to use it or lose it.

Research shows (Yes, research. I have a lot of free time to read, research and develop neumonic devices to help slow MA memory loss. My schedule is flexible even if my spine is not.) if you want to enjoy sex more - enjoy more sex!

'Survey says' the sexually active body gives off pheromones (think: sprite on pixie orgy soundtrack - fairy moans) to attract the opposite sex. Sex produces estrogen in women to help their hair shine and skin glow. Sex stretches every muscle in your body, burns calories, and is ten times more effective (helping you relax) than Valium. Sex is the safest tranquilizer ever.

Sex releases endorphins into the blood producing a sense of

The Incontinental Divide

well-being and euphoria, (think: the opposite of what it is because it sounds like something nasty requiring prescription ointment - Eewwe4 E Ah) so sex is a cure for mild depression. I'm happier already. Sex can relieve headaches by releasing tension formed in the brain. Finally, (this is my personal favorite) without having to spray anything up your nose, (unless that's what floats your boat during the regatta) sex is a natural decongestant.

Sex is a cure for the common cold!

Okay, maybe not a cure, but sex can unblock a stuffy nose. Move over Vicks Vapo-Rub!

If I feel a sexpiration date approaching my MA self, I won't panic. I've decided not to worry that things are not as they once were, where they once were, moving as they once did. My MA body is part of one of those 'use it or lose it' deals. As long as I keep moving and enjoy what *is*, my research will pay off and I'll never reach a sexpiration date.

Once I left the Front, I experienced some minor technical difficulties, but I still feel no need to panic. I'm old enough to be an MA Queen so I'm old enough to weather almost any crisis — especially the fun ones.

I'm working on a fun crisis. Men who buy Porsches or Jags at my age are rumored to have compensation issues. (Women *have* no penis; so they have no compensation issues. Women who want, but *get* no penis have compensation issues.) There is probably some MA crisis brewing when I'm considering buying, not a sports car, but a Harley.

I have the money and the questionable fantasies - enough of each to justify the purchase of a motorcycle. Like the comedian who does the bit about having 'stuff' I too, have lots of stuff. I have stuff I don't need, stuff I don't know how to use, stuff I like, stuff I use all the time and stuff I'm keeping until I can replace it with other stuff. It's not that I need a Harley. I want one. (Wind in my face - hot, leather-clad steel and chrome rumbling between my thighs.) When I was twenty five, I would have grabbed a vibrator and turned on an oscillating fan. Now, I want more stuff.

Oh, sure, I've got a Dual-head-twin-action-12-speed-four-on-the-floor-fuel-injected-humming-hemi-carb-burnin' vibrator that rides *like* a Harley. When I introduced myself to my new best friend, the package said his name was Big Boy. Marvels of modern science and ain't technology grand? — I almost passed out. *He* may not replace the kisses on the back of my neck that make my outsides tight and my insides liquid, but Big Boy will do in a pinch. I like that pinch. Paramedics will probably find me on the day bed in the spare room, spread eagle, flowing like a mountain stream and grinning from ear to ear. They'll shake their heads and sadly tsk, tsk, "She wasn't wearing a helmet."

Twenty-five or fifty, it's nice to make new friends but I still want a Harley. It's got all the right stuff. Size *does* matter when you're cruising through a use it or lose it life. And honey, if you ain't cruisin', you're losin'.

Don't Think

Regardless of size, regardless of age, no human beings should think about how they look during sex. We look stupid. You look stupid. I look stupid. With weird sounds, messy fluids, eyes rolling, parts flapping - everyone looks stupid during sex.

Not long ago, I dropped a mirror on the ceramic tile then strained to pick it up, surprised and pleased it didn't break. I caught a less than flattering glimpse of myself in that mirror and had a revelation. That's what I look like during sex! Surprised, pleased and strained, with all of my loose-skinned body parts swinging forward. If I thought about how sex looks I would never enjoy sex again.

Sex, at any age, is all about how it feels. When I'm all lathered up and steamy and I slip and fall out of the shower I shared with my lover just seconds before landing backwards on the toilet, cracking the porcelain and my ribs, I can't think about how silly I look laying with my partner on the floor next to me. He's worried. I've got the wind knocked out of me, legs up over the side of the tub, and water is spraying all over the bathroom. If I could catch my breath I'd laugh at how ridiculous we look and I'd forget all about the lather and the steam that got me there in the first place. MA sex *has to* be about how it feels, because sometimes, the visual just isn't pretty.

I refuse to think about how I look during sex. While I'm wasting time thinking, *I wonder if my jiggly thighs and buttocks are unattractive?* he's thinking, "Score! Thighs! Ass! Score!" He may not be the chiseled-I just want to cuddle-millionaire-poet rubbing my feet after an evening of ballroom dancing, as we discuss the program we're watching together on Lifetime, but I'm probably not the mute-super model-nymphomaniac-liquor store owner he was hoping for either. I'll get over it.

There are thousands of things a person can do to stay interested in, and entertained by sex. Games and stories we enjoyed as children can be adapted to fit our adult life styles. Since life is all about change, I've tried to adapt.

I can put on a blonde wig and read, *Goldilocks and the Three Bare Ass Nekkids*. Or I could try, 'Little Red Riding Hood'. "My, um, Grandmother, what big BVD's you have."

Naked Twister: Much more fun as a nude adult than it was at my eleventh birthday party. Left hand green. Right foot red. Twister! That's not your foot! And *that's* not a blue circle! Puts a whole new spin on the game, don't you think?

Hide 'N' Seek is self-explanatory.

Chutes and Ladders can't be explained without pictures.

Strip Racko? He'll cheat. I can't prove it. He's never won a game of Racko before, but the minute *my* clothing is at stake, he wins every round. What's up with that? I did win a Strip Racko match by default one evening when a half crazed field mouse, poisoned by the bait I set out in the garage, ran into our living room. As I sat naked (except for the afghan draped over my shoulders) with my husband, who had yet to lose his underwear and loose-fit pants, frantically lining our Racko cards up in numeric order, the rodent circled us. I jumped onto the couch with my cards and blanket. Ric tipped his card rack over and screamed like a hot tea kettle when the mouse ran up his pant leg as he tried to strip. Racko! I won! He was naked first!

When childhood entertainments just don't cut it for me as an adult, I try a new locale or a new outfit or a little role playing or all of the above.

I can come home from work, tired and hungry, in need of some attention and still make dinner. He can come home from work, tired, hungry and ornery, plop down on the couch totally oblivious to the beautiful woman (me) in the kitchen, turn on ESPN and sit complaining about his less than lovely day. He doesn't greet me or touch me. He doesn't ask about me at all. I suck it up, try a different approach, take his dinner to him and smile. He continues his tirade and complains about the meal. My ancestors begin whispering to me. "Hay's ahn eejit."

I know. I also know a sure fire way to help us both relax. I invite him to join me. He looks past me and yells something at the television. I shower alone.

"Da man must be daft."

He is.

I emerge from the bathroom, looking great, smelling delicious. The minute he hears the door open, he resumes the harangue. He isn't speaking to me. He is simply speaking in my direction. He talks about my widowed friend - how tired *she* looks, how stressed out *she* must be, the yard work *she* needs done, how tired *he* is, how hard *he* works, on and on and...

I spoke with my friend a few hours ago. She *is* tired and stressed. But she's not here. I am, in the moment, in the flesh. I tell him I don't want to talk about my friend right now. I stand in the doorway, backlit by candles. I call out, "Here, kitty, kitty." We don't have a cat.

He rambles on about house repairs and my friend.

My ancestors whisper, "Hay should shut has mooth ahn open has oyz."

I meow. I point my black, silk-gloved finger at him, curling, inviting. Come here. "Here, kitty, kitty…"

He mentions my friend's weed control problem so I tell him to stop talking, *now*.

"Da man must be deef ahn domb. Tis woeful."

I try, one more time, to get his attention. I blow out the candles and mew gently. I meow. I purr - a deep, throaty, moaning meow.

He yells something at the referees on ESPN.

My ancestors yell, "Daft EEJIT!"

I yank the cat ears from my sweet smelling hair. I know he can see my well rounded curves; my moist, soft skin beneath just enough black satin to cover my pink parts, as I move catlike past the doorway to storm upstairs.

"Wait! Whoa! What are you wearing? Hey, wait. Honey, that was great! Let me see what you're wearing! Wait!"

"Bite me, tom cat!"

Guns were smokin! He took a shower fast enough to break the sound barrier, but by the time Marshall Dillon came to bed, Miss Kitty was one pissed off pussy. Maybe that's why my mother always told me not to go to bed angry. Not because anger will ruin my sleep. Not because I'll still be resentful in the morning and treat my mate to a variation of the old 'silent treatment' joke. We don't speak to each other, but exchange curt notes for rudimentary communication.

HIM: Wake me at 5:00. I have an early flight.

ME: You're leaving town? Hooray! When he wakes at 9:00, he sees my note on his pillow: Wake up Honey. It's 5:00!

I won't go to bed angry because I'll wake up satiated, (next to my snoring husband whose backside is mysteriously impaled with a cat ears headband) but I'll be paralyzed with pain. Did you know women could bruise their ovaries? We can. Sing along with me girls, "Anything he can do I can do better." Bruising ones ovaries is the female equivalent of getting kicked in the testes. Hard. You do the math, draw the pictures, and write the notes. If you go to bed angry *and* horny you can cause permanent structural damage to your MA self.

If you have to think, no righteous MA Queen should be thinking about anything but sex, during sex. Just because we females have all that connective tissue between the two hemispheres of our brains, doesn't mean we have to use it. I've got a snow cone maker and roofer's knee pads too, but I don't have to use them... hmmm... a little shaved ice... someone on their knees... (Ooh, sorry, I digress.) Just because I have options doesn't mean I have to use them all during sex.

When I can't help but let my mind wander to tasks other than the one at hand, I know I'm missing *the* point of pleasure. This is all I get! This moment is it! Enjoy! During sex I force myself to forget the oil change in the mini van or the new wallpaper samples, unless I'm planning to haul supplies to redecorate my G-spot.

There are times I insist on using *all* of my time efficiently. Sometimes I'm really 'into' multitasking so I read the Kama Sutra. The Kama Sutra is *all* about doing fifty different things *all* at once. Just look at the pictures:

"Look at this one."

"Upside down."

"I can't do *that* upside down."

"The *book is* upside down, Dope."

'You want me to put my foot *where*? So you can put your arm on *what*? You think *that* will fit *there*? Facing the headboard? But I have errands to run in the morning!'

Now that I'm MA I think I'll stop thinking about things that require more feeling than thought. I like the thought of not thinking. I think.

World Piece

⚡

I know no valid reason to deny myself or my partner, the gift of sex. If we're just not in the mood, fine. If someone is ill or injured, okay, we'll take a rain check. But, if I withheld sex from my partner as a *punishment* because *I* was angry about something - well, that would be goofier than the goofy way we look when we're goofing around.

My man won't understand how a 'compliment' like, "I married you because you're a natural. You're not all skinny and made-up like other women." might affect his sex life. He will *never* make the connection between his being naughty, and my reluctance to be naughty with him, because he has a 'pain release' lever to prevent my anger from reaching his brain.

Pull The Lever. He feels good. It's that simple.

A standard-issue piece of equipment for men, the Pain Release Lever is durable, pliable, washable, portable, and certain 99.9 percent of the time, to make him feel better when activated.

His bad day at the office is a great night at home, if you just pull the lever. When his team doesn't make the playoffs or win the pennant, simply pull the Lever and he'll cheer up. Pull the Lever, then order a pizza? He'll forget about ESPN. If you pull the Lever and deliver that

The Incontinental Divide

pizza with a cold beer, you can eliminate hunger in the world. Deliver that pizza and cold beer *naked?* Pull the Lever to achieve World Peace.

Women may hesitate to attain world peace, because operation of *our* machinery can be complicated and time consuming. Female equipment is compact, built in to several control panels with a series of buttons to push and bells to ring to make her feel good.

This is not a design flaw. If females had an easy access button, the world population would explode. Everyone would be pushing buttons. No one would do the shopping and our economy would collapse. Deafened by the constant high-pitched squeals of women all over the world screaming, "Oh Yeah! That's the button!" neglected children would be scouring the countryside, drinking warm beer and foraging for leftover pizza. No one would stop to ask for directions, so as a species, we'd be lost. We females are complicated for good reason.

Some women need a brilliant engineer with a Ph.D in button pushing to light up those control panels. More women could use the services of a gifted machine operator to blow the whistles and flash those lights. But, most women are paired with a basic mechanic. He has general knowledge of her working parts, some button manipulation skills, and of course, the Lever is in his toolbox.

If you're avoiding use of the Lever because *your* control panel is gathering dust, fetch the operator's manual from your glove box and learn to work the buttons yourself. Then, show your mechanic what's under the hood. Once he discovers his button pushing skills can only enhance operation of the Lever, you'll both be driving finely tuned machines.

Withholding sex because you're angry that he used your grandmother's quilt to sop up the overflow when he changed the oil in the truck, is a silly gamble. No machine operator's manual lists, 'old blanket' as a reason to abstain. Unless you're into angry sex, one has nothing to do with the other.

Your machinery and his equipment were designed to work together. With the right combination of button pushing and Lever pulling, lights *will* flash, bells will sound and wheels will spin for both of you. Push the buttons and pull the Lever *together* – and Ding! Ding! Ding! You've got a slot machine with a jackpot payoff no Vegas casino can rival. If you play the slots often enough, you might *come* around to his way of thinking.

Because 'No Sex For Him' is punishment for me, when I'm angry with my spouse for some perceived transgression, I make him read the instruction manual to program my new DVD player. He suffers righteously while I watch a movie. When he leaves the toilet seat up, I use his souvenir Wayne Gretsky hockey jersey to dry my bum. If he forgets Valentines Day I just draw hearts and flowers *for* him – maybe on his face, with permanent marker, while he sleeps, but I will not be punished for his crimes.

What happens in Vegas, stays in Vegas, because I want my piece of world peace.

Play Through The Pain

The lighting is poor and there is no cheesy soundtrack. We don't have clever stage names like, Poppy DeCherry and Jack Hammer. No surgically endowed extra waits in the wings to step into the shot in case of equipment failure, because real sex is not like a porno movie.

Sex is more like a sporting event. In real life, when real bodies engage in real sport, there is a real possibility that one of the athletes will cramp up and keel over. Because I'm MA, I sometimes skip foreplay to do gentle stretching exercises instead.

Staying 'warmed up' 24/7 may be the secret to a long-lasting marriage, but sports injuries can happen even if a person has done proper warm ups. If an MA wife and her MA spouse take a joy ride on an All Terrain Vehicle, as the rhythm, speed and intensity of the ride increase, so does the potential for injury. Even if the ATV is parked in the middle of a cornfield, and the engine is no longer running, and the lights are off, injuries can occur. If *she* is warmed up and *he* has his lights on, when spine repeatedly meets roll bar on the back of an ATV, sports injuries happen.

Real life, every day, run-of-the-mill injuries, can further elevate the risk of sport injury.

In a porn film, Jack wouldn't slip a disk while doing a happy dance, having just finished the job of shoveling a ton of limestone gravel around the calf hutches at his farm. Poppy wouldn't break her wrist as she wrestled with a jammed switch on an emergency spotlight. But, if Jack and Poppy were *real* MA athletes, in a real sporting event, they would have to play through their pain.

Because of his back injury and her broken wrist, Poppy and Jack hadn't spent any quality time together between the sheets in more than a week. The couple measured sexual frequency in dog years, so a day was actually a week and a week was seven months, or seven years or, oh hell. They were horny and hurting so they brought in reinforcements. Big Boy, the vibrator joined them for an evening of fun and games.

Santana music played in the background. Candlelight danced across the ceiling. Warm, sweet flesh on crisp linen promised a wonderful time, but something was off.

"Big Boy needs lubricant" Poppy said.

"Already used some."

No, something was not right. "Try some more."

Spritz, spritz, spray, spritz. Carlos teased the guitar strings. Drum rhythm quickened.

"Yes. That's better. But. But, *we don't have any SPRAY lubricant! What IS that!?*"

"I don't know. It's lubri… It's, I can't read it without my glasses!" He flipped over to show her the bottle in the dimly lit room and laid his full body weight on her broken wrist. She screamed in pain. Startled, Jack jerked sideways and threw his back out again.

"Sorry honey." Jack moaned, "It was this. This is, oh my God! I'm so sorry. Are you all right? Are you all?"

Snore No More! Peppermint oil spray to numb the back of the throat so the soft palate doesn't vibrate as you wander dream land! Peppermint cools and numbs soft tissue.

By God, it did just that!

He couldn't move. Her wrist (not even close to the target area) throbbed. Big Boy hummed and gyrated in a happy little circle around the middle of the bed. Jack lay writhing in pain as Poppy made a bowlegged-cowboy-dash for the stairs. Holding her thighs apart, she teetered into the bathroom. Numb from bum to belly button, she felt only the unprecedented urge to douche with Drano or Lime Away or some toxic chemical that might restore *any* sensation to her, definitely not vibrating, soft tissue.

She took an emergency shower. She thought about the true athletes who play through their pain. *Never quit. It's not over til it's over. No pain no gain.*

She thought about her sister Vickie, whose trip to the emergency room after an evening of fun and games, (when she wrenched her knee on the dismount) could serve as inspiration to any Olympian. If mild-mannered Vickie could play through the pain, with Kerri Strug's Olympic spirit and style, (arms extended - all of her weight on one foot) the wild-mannered little sister could try. *Try again. If you snooze you lose, so snore no more!*

With my good hand, I grabbed (I mean ah, *Poppy grabbed*) a pair of reading glasses, a flashlight, some soothing lotion, and then ran back upstairs. The Santana CD started over.

There was no improvement in the lighting, but the soundtrack was great.

Pay Back Time

I've crossed the Incontinental Divide and there is no crossing back, so I never know when life will smack me upside the head with an ache or pain, or piddle. I have to look for comfort and joy anywhere I might find it.

I haul my MA butt to the proctologist's office for my first ever, colorectal screening. *Won't this be fun?!*

I am not a bad person. I believe God is merciful and positive. I believe we have free will to choose yes and no, informed and foolish, but I don't believe in sin.

However —

When I enter the Special hemorrhoid room with the Special hemorrhoid table in the Special surgeon's office — I beg God for a hall pass on my sins, past and future, and those of my ancestors in case the doctor believes I need to repent.

Yes, back at the Front, in a church, during a funeral, I tallied a 'Biggy' on the Catholic Sin-O-Meter. I wanted only to say good-bye to my loving father-in-law. I did not want my tears to further upset my family, my husband, (already beside himself with grief) and friends. I delivered the eulogy from the choir loft where the rest of the congregation could not see me cry. I wanted to deliver the tribute I'd penned,

The Incontinental Divide

with the same love, respect and good humor my father-in-law gave the world, but every time I opened my mouth to speak, the portable microphone moved and screeched. I wanted to say goodbye. I wanted the microphone to stop squealing. As I sobbed, the microphone hissed. As I spoke, the microphone wiggled and wailed, echoing back at me. In frustration and grief, I flipped the microphone switch off. Through tears and clenched teeth, under my breath, I cursed, "Oh, Jesus Christ."

He heard me.

Everyone heard me.

Because I had flipped the 'on' switch for the surround sound speakers, rather than the microphone 'off' switch, all of God's Kingdom heard me loud and clear. They heard me sniffle. They heard the long pause as I thought about sin, the Third Commandment, and going straight to hell. They heard me catch my breath as I waited to die, right there, in the choir loft. They heard one last sob as I cleared my throat. Then all of God's Kingdom heard me pay tribute to a man I loved. With the clarity of angel song I delivered a beautiful eulogy. According to church doctrine, I was damned to Hell for all eternity, but I got to say good-bye before I left.

As embarrassed as I was, I couldn't pray for forgiveness for a sin I didn't believe in. But positioned on my knees, on a step, on a table, up in the air, bent at the waist, cheeks spread, arms above my head, face pushed into a disposable pillow, with my butt at an angle 180 degrees to the floor — I know it's pay back time for something!

There is no way to do this in a dignified manner. The exam is like the Brazilian wax job I had. Once. Lamaze breathing techniques will come in handy and the use of inappropriate humor may or may not get me through the moment.

The nurse and doctor are calm and patient. She pats my hand reassuringly. His voice gently rolls out his intentions.

"I'm going to be probing now."

I reply with the only appropriate sentence, given the circumstances. "Yep."

"Now a scope. This will be a little deeper."

"Oh, yep."

"A little more pressure here. Doin' okay?"

"Okay. Oh. Yep." I wish he'd stop talking.

"Now, I'm sorry. I have to push here."

"Yep." I picture my ancestors: Powerful Druids and fierce Celtic warriors, standing silent, butt cheeks clenched. They can't help me with this one.

"I'm going to get a better look here… with the scope again."

"It's not a do-it-yourself project for me, Doc. Just do whatever needs to… Oh, okay."

"I'm going to use…"

I don't care if Geoffrey the Toys-R-Us giraffe is buried up to his shoulders in there. From this angle... "Yep." *...in this position, on this table, in this room, it doesn't matter what's probing. A probe is a probe!* "Ohh-kay!" *Just hurry up and be done!*

"Done."

"Oh, good. We're done? Good. You sure? Done? I'm done. Good."

"Are you okay?"

"Yep." *Unless you want to cuddle.*

I find comfort and joy when the exam is finished. I discuss treatment options with my doctor. I can try medication or I can have surgery to rid my MA self of the "outies" and jagged scars plaguing me since my last child was born twenty some years ago in our living room. Had I delivered my baby in a non-emergency situation, in a hospital, like other baby boomers, perhaps I would have no need to seek an alien anal probe. At a hospital they would have given me nice drugs and made neat little incisions to open the doorway to the new world for my offspring before any structural damage occurred. But, I didn't make it to the hospital twenty some years ago.

Sunday Morning

In 1982, I made it to the toaster and the tea kettle for a sunrise breakfast to calm my upset stomach. I made it upstairs to wake my three year old and inform my husband that 'sleeping-in' was not an option that beautiful Sunday morning.

With flu-like symptoms, I made it to the bathroom. My three year old also made it to the bathroom to tell me to get off the toilet. Kelby began his usual morning prattle by asking if he could have my toast.

I nodded.

"When does Underdog come on? Can I turn on the TV myself? Where's my cape, my Underdog cape?"

I pointed.

"Why's Daddy still home? Who's milkin' our cows? You should get outta here Mommy. You been here all day. Can you put jelly on the toast? I'll bring it to you."

"Ric!" I drew controlled breaths through a wicked set of contractions too strong and too close together to be early labor. "You — need to get Kelby to your parents'."

"Already?"

"Yeah. Already."

"But Mommy, Underdog's on! You said I could have your toast! You said."

"I know — Honey. You can watch Underdog with — Grandpa. Go with Daddy, now."

"Why?"

"Because our baby's — coming today." I took a deep breath at the end of the contraction.

"Can't I live here when the baby comes?"

Ouch. Jeez, stab me through the heart why don't ya?! Labor pain's got nothin' on this kid. "Oh, Kelby, of course you can. We talked about this already, remember? We love you. We'll always love you, no matter what, no matter where. We have so much love we're gonna share our love with a baby, too. Remember?"

"Yeah. Share love with the baby, but not my toys."

"That's right. Some things are just for you - like these." I blew kisses to my confused toddler then motioned him out of the bathroom.

"You need to hurry, Ric."

"Re-re-really?" Color flagged his cheeks.

"Yes, re-really. Don't panic. You don't get to freak out. Just get Kelby outta here and hurry back for me."

"Okay." Ric scooped our crying, protesting, pajama clad toddler into his arms and ran out the front door.

Before waking my family, I called Dr. Start Without Me, to tell him I had the flu. He suggested the tea and toast, and reminded me, this labor might be different from my first. Oh? Re-re-really? For hours, I'd been telling myself I had the flu. Wanting to hold on to this pregnancy as long as I could, knowing this child would be my last, fearing I may enter the hospital and never leave - because I had cervical cancer - battling the flu was easier than facing the truth. Two earlier pregnancies had ended in miscarriage. Because I fought so hard to bring this pregnancy, this baby, *my* baby, to term – lying to myself was crazy.

I didn't have time to be nuts. Muscle and sinew flexed across by lower back. My pelvis, my hips, my thighs... my goodness! My body

The Incontinental Divide

tightened, as my baby reminded me to get with the program. You're in labor. *Now! You're in labor NOW! You Dope! Get it together!*

I pulled on a pair of shorts, walked to the living room closet to grab my already packed, overnight bag when a wave of muscle contraction hit me so hard I doubled over. BREATHE IN. Good Gravy Marie! BREATHE OUT. What the hell was I thinking? BREATHE IN. Try to get to the couch. BREATHE OUT. No, not the couch. It's brand new. BREATHE IN. Lay on the floor. BREATHE OUT. No, not the floor. BREATHE IN. I just had the carpets shampooed. BREATHE OUT. There's a towel. BREATHE IN. It's Kelby's Underdog cape. BREATHE OUT. It's really just a towel. BREATHE IN. Lay down! BREATHE OUT. BREATHE IN. BREATHE OUT. And relax.

Ric burst through the front door. "Mom and Dad were at church. I took Kelby to the farm."

"By *himself*?!" I rolled to my side as Ric helped me stand.

"No. Roger's there. I'll put your stuff in the car. I parked by the porch."

"Oh. Okay. Kelby's okay?"

"Yeah. He's mad, but he'll be fine." Ric disappeared through the door again.

I took two steps and... the baby began his descent.

Ten steps through the room, out the door, two steps off the porch, and I would have been *so there*! I would have been *So*, in the car and on my way to natural (in a hospital) childbirth, like all of the other sane women in our industrialized nation. *American Woman, you are So screwed!*

"Are you ready? Need help?"

"Call an ambulance."

"Why? What? Shit! What should I do? No, shit? What do you...?"

"I'm not gonna make it to the hospital. Call an ambulance. Then you need to look and tell me what this is between my legs." My 'winter insulated', unshaved legs were testament to the fact that I hadn't been able to see below my belly for weeks.

"It's a baby, isn't it? What else could it be, Chris?"

The look on his face (terrified/quizzical/humor/horror) made me laugh aloud, "I know it's a baby but if it's the baby's head you'll have to help me here. If it's the bag of waters we'll be okay for a bit longer. You need to look so I know what to do."

"Don't you *already* know what to do? Stop laughing. This isn't funny, you know." All color drained from his face. Ric sprinted to the phone as I pulled my shorts and panties off. I lowered myself back to the towel on the living room floor.

From the kitchen, he called out, "What's our fire number?"

"180!" My giggles were replaced by heavy breathing and panting.

I could hear him on the phone. He was relatively calm. *He's a dairy farmer. He can handle this, right? He's delivered thousands of calves before, right?*

Calves? Right. Wife and unborn child in peril? Wrong. Wrong. Wrong.

Ric trotted into the living room repeating, "ten or fifteen minutes." He bent over, took the mandatory beaver shot, straightened himself, turned green, and said, "It's the bag of waters." Then he spun on his heel, ran into the bathroom and threw-up.

Oh. BREATHE IN. Okay. BREATHE OUT. BREATHE IN. BREATHE OUT. I can do this. BREATHE IN. Alone. BREATHE OUT. If I have to. BREATHE IN. BREATHE OUT. BREATHE IN. Hope I don't have to. BREATHE OUT. Little breath. And relax.

When my husband returned, pale and perspiring, he gently covered my nether regions with a bed sheet and asked, "What do I do next?"

I am an exception to most of the Irish clichés. I can't sing. (I *do* sing - badly.) I can dance, (with gypsy abandon.) And I don't really like to drink alcohol. I can hold my liquor as well as the next leprechaun, but there are so many other beverages that taste better than booze. I'd prefer to quench my thirst with something that won't tip me over or turn my complexion the color of the Emerald Isle.

I read somewhere (probably in a Marvel Comic) that a shot of whiskey could slow a woman's labor. I was already a little green around the gills and I couldn't tip over any farther than the floor I was on, so I sent Ric off to fetch some liquor. I panted and breathed through the next round of contractions.

A wave of nausea passed over me as I got a whiff of the half gallon jug of booze my husband placed next to my face. My eyes watered and my nostrils burned. "What the hell? What is this, Ric?"

"Grogg."

"What's grogg?"

"Snowshoe Grogg. I don't know what it is. It's all we had that smelled strong. I put some other stuff in, whiskey and vodka and, it's Grogg and stuff."

"Oh-kaay, thank you." *I think.*

"What else can I do? What do you need? It's been ten minutes. Where the hell are they? I'm sorry, Honey. Don't worry. How you doin?"

He was so genuinely concerned and sincerely frightened that it showed on his usually stoic face. I had to keep him busy or he would flip his lid.

"They'll be here soon enough, Ric. Could you get some ice chips for me to suck on? My throat's a little dry."

"Oh. Sure! Sure, Honey." He ran off to the freezer as I rolled over to move my 'shot glass' (without spilling it on the clean carpet where it would surely burn a hole) as far from my nose as possible. I was hoping for a shot to slow labor, not a liquor induced lobotomy.

I fought the urge to push. I panted through the contractions, one on top of the other, wave after wave, breath after breath, again and again until my muscles relaxed.

There was a cacophony of noise from the kitchen. Doors slammed. Ric swore, "Ouch! Shit!" Ice trays crackled. Hammers pounded. Bang! Thud! "Dammit!" Smash!

Sounds like he lost his wallet. Something's dying out there. I hope it's not my Breathe Honey, coach. As I lay speculating, my breathless spouse lugged, not a mere cup of ice chips, but a bath towel full of crushed ice into the living room. He was far too excited for this *relaxed* portion of the program.

"Don't push. Are those sirens? Don't push yet, Honey. Can you hear them? They're going away from us though. They're going the wrong way. Oh, sorry, Honey. Is this enough?" He spread the towel out next to me and disappeared.

There was enough ice to chill that half-gallon jug of Grogg. I could have a nice, cool toast to celebrate the birth of our second child, which felt like it would happen in about five minutes. I resisted the urge to push. I resisted the urge to panic.

I began to envision my Celtic ancestors; strong, brave, Gaelic beauties laboring through labor in a peat bog, pausing to squat and drop out a bonnie bairn. *AAGHHH! Back to work!* I was hallucinating. I was hyperventilating. There was commotion at our front door.

I was in desperate need of oxygen because the paramedics we expected, looked exactly like my husband's brother, Ron and his wife Connie. I slowed my breathing so I didn't pass out. Lightheaded and hands tingling I called out in the direction of my hallucination, "Ric? Somebody? Can I have a paper bag?"

I was not as close to the edge of the abyss as I suspected. Connie and Ron *were* there with the cavalry right behind them. Ric and Ronnie held the front door ajar as the four, hometown EMTs following my sister-in-law, wheeled a gurney up the steps.

All right! If my sister-in-law's here, even if she doesn't know what to do or how to do it, something will get done.

Connie got more work done in less time than it took me to scribble a to-do list. If there was a job she couldn't do alone, she coerced (or nagged) Ron, into getting it done for her. Connie was a small package of pure, raw, kinetic energy who spoke faster than most people blinked, and worked harder than most people twice her size. On a slow day, she wouldn't pause to take a breath. When she was excited, like when she was about to participate in the birth of her niece (or) nephew, in her brother-in-law's living room, before church on a Sunday morning — Move over, Juan Valdez! Señora no need no caffeine bean!

"Chrissy! We heard on the scanner that an ambulance was going to one eighty not turn a one-eighty but one eight zero on this road that's Larry & Eva's address we thought maybe Larry was having another heart attack so it scared us but when we heard they were coming to deliver a baby we got right in the car we knew they were going to get lost they're here now but they were going down the wrong

The Incontinental Divide

road so we flagged them down and brought them here you didn't make it to the hospital huh so how you doing can I get you anything here they come you said you wanted a paper bag here they are with the stretcher I'll get that bag."

I thought, "Breathe, Connie. Here, do it with me." Breathe in. Breathe out.

I (with Connie) moved past the 'relaxed' portion of the program. I (with baby) leapt out of the 'controlled' portion of the program into the endurance phase.

Connie handed me a brown paper bag. I had no idea how or where she found one so quickly, but before I could thank her, she turned to supervise the removal of the macramé plant hanger blocking one of the doorways to the living room. The EMTs made introductions before realizing the gurney would not fit.

Sporting matching, red volunteer-rescue-team jackets, the sleepy-eyed, Emergency Medical Technicians brought the stretcher in from another angle. One man and three women arrived just in time to perform a medical service for a stranger. The EMTs were excited, but professional. For fear I'd wig-out then try to waddle down the road, the excited, professional EMTs didn't mention this would be their *first ever*-deliver-a-baby-medical-service, until the deal was sealed. They were efficient. They gently moved me to the stretcher then stated, "You're in charge of the agenda."

Emergency childbirth in my living room was not on my, 'To Do' list, but there was no time to quibble.

I waged war against the urge to push. I couldn't speak, but introductions were right on the tip of my tongue, *Well, Hello! Good Morning, strangers. Nice to meet you. That's Connie and Ron. The pale man is my husband, Ric. I'm Chris, by the way, and... and this is my vagina! She's a little stressed right now. Hope you don't mind if she doesn't shake your hand. Hope you don't mind if she does!*

As one technician radioed the hospital, another opened the birthing kit to extract a clamp, an aspirator bulb, and a thermal space-blanket the size of a washcloth.

Disappointed there was no catcher's mitt, I blew out a deep breath. "We won't make it to the hospital!"

All heads turned to me.

"The baby's here — NOW!"

Like a surreal game of freeze-tag, everyone stopped dead in their tracks - FREEZE then players skittered and chattered all at once. Ric said, "No! Dammit!" and moved to my side. Connie moved to his side. Ronnie ducked outside. The ambulance driver stood ready in the doorway. The female EMTs positioned themselves around my feet.

One woman readied supplies. Another was on the radio, telling 'Dr. Start Without Me', that I started and was apparently going to finish, without him. The third woman held the position and the view only God, my diaper-changing mother, Dr. Start Without Me, and my husband have had in broad daylight. I prayed the woman could catch.

Ready. Set. Go Away! Ready. Set. Go Away! Ready. Set. Go! GO! GO! GO!

The drama queen in me was silent. I did not allow myself to scream in pain as bones shifted and tissue ripped. *This is too fast. This is too hard. This is gonna' leave a mark!*

"Is he breathing?"

"It's a boy!"

I snapped, "IS he breathing?!"

"Yes, Chris. He's breathing. He's beautif…"

"eeww." My baby made his first sound.

Figures.

Someone kissed my forehead. Someone cried tears of joy. Someone radioed the hospital. Someone stepped in the pile of ice. Someone placed my child on my chest and I held him to my heart. I whispered to my little man, "You made it. 'Tis Himself. Nice to meet you."

"wheewweh." He yawned and stretched.

"You're tellin' me, whew!" I lay my head back on the stretcher.

His wife and child were not yet out of danger so Ric was quietly losing his mind. When the EMTs radioed the hospital regarding tissue damage and hemorrhaging, Ric joined his big brother on the front porch for the fresh air he'd get by chain smoking. Poisonous fumes

The Incontinental Divide

were preferable to the stress in the living room. The men shuffled and paced, waiting for the EMTs to prepare me for 'transport'.

I didn't really care about damage and bleeding. I was concerned my naked infant may be cold. "Can we cover him with something other than this Astronaut Barbie blanket?"

"Newspaper is sterile I read that newspaper is sterile wrap him in newspaper where's the paper?" Connie ran off to grab the Sunday Gazette from Ron.

Newspaper? Whatever. He's pink. He's breathing. He's moving. He has all of his external parts intact and the two of us didn't die!

I may have been bleeding to death as I pondered the best swaddling for my newborn, but *in that moment* I didn't care. I was the Happiest Girl in the Whole USA. *Zip-a-dee-do-dah, and thank you Lord for ma-kin' him for me.*

The moment I plastered sheets of newspaper to my gooey infant, I realized the error of my ways, "Eewwe. Gross! It's sticking to his head." Like a wiggly parcel of fish 'n' chips, the baby protested his 'wrap.' I giggled, "I'm sorry, little guy. We'll wrap you in something else. Aunt Connie, there are clean linens in the upstairs clos…"

Connie was off and running before I finished my sentence. She returned with an armload of sheets and towels before I finished peeling the newspaper from my baby's little body. "Sorry about that that wasn't my best idea ever here let's get you two bundled up super job Chrissy super that was wild!"

With congratulations and thank-yous all around, there were more tears and smiles, hugs, nervous laughter, pats on the back and a quick reminder (from one of the responsible adults) that I needed to get to the hospital.

I was still the CEO and director of the production company. Power is intoxicating.

"Wait." Everyone stopped. "I want a picture. Can we take a picture?" Everyone scrambled.

Ric fumbled with my complicated camera, attempting to photograph his wife, child, and the 'Save-Their-Lives-Please-Team' but he couldn't do it. He was a little stressed.

When not on call, scraping bodies off the highway or delivering babies, the ambulance driver worked as a local photographer. He rescued the camera and snapped a picture of three grinning EMT midwives, a beaming Aunt Connie, a wound-up new Daddy, this smiling Mother and the, 'Speedy Delivery' still warm, fresh from the oven, honey bun. The camera flashed. The baby said, "eeww."

Thirty-eight minutes after calling emergency services to the wrong address, I cradled my son in my arms, en-route to the hospital. Ric followed in our car. Ron and Connie stayed behind to clean up. I imagined Connie would have our furniture and room accessories put back in place; carpets shampooed, plants watered, lawn mowed, house painted, breakfast ready, laundry washed, phone calls made and be seated with Ron enjoying a nice chilled glass of Snowshoe Grogg, before I reached my destination.

I stroked my baby's tender skin. I kissed his soft cheek and read the Sunday comics transposed on his forehead. Dr. Start Without Me, met me in the ambulance bay.

"So you didn't have the flu?"

"No, guess not."

"What *did* you have?"

"A boy."

"Let's get you fixed up."

Sunday morning I had a baby. Monday morning I had something different. Monday morning I had surgery to rid my body of the cancer threat. My childbearing years ended that morning.

At the ripe old age of twenty-five, my life changed - again and again and again until another morning – when I was MA.

I was discussing butt surgery with Doogie Howser, in his 'special' office.

"What kind of recovery time are we talking here?"

"Well, that depends on your overall good health, tolerance for pain, and whether or not there are complications."

"What kind of complications?"

I stopped listening somewhere between abscess and overdraw my checking account. I heard: pain, infection, pain, peel your wallpaper, pain, puncture your colon, pain, IRS audit, pain and probable *pain*. I opted out of surgery to take the medication route.

Before I left the Special office, with my Special prescription for Special medication, for the Special scars-hernia-south of the border-malady I got during a Special home delivery, I had the surgeon sign an affidavit stating: My head, in fact, is not up my ass and I do not, in fact, have Circling Disease. I'm Special.

Run, Bambi. Run!

When the life I love, loves me back too hard, I try to get outta' Dodge. I periodically use my life savings to check out a new locale and expand my gray matter. I take a vacation.

Vacations are a blast when you're beyond the age when you have to take the kids. No more arriving at the gates of the Magic Kingdom, locked and loaded with everything but our tickets for admittance so I get back on the shuttle ferry, spill a soda in my lap, make the uncomfortable, hold-my-purse-below-my-navel-walk back to our hotel room, get our tickets, use the mini hair dryer on the maxi wet spot on my pants, get a little too close to the fabric, short out the dryer, cause a power outage in our hotel, sneak out through the dark lobby back to the boat landing, re-cross the magic waters, head back to the gates of the 'happiest place on earth' to find my extended family has gone on ahead and my kids are trying to wrestle my new, "No-I-don't-know-how-to-use-it, but-it-cost-three-hundred-dollars," camera away from each other during a Kodak moment of my husband groping Snow White.

No more.

Vacations are so much fun because an entirely new world of stress

The Incontinental Divide

opens to me. The pressure of planning, participating in and paying for a *relaxing* vacation is intense. I usually need a vacation after a vacation.

Back at the front, I tried a hunting/camping vacation with my spouse. I felt it was important to our relationship to attempt to participate in activities he enjoyed. Today I feel differently. I now know it is important to our relationship to do as little together as possible lest there be bloodshed. Naive, thirty-something Princess - I tried to enjoy the experience.

I took target practice with my spouse. When he discovered I knew how to handle small firearms, comfortably and accurately, all of the accessible handguns mysteriously disappeared from our home. He, of little faith and Me, of hair trigger temper, required no further target practice – together. In an effort to maintain enthusiasm for our upcoming trip, I didn't mention the fact that I didn't know diddly about shotguns. Rifle; BB Gun; Tomahawk missile launcher; whatever! A gun's a gun when you're going hunting with your husband.

I sat through my spouse's lectures on maintaining silence in the woods. I agreed to forego showers, shampoo and perfume so no woodland creature would be frightened off by my chemically enhanced human scent. I declined the offer to smear 'deer estrous' on myself to lure the big bucks my way. I would not purposely spread a glandular secretion from a doe in heat, on any part of my human self, even if the big bucks I attracted were the type I could spend. I purchased the required license and a blaze-orange deer hunter's wardrobe. I tried on boots heavier than the spare tire in our car. I tried to enjoy the new experience.

My husband was *so* excited, *so* happy, at the prospect of doing something *so* fun, together, I didn't dare burst his bubble. When I woke the morning of the hunt, technically, it wasn't morning and technically, I wasn't awake as we arrived at our stand before sunrise. I woke with the worst cold of my life. Technically, I was convinced I was dying, but the hunt would go on. I would go on the hunt. I took an antihistamine.

I looked like the Pillsbury Dough Boy in a prison jump suit. Breathing through my open mouth, wearing two pair of thick socks inside my heavy combat boots, sneezing, carrying a fifteen-pound pack, stumbling, coughing, lugging a loaded firearm longer than my legs, I tried to silently tiptoe into the dark woods. I was as quiet and graceful as The Hulk on Dancing With the Stars.

At the edge of the black woods in a secluded, camouflaged, semi-circle of a clearing, I placed my belongings near a fallen log. When my smiling husband whispered good bye and good luck, I experienced a moment of confusion and panic. "I thought we were hunting together?!"

"We are hunting together. Isn't this great? But I'm not going to stand right next to you. That would be silly. I'm going to *my* stand at the other end of the woods."

"Yeah, that would be silly, hunting together, together."

I plopped my padded orange butt down on the fallen log to wait for sunrise, alone. The forest was spooky. All alone in the dark woods I heard the rustle of each and every leaf. *Lions and tigers and bears...* my eyes tried to adjust to the dim light *...oh my...* crickets chirped. The hair on the back of my neck stood at attention when a twig snapped somewhere behind me. Every God-given protective instinct in me kicked in, telling me evil waited behind me. Sitting with my back to the woods, unknown danger lurked in the dark. The gun was useless because hunting season didn't open until sunrise. I didn't want to break the law and go to DNR prison, but… A leaf fell and brushed my cheek. *Lions and Tigers and Bears, Oh My!* Adrenaline coursed through me. I breathed hard and heavy. My heart pounded. *Protect yourself!* I didn't survive electrocutions and lightning strikes and three miscarriages and child birth in my living room and cancer and assault and addiction and overdose and… *and* a paper cut in my eye just to be taken out by some namby-pamby forest freak! *I will protect myself!*

I slid to the ground pressing my shoulders against the log as a tree branch moved above my head. I untied my laces, then yanked the heavy boots from my feet.

When the sun finally broke over the horizon I was seated on the damp ground, jaw locked, fists clenched around my twenty-pound boots, poised to beat Thumper and Gentle Ben to death. The happy little squirrel above my head chattered "good morning" to me. Maybe I should have tried decaf.

My feet were wet. I thought about the probability of catching

The Incontinental Divide

a *worse* cold from wet feet. I'd probably go hunting anyway. Sitting alone and frightened on the dark forest floor, sucking air through my open mouth, swinging a combat boot at Chip 'n' Dale as they scurried around my wet feet, things probably wouldn't get any worse.

I checked the contents of my backpack, searching for a bottle of water. I found a box of shotgun shells I didn't recall packing, and a gigantic sandwich on white bread. I didn't like white bread. I must have put spouse's sandwich in my bag. I dug a little deeper and pulled out five small bottles of, *what the hell?* Four airline shots of whiskey and a vial of 'Doe-In-Heat'. I had my husband's backpack. Hunting was *so* fun!

I couldn't breathe through my stuffy nose. When I shoved my hands into the pockets of my coveralls to locate the hunting contraband - mentholated cough drops - I had stashed there, I discovered the other decongestant/antihistamine tablets from the pack I opened earlier. The survival gear of choice for a Princess in the woods: drugs. Numbing drugs. Lovely drugs. It wasn't exactly a blotter acid blast from the past, but I was a happy Princess.

The pills were covered with pocket fuzz. Since it felt like my head was plugged with pocket fuzz, I made a decision based on statistics and probability, to pop a pill into my mouth. A second pill probably wouldn't hurt me. It was part of a multi-pack so I was supposed to take multi-pills, right? I probably wouldn't be able to taste it. I had a cold and everyone knows you can't taste anything when you have a cold. I could probably swallow the lint I couldn't peel off, right? I was an art major. Statistics and probability were not my strong suit.

"Gghyak!" I coughed and gagged as the bitter pill melted on my tongue. I frantically opened what I thought was a mini whiskey bottle, took a swig, "Gghyak! Oh Gawd!" I threw the half empty vial of 'Doe In Heat' on the ground, wrestled the top off the whiskey and drained the liquor into my throat. Statistically, I should have thrown up just then.

I plunked down on the log as the burn in my chest hit my empty stomach.

I scraped my tongue with the back of my glove. The clearing was heating up. I fanned myself with the flap on the backpack before extracting the behemoth sandwich from the bag. When I picked off the tomatoes and tossed them into the underbrush, I was not littering. I fed the bugs. Raw tomatoes cause an allergic reaction in me, similar to that of eating peanuts. Already struggling to breathe, I chose to eat around the parts of spouse's sandwich touched by the offending tomatoes. If my husband was enjoying *my* turkey/broccoli sprout on whole wheat, I hoped it was giving him gas.

I opened a second bottle of whiskey and took a shot to wash down my breakfast. After polishing off half the sandwich, I polished off the other bottles of whiskey. I popped a mentholated cough drop into my mouth for dessert.

Oh, whatever! I wanted the deer to catch my human scent. I wished I hadn't spilled the Doe-In-Heat so close to where I sat. I didn't actually want to attract a buck or *shoot* something while I hunted. That would be silly, hunting while I was hunting. It was also silly to drink the other bottles of whiskey, but I did it anyway.

I watched the bugs and creepy crawlies on the forest floor. I wished I'd taken a shower. I watched the squirrels and chipmunks skitter about. I wished I had a camera to shoot with. I listened to the birds sing. I wished my lips weren't swollen from the tomatoes on that sandwich so I could whistle for spouse to come rescue me.

Less than two hours into the hunt, the last wish I recall was for a fluffy pillow. I didn't feel very sparky. I was sweating. I was dizzy. I was — crocked.

I peeled off my blaze-orange jump suit and peed near the fallen log. The music of a songbird moved me to dance and spin around the camouflaged clearing. I swayed and swiveled with my jumpsuit dragging around my ankles. I tripped over the fallen log and took an unscheduled nap.

Twigs and leaves jutting out of my hair, my drool-wet chin was planted in the mud. I woke as shots rang out from the other end of the woods. When I spotted a small herd of deer running toward me, I stood, raised my gun to my shoulder and took aim. I couldn't find the safety release. I couldn't find the trigger. My gun was upside down.

Run, Bambi! Run! There are crazy people in the woods under the influence! They're wielding upside down firearms! The menthol-smelling, naked, dancing

The Incontinental Divide

one can't hurt you, but a real *hunter might shoot while you stand laughing! Run, Bambi! Run!*

There *were* parts of the vacation with my spouse I enjoyed. I liked the sitting around the campfire, laughing part. I enjoyed the rolling around on top of our sleeping bags together, part. I came home *itching* to talk about my woodland experience.

"Chiggers!? What are chiggers, Doc? From the woods, you say? They hop *and* bite? I remember some jumping and nibbling. In the grass, you say? Huh. Chiggers."

I tried R&R his way. Now, it's my turn.

Christina Crall-Reed

Give Way

I was going on *my* vacation of choice. Spouse was going with me - like it or not. *Stop whining. I know you don't like the beach. Yes it will be hot. So, I'll teach you to swim. Yes, you can take time off work. No, it's not a punishment. Stop whining and have fun! We are going and we're going to have fun, dammit! I mean it! Shut up and have fun!*

I made reservations and arrangements draining both my Harley fund and 'emergency' fund of every penny, because I needed a break. It was an emergency. My ancestors nagged me for months. 'Find Herself a beach, ahn a pint wid an umbrella bafoor she kells him.' All of life's signs were pointing to the need for a break.

One of my quirks (I have a few) is to go on vacation and photograph funny signs. *Any* tourist can photograph a loved one on a donkey at the Grand Canyon, but I have a picture of my sister Liana, outside a shop in the Cayman Islands, smiling sweetly, sitting on a clean, white bench beneath a "**REST ROOMS**" placard. The sign above my sister's head is complete with the familiar international symbols for, bathroom: (stick figure - he pee - she pee - all pee here) and a directional arrow pointing straight down to the bench.

Millions of people may have seen the same signs, but I stopped on old Route 66 in Albuquerque, New Mexico, to knock on a stranger's

The Incontinental Divide

front door in search of a 'quickie' having just photographed the "**SPEED HUMP**" sign outside.

Advertisements, posters, announcements, street signs; if something is a little left of center, like my imagination, I take a picture of it.

During my commute to work I see a roadside sign announcing a, "**HUGE MARINE SALE.**" I begin to ponder the possibilities. For the remainder of the drive, I think of nothing but vacation and the Huge Marine Sale.

The ocean is hours away. There is neither lake nor river for miles, so I have little use for a boat, but I would *love a Huge Marine!* I could trade in the spouse on the couch for one of America's finest fighting men. A Marine could patrol my territory and secure my perimeters. Oohh, yeah! If I tire of playing with him he could help me move heavy furniture. Semper Fi! Since spouse and I have been fighting for months, perhaps the "**HUGE MARINE SALE**" billboard is a 'sign' it's time for Marshal Dillon and Miss Kitty to get outta' Dodge.

I pack my bags. Spouse currently tops my short list of irritating-individuals-to-be-maimed-later, so I don't pack his suitcase. He can pack his own bag. I'm an MA Queen, not his queen mother. I do the laundry, stack it (as I always do) on top of his dresser, leave a list of items he may need on vacation, on top of the empty suitcase I've conveniently left next to the dresser (so he can find it) and I take my bags to the car. I know he'll be beltless, wearing heavy jeans, no underwear, tennis shoes sans socks, and some 'Girls Gone Wild' t-shirt, (purchased from a street vendor) for the duration of our vacation.

I am thoughtful (self-absorbed) enough to bring his wallet. One of us should know where his identification is so we can *both* board the plane. He'll need money from his wallet for a toothbrush because he won't be using mine. Ever, never, ever. I'll arrive at our destination with bags locked and loaded for fun in the sun. He'll check into the hotel and go straight to the gift shop to purchase *his* vacation essentials: soda, chips, candy and a magazine. I'll unpack then don some appropriate, 'explore the beach' attire. He'll have nothing in his suitcase to unpack so he'll undress and crawl into bed with the TV remote. I get the beach. He gets to sleep. Paradise for two.

As my husband munches chips and M&M's in our bed while watching cartoons, I stress about fat thighs. I stress about covering and uncovering my less than perfect body. I step out onto the white sands overwhelmed by the beauty of the aqua sea, the dancing sunshine, and the rolling waves. When I spot a two-hundred-plus pound woman with a larger hangover than an elephant on a footstool, clad in a two-piece, blue bikini, I am overwhelmed with perverse pleasure. It's the same swimsuit I'm wearing. But, (this is a Big Butt, but) my fashion doppelganger wears that suit like she has a prescription for it! *She* is having fun!

I feel momentary guilt for indulging in self-doubt. Suddenly, I don't feel so bad about a little cellulite. In fact, I feel pretty good. In fact, (My goodness! Nice gams!) I toss my cover-up on a beach chair and go splashing off into the water. What a great beach!

I paddle around in the ocean long enough to relax. I go ashore, dry myself and head out in search of a beverage with an umbrella. On the beach, there are plenty of sites I'd rather not see. I knew before I made reservations, before I packed my bags or got on the plane, any Speedo sightings would cause me unnecessary stress. From my seat near the hot tub, I can observe men and women in various stages of undress and easily conclude, Speedos should be against the law. If I wanted to check out some man's package I'd have called the UPS guy. He's got a whole truckload of stuff.

I watch the hairiest, Speedo-clad, potbellied man I've ever seen, drag a screaming demon child away from the Jacuzzi toward the seashore. *Eewww.* Here comes that complimentary continental breakfast for a repeat performance! I close my eyes hoping the disturbing vision is not permanently etched on my retinas. I swirl the umbrella around my glass. I listen to the sounds of the surf and the happy voices of my ancestors, 'Tis a lovely marn. Tis a foin tang. Tis Herself, relaxin' ahn glad to bay here.'

With my drink in hand, I stroll back to shore. My ancestors stop cooing when I discover the hairy guy stole my beach chair and left my belongings in the sand for his cranky, snot-nosed, six-year-old to use as he pleases. The kid is burying my damp towel, book, and water bottle under a mountain of sand, topped off by a huge conch shell, which still has some half decomposed creature hanging out. I know immediately, my remedy/revenge options are limited.

If I move my stuff the kid is going to scream bloody murder.

The Incontinental Divide

If I braid the man's back hair while he lounges in *my* chair, I'll get deported. Regardless of my motivation, the moment Mr. Sasquatch S. Peedo complains, the authorities will kick me right off the pristine, Caribbean beach, back to the states where the closest I'll come to the aqua sea is the greenish-brown puddle at the edge of the lawn where I left a leaky hose running.

As I assess the situation, my swimsuit twin stomps across the sand like a Soprano's hit man, hell-bent on whacking someone. She faces the hairy man, cusses him out, grabs my possessions away from the child, and then gives them both, "The Look." She turns to me and smiles so brightly that I have to squint. "They did that to me yesterday. Ape gave that little brat my margarita glass to dig with! Can you believe that?"

"Do you know them?" I ask.

"They know me now." As Hairy Tourist drags his screaming offspring away, the woman puts her hands on her voluminous hips, assuming the classic, 'Don't *Even*' pose. She calls after the retreating males. "That's right. You *GO* complain. And put some clothes on while you're at it!" She turns to smile at me again. "Can you believe that? Man's thang just right out there for the whole world to see. Give me a pain."

"Yes." *Kindred Spirit.* "I feel your pain." The woman's mannerisms remind me of my friend, Sherri. We introduce ourselves, feel a bond like we've known each other since conception, compliment one another on choice of swim wear, then set out in search of margaritas. At a little table by the pool, we talk. We talk and we talk and we laugh and we talk and we laugh some more until my new pal's vacation mates send out a search party to locate us.

My new buddy, Mary, is vacationing with friends and celebrating her lover's divorce. "We've been together since Moses was a baby, but now it's official. He's *my* man. There he is. There's my Joe." Mary gazes lovingly at a homely, skinny, balding man stumbling across the sand, holding his shorts up with one hand, clutching a beach tote in the other.

Oh-kay. I try to picture them in the throes of passion. When Joe stumbles out of his flip-flop, bends over to put the sandal back on his foot and exposes his 'plumber's crack' I try *not* to picture them

169

together. Mary can see the wheels spinning in my head. She leans across the table. "He treats me like a queen."

I smile and understand.

"And he's hung like a horse."

Aaagh! Too much information! I have no choice but to picture them playing, Chutes 'n' Ladders and Naked Twister together. Jesus, Mary and Joseph, I need another margarita!

Joe greets Mary with a kiss behind the ear. She flashes that blinding smile at him. The chemistry between the strange pair is so palpable I can smell it and taste it and feel it in the air. In their universe, on their planet, in their space I am an outsider. When I excuse myself to leave, Mary and Joe are leaning together, holding hands, giggling about his loose britches.

I envy this odd, compatible as cookies and milk, duo because they've got It. They are lovers *and* friends. I've always wanted It - never felt It. I've lived without It all these years so I envy It when I see It in other people. I *am* grateful for the ocean, the sunset, and the lush, tropical paradise I enjoy the sea breeze caressing my skin. God gave me the Caribbean for five nights and six days. I wish it was enough to get me through the other three-hundred and sixty nights I spend with someone feeling alone, because It isn't there. I sigh and count my blessings as I ride the elevator back up to our room. I don't doubt my husband's love for me. I choose my poisons and I count my blessings.

Paradise is full of surprises. Spouse is *not* sitting in his underwear, scratching himself, watching ESPN. He is clean, shaved, dressed for dinner, (or dressed for undressing) rearranging the flowers on a room service cart. Suh-Weet! I don't know who this guy is or what he did with my husband, but this stranger is gonna score! (Okay, I'm going to pretend he's a stranger. Even if my husband encouraged me to *date*, I couldn't *sleep* with a stranger on vacation. The angry bulldog look on my 'sleep' face and my jet engine snoring would generate complaint calls to the front desk. A potential slumber party guest would blanket themselves in 'Do Not Disturb' signs and run screaming out into the lobby.) I enjoy an evening of fun and games with my husband/stranger.

Vacation sex for the established couple is similar to shopping for real estate. It's all about location. Location, Location, Location.

The Incontinental Divide

Different locations; different room, different bed, different carpet, bath tub, night stand, elevator, window sill, the vibrating air conditioner unit outside the window, on a beach chair, in the mangroves. Vacation sex can put us in the true, 'happiest place on earth' if we follow a few simple rules.

Rule number one: (This is the only rule. We're on vacation, remember?) Rule number one: practice safe sex. Even long established couples should practice safe sex. We're not talking, 'no balloon - no party' safe sex. We've been together long enough to know we're not playing, 'Plague! You're it!' To be safe on vacation, the established couple must move the bed away from the wall so the headboard doesn't bang a hole in the plaster, then dead bolt the door to avoid an, oohhbabyoohhbabyoohHouskeeping, situation where I open one eye to see the maid standing next to our bed with an armload of fresh towels. Safety First!

When I'm not busy safely exploring new locations with spouse, dining with Mary and Joe or avoiding direct eye contact with Hairy Tourist, whose room is right across the hall from ours (I *know* he steps out of his room, in his birthday suit, to steal my morning paper) I am out photographing signs.

"**New Roundabout Ahead.**" I've never seen the 'old' roundabout but if there is a new one up ahead, important enough to warrant a sign, I'll check it out.

"**No Parking. No Stopping or Landing Off People Around This Area.**" I can't figure this one out. Perhaps the sign has something to do with too many umbrella/rum drinks. If I park, stop, stand and read the sign I'll probably be okay, but if I park, stop, read the sign, tip over and bump into someone else, I'll get deported? I'm pretty sure if I park *then* stop I'll blow the transmission in my rental and get kicked off the island anyway.

The cold, rude American, 'YIELD' sign has a gentle Caribbean equivalent: "**Give Way.**" Give Way is a polite suggestion. Give Way is a well-mannered rule. I take scores of photos because "Give Way" is my new catch phrase.

Spouse hogs all of the blankets? I whisper, "Give Way" before I tuck and roll into a cozy ball under the covers on my side of the bed. The boss is riding me about the unfinished business cluttering my desk? "Give Way." I'm on coffee break. The moron ahead of me in the express checkout line has a cart full of unmarked, unweighed, unpriced fruits and vegetables? "Give Way." I've gotta' pee. Wouldn't life be grand if everyone would just, "Give Way" *my* way?

By the last day of vacation I am refreshed and relaxed. We are so relaxed, spouse and I have become 'those people' we'd rather not see on the beach. My husband wears an orange, Hawaiian-print shirt over the baby blue, Richard Simmons short-shorts he purchased (without adult supervision) when the only two outfits he packed were dirty and I refused to wash *his* laundry on *my* vacation. He sits in a beach chair, jealously watching me over the top of his new, bigger than his head sunglasses. I am one of 'those' women swimming around, wearing some thong-string-thing impaled in my backside. So, I should have cleared it with customs before I put it on. I am relaxed.

It's 'de Islands, mon.' I'll have to do my own cavity search before leaving the country so I won't get arrested trying to smuggle anything out, but hey, Give Way! I had a good vacation.

Slow Starters

Refreshed and relaxed, we return home to our empty nest. In reality, there's no such place. Our kids grew up and moved away, but this nest is full of so much useless, collected crap there is hardly room to walk around the stack of papers and magazines I've meant to sort through since Reagan's first term in office.

This is our 'starter' house. Apparently, we are slow starters because we've lived here for more than twenty-five years. We moved into our fixer-upper with a lawn chair and an ashtray a month after we got married. We were in 'loovve.' For the first year I didn't mind that the house was too small, had no closets and the windows were painted shut. I dealt with worn out plumbing and wiring, crooked floors, asbestos insulation, lead paint, a dirt floor in the cellar I had to go outside to access, and a yard full of run-down outbuildings left over from the farm operated here in the 1800's - because we were in 'loovve.'

With newlywed enthusiasm, my groom and I fixed up what we could, threw away the rest and settled into our love nest for a few short years. More than a quarter century of short years later, we're still here, the house is decrepit, and I think my groom is an ass for forgetting our twenty-sixth wedding anniversary.

I console myself with the fact that the house is paid for and it's full of memories. I partied here and I mourned here. I sweated and primped, laughed and cried, sang and screamed, and I overdosed and died here. I came back to life to raise my children here. My son was born here. I spent my adult life here. The house is like my marriage; like a thunderstorm; like aging - I don't always like it - but it's familiar so I stay in this house.

Yes, I've made a little progress. I spackled and plastered and painted my way through mental illness. I've redecorated. The cellar floor (we still have to go outside to access) is cemented. The 'Farmer In The Dell' outbuildings (chicken coop, milk house, pump house and root cellar) are gone. We have a new garage and the house is paid for.

But the doors don't close. The windows don't open. The roof leaks. Wind blows through cracks in the siding. The floors are so crooked if you spill water in the living room it runs downhill to puddle in the kitchen, and the wiring is, of course, toasted. The electrical anomalies in my house (and in me) are legendary.

Six lightning rods on the roof, more than a dozen heavy-duty surge protectors, back-up batteries and ground outlets can't protect this 'Little House On The Prairie' from lightning strikes or me. It's fitting that I live in this house. It's *irritating* that I live in a house with so many electrical problems, but it's fitting.

Coming home is a treat. The day I return (refreshed and relaxed) from vacation, unlock the front door and the knob falls off in my hand, I enter our castle anyway. The bulb burns out and pops when I flip the light switch. I retrieve a flashlight, turn, smack into the corner of the table, cut a gash the length of a boa constrictor in my tanned shin, turn on the flashlight to see my breath because the furnace stopped working while we were away. The pipes froze and the kitchen flooded. My leg bleeds into the icy water I'm standing in, but I am *still* full of optimism. It's paid for. It's paid for. It's paid for!

I hide in the bathtub with the dog, while Ric fixes the light and changes the bulb. Only in a coma, would I be relaxed enough to hang around for a standing water/electrical repair. When it's safe to leave my hidey-hole, I bandage my leg and sop up the mess on the kitchen tile. Ric thaws the plumbing and re-starts the furnace while I attempt the doorknob repair.

The Incontinental Divide

I'm happy to be home, such as it is. Even after my dog, (overwhelmed with joy at my return) gooses me, and I jump, slip and crack the front window with the screwdriver I was using to repair the doorknob - even then, I am motivated to tackle *the* renovation project I've been avoiding for more than a year. I am a slow starter, but Give Way! I am going to redecorate our sons' room.

Christina Crall-Reed

Ladies Home Companion

I've formed a basic plan of action. If something (in the room) doesn't enhance my life, I'll get rid of it. That's the plan, anyway. I jot down a simple checklist of the things I'll need to get started. Organization. Time. Creativity. (I'm an artist who doesn't wear a watch so theoretically, I have all the time in the world to get organized.) I've been doing projects in this house long enough to know I may have to add a few items to the list or modify my plans, ever so slightly.

This is '*The* House That Jack Built' so one project leads to another. Hanging a picture on a wall in our home takes three and a half weeks and costs, $4,472.00 dollars (plus tax).

I pound a nail to hang a picture and I knock plaster loose. I find the putty to plug the hole I knocked in the plaster, but there's no putty knife in my toolbox. I don shoes and coat to go outside in the rain, to give myself a hernia opening the heavy storm doors, to venture into the creepy-crawly infested cellar in search of the putty knife, which isn't there. I flail at the cobweb that touches my face as I stomp back up the cellar stairs to close the heavy storm doors, which give me a double hernia. In pain, I let the doors slam and the vibration causes a crack in the window on the front porch next to the recently taped window that cracked when I smacked it with the screwdriver I

The Incontinental Divide

used to repair the broken knob on the front door. I walk in the rain, doubled-over in pain, to the garage to find the putty knife hanging on the peg-board wall above my head. I can't stand up straight so I grab a hoe to swipe at the peg-board to knock all of the tools on the floor where I can reach the putty knife, to put in my pocket, to walk in pain, in the rain back to the house. I can't remember where I left the putty, so, wet, wounded and wondering *why* I live in a house Jack built, I go to bed.

When I wake the next morning my stomach feels better but my husband is angry because he's late for work because he has a flat tire because he drove over a hoe that *someone* left on the garage floor with his tools. While he changes the tire I make a note to fix a special dinner for my husband after I fix the cracked windows after I putty the hole in the wall, which is much larger than I remember. Ignoring the tiny crack above, I fill the hole, get a new nail to pound a new hole next to the old hole, hit the new nail once with the hammer and the tiny crack above the old hole widens and spreads. The plaster around the old hole and the new hole caves in to make a newer hole, bigger than my head. Charter member of Mensa that I am, I think it would be a good idea to stick my head in the hole to see what's inside the wall.

So I do.

And it's not.

It's not even close to a good idea.

With my head stuck in the wall between the broken slats and my hair twisted around an old nail I have free time to let my eyes adjust to the dim light. I spot some odd insulation. Are those *magazines*? Those *are* magazines - old magazines that I must reach. If I stand on my tip toes and push my fingers into the hole next to my face I might be able to — get my fingers stuck while the strain of standing on my tip toes, trying to reach down into the wall, stretches my hernia causing me to scream out in pain. I jerk my trapped head back yanking hair from my scalp and scratching my cheek with the rings on my previously stuck fingers. Got it! I shake the hundred year old hickory nut shells, plaster, mouse poo and bugs from my hair and gaze sideways, because I can't stand upright, at the new and improved, size of a dishwasher, hole in the wall.

1946, <u>Ladies Home Companion</u>! I peruse the moldy, dusty, brittle magazines to see that more doctors recommend smoking Lucky Strikes over any other brand of cigarettes. Chesterfields may improve my general health and well-being because I'll *enjoy* the smoking pleasure so.

As I punch in speed dial for the farm, to summon my husband to drive me to Urgent Care, I turn the pages and feel inadequate for not owning the new, 1946, Speed Queen, wringer-washer that would make my dreams come true.

According to the ads and articles in the magazine I should wait on pins and needles at the front door, for the homecoming of the hard-working man of the house. I try to imagine myself, sixty years ago, in this house, <u>Ladies Home Companion</u> style.

I've prepared his before dinner cocktail; arranged the children and arranged the newspaper next to my husband's favorite chair and ottoman, which are, (according to the ad in <u>Ladies Home Companion</u>), available at fine furniture stores near me. I've arranged my hair, checked my make-up and smoothed the new dress I wear, over my Playtex girdle, and poke-an-eye-out-bra, which are available at Montgomery Ward. Aprons are also available at Montgomery Ward, but I, of course, stitched my own on my Singer (with button hole attachments) Sewing Machine. I starch them with Argo, for that crisp, clean look, and press them with my new G.E. Iron, just as the other happy women featured in <u>Ladies Home Companion</u> do. I should remove my apron before serving the fine, four square, meat and potatoes banquet I have prepared, hot and tasty, ready and waiting on the table for my husband's homecoming. Wouldn't I be just *the* happiest little woman?

I would be happy because the featured article in the magazine states, 'a woman should be smiling and pleasant when her man comes home.' Do not bother him with your little questions or concerns. He will have more important things on his mind. He works hard. He will be tired. Do not be cross if your husband is late. Do not be cross if your husband does not come home at all. He has important business to take care of. He may need time alone to unwind before coming home to you — you, *happy* little *woman*, you!

No wonder the magazines were in the wall! After chopping down the trees to saw the wood to make the slats to build that wall, one of my homemaking predecessors probably hid the magazines there before she plastered over the hole. I pen a note on a Post-It, date it, sign it, stick it to the cover of the magazine and drop the old publications back into the wall. Perhaps, sixty years from now, one of my descendants will rediscover the magazines and read:

"Dear Ladies Home Companion... Bite Me. **Kiss my** *-* 9 to 5 workin'; too tired to cook; Chinese take-out, eatin'; don't care what's in the sports section of the newspaper, readin'; his dinner's in the microwave and he *better* empty the dishwasher; I'll call him from my cell phone to tell him good night because I'll be home when I get there; went out dancing with my friends; low-rise jeans, dry clean only jacket purchased with my own money, Wonder bra, thong, no girdle, wearin' - **ass**. *Sincerely, C.C.R., 4/10, 2004."*

I call the farm again to nag my husband to hurry. I wait, on pins and needles, at the front door, for the homecoming of the hard-working man of the house.

Three and a half weeks after first attempting to hang a picture on a wall, I return home, groggy and sore from hernia surgery. The carpenters who repaired the cracked windows and the wall while I was at the hospital, left a bill and a note taped to a plastic bag, on the coffee table. I tally the costs of attempting to hang a picture.

CARPENTERS: (Wall & Window Repair) Materials and Labor = $ **960.00**
URGENT CARE: (Antibiotics & Tetanus) Insurance Deductible/Office Visit = $ **375.00**
TIRE REPAIR: (Hoe Damage) Husband's Car = $ **93.00**
SURGERY: (Hernia Repair) Happy Little Woman = $ **3,044.00**
TOTAL: (Hanging Picture, Which [laying on the table] Remains, Unhung) = $ **4,472.00**
(plus tax)

Then I read the note taped to the plastic bag, *"We found these in the wall. Your husband said you might want to keep them. They're from 1946!"* Whatever.

The Nursery

It's time to redecorate. I stand at the door to the empty bedroom trying to psych myself up for this project. My cleaning supplies, toolbox, 'to-do' list, and a big jug of coffee are on hand, but I hesitate. I tell myself, "You can *do* this. You're a big girl, Chris. You're prepared. Your mother would be proud - you've got a Kleenex tucked in your pocket." I pause. "You *can* do this! It's time to redecorate! You've been in this room thousands of times!" The problem is – I've been in this room thousands of times.

This is the room, too cold that long ago February night, for our newborn baby to sleep in. Ice covered the windows inside and out. A cold draft blew from the floorboards. After seeing my own breath as I stood in this room, I lay my infant son in the bassinet then took bed, baby, blankets and all, on the first of many 'road trips' across the hall. Kelby slept in the bassinet at our bedside. I lay awake, watching him breathe. The blizzard raged outside for days, but the three of us lay clean, soft and naked on the heated waterbed. As they dozed, I watched both of my men breathe. Life was good. I closed off the nursery until I'd caulked the windows, carpeted the floor, and stitched window quilts to keep the brutal Wisconsin winter at bay. When the nursery was warmed and redecorated, I rocked my baby to sleep there.

The Incontinental Divide

Getting our baby to sleep through the night was a challenge. Getting my husband to stay awake through the night so I might find a few hours rest was a bigger challenge. After three months of baby care, housework and sleepless nights, I found myself exhausted, and pregnant again.

Perhaps it was a little too soon after my first pregnancy to be excited - but I was. Perhaps I shouldn't have told anyone our good news - but I did. Perhaps the pain of losing something I never really had is different from other heartache. Perhaps not. When I miscarried, I mourned the loss of a child that was never meant to be. I held the child I *was* blessed with, to my breast. As I rocked and I cried, exhausted and devastated, I held my baby in my arms. We cried ourselves to sleep in the cozy nursery.

The room changed with the seasons. When I discovered I was pregnant for the third time, my toddler and I redecorated. I chose a circus theme in rainbow colors.

"Won't it be fun, Kelby, to have a new baby *and* a new room?"

"*This* is my room."

"I know but we're going to make it better looking so you and the ba…"

"This is *my* room."

"Yes, honey, this is your room but your room needs a little fixing up so it will be…"

"This *is my* room."

The polka dot fabric on the walls and the brightly striped window shades put me in a good mood despite Kelby's lack of enthusiasm. I whistled and hummed while I painted the dresser and bookshelf. When I left the room to answer the phone, my son redecorated the redecorations by painting the red carpeting, the bookshelf and himself, a lovely shade of blue.

"Oh, Kelby, what did you do?"

"This is *my* room. **My** room is blue. That baby can have some other color."

To avoid the explanations and uncomfortable condolences if something went wrong, I kept the news of my pregnancy quiet until

I was past the three-month mark. When I shared the news with my friend Peggy, she was so happy for us, she shared the news with a few of our other friends - who told a few friends, who told a few friends who were excited for Ric and me and our expanding family. Friends celebrated 'our' pregnancy into the night.

In the middle of the night, I woke thinking our waterbed was leaking. It wasn't. I was bleeding.

"Ric, wake up."

"What?! Jee-zuz! I just got to sleep. Leave me alone."

"I need to go to the hospital."

He opened his sleepy eyes wide, trying to focus. "What's goin' on? Jesus Christ! What happened? What the hell?" Backlit from the hallway, he could see I was covered in blood. "What's goin on, Chris?!"

"I don't know. I don't... I'm bleeding." I clutched my stomach, seized in pain.

Cramps and dread tortured me enroute to the hospital. *How could this be happening again? Why? I did everything right. Why now? What's wrong? Please God, don't let this happen. Can't I please keep this baby? Please, God, help me!*

By the time I got to the hospital, God had answered all of my questions and pleas. The answer was no.

After a night in the hospital and an emergency procedure to stop the bleeding, I returned home, numb. I was not pregnant, not thinking, not grieving, not anything but numb. Peggy brought us dinner, offered her condolences and wept for our loss. I did not. I hugged my friend, thanked her for her kindness, ate the chicken casserole and went to bed.

I allowed myself to feel little more than empty. I cleaned and scrubbed our home, took care of our child and slept. I went through the motions of my life, hollowed, without connecting my soul to task. My only thought was to keep moving. When I was awake, I cleaned. I scrubbed walls and floors, drawers and cupboards. I dispatched, filed, folded, sorted, polished, fixed, tossed or organized every scrap of paper, article of clothing, spare key, button and photo in our home. I moved furniture, repaired windows, vacuumed, pounded, painted and dusted. When I managed to sleep, I was too spent to dream. If I suppressed the joy in my life, I might be able to keep the anger at bay. As long as I felt no pleasure, I would feel no pain. Until I did.

I scrubbed the dried paint from the carpeting in the nursery. Surrounded by buckets and rags and cleaning supplies I found a dry patch of carpeting and sat, exhausted. As I leaned against the polka dot wall, Kelby climbed onto my lap.

"Are we done now, Mom?"

I kissed his mop of blond curls. "I think so."

He stroked my hair and my cheek with his little hand. "Mommy, if you don't be sad anymore, the baby can share my blue color."

My breath caught in my chest.

"The baby can share my room."

"The baby's gone, Kelby." My eyes welled up.

"Where did he go?"

"Maybe back to heaven."

"When is he coming home?"

"Someday, honey. Someday, I hope." I cradled my son in my arms and I cried.

I finally cried.

Stack Em Up

Someday came a year later with the birth of our second son on the living room carpet. Maybe my boys were destined to mess up the carpeting. So be it. I had a hard enough time balancing the checkbook let alone figuring out God's plans for flooring.

Our sons shared every color in the spectrum *and* the little bedroom. They played, cried, laughed, and slept, argued and shared secrets in their cramped room. They grew, then they grew some more, then they grew and grew and kept growing. When larger beds were called for, but a larger room was unavailable, I decided bunk beds would be the solution. Wouldn't it be fun for them? Sharing bunk beds like my sister and I shared when we were girls.

I liked the bottom bunk. I could make a dark, cozy, cave-tent by hanging blankets from the bed above. In my little cubby hole, using the flashlight I'd hidden under my pillow, I could read in the middle of the night without waking my sister. It was even more fun to lie on the bottom bunk and push the soles of my feet into the box springs above trying to topple Vickie to the floor.

"Quit it."

"What?"

"Cut it out. Quit kickin' my bed."

"What? I'm not doing anything."

"I *said* quit it!"

"Quit what?" I put my feet down. "Hey Vickie, are you sleepin?"

"Yes."

"No you're not."

"Yes I am. Now, go to sleep."

"I can't. I'm bored."

"Good. Sleep is supposed to be boring. Now, be quiet."

"Hey, Vickie?"

"What!?"

"Goodnight."

Once my sons' bunk beds were delivered and set up, I lay on my back on the bottom bed, feet on the mattress above my head, pushing, to see how Bailey might knock Kelby to the floor. With one push, the seventy-pound box spring/mattress assembly fell on me, scraped my arm, and crushed my fingers. *This can't be good.* The whole point of trying to push the occupant of the top bunk to the floor was to cause annoyance. 'Death by Bunk Bed' would take all of the fun out of the game.

I, of course, reported the problem to the furniture store. The furniture store, of course, told me it was not their problem. When I contacted the manufacturer to report the problem, they told me the responsibility for the problem was with the furniture store, which told me, it was not their problem. When I lodged a complaint with the Wisconsin Department of Consumer Affairs, the furniture store *and* the manufacturer contacted me to set an appointment (at my earliest convenience) to fix the problem. Taa Daa! My sons had safe, new, try-as-they-might-but-couldn't-push-the-box-spring-mattress-assembly-to-the-floor, bunk beds.

With my sleeping children stacked up in the corner, the bunk beds made life a little easier. By organizing and safely storing my sons in one location, it was efficient to peek in on them in the middle of the night without turning on the lights. In the dark, my pre-storm preparations were fast and businesslike. If the boys misbehaved while they were supposed to be asleep, bed checks were made with a stealth and speed unavailable with the lights on. When I needed to look at my sons just because I loved them (every night) I could peek into the little room where they slept, so sweet, so precious, so — piled together in the corner. Stacking my kids in one place gave me free time to enjoy other things, like life. The beds gave my sons a base of operations for the next fifteen years.

The Jungle

During my sons' teen years, the bedroom frightened me. I tried not to enter the teenage jungle unless I had no other choice. When that dirty gym sock odor wafted downstairs invading the other rooms in our home, I would lug cleaning supplies upstairs, then push the door to the jungle open with the vacuum cleaner.

I'd hold my breath while my eyes adjusted to the dim light. The heat was oppressive. I could almost hear monkeys chatter and exotic birds call out, 'Caw! Caw!' I would traverse the expanse of jungle, swinging from stereo wire vines, imagining lizards and snakes skittering and slithering beneath my feet, mosquitoes buzzing my sweaty brow - all while praying my sons were still alive in there - somewhere in the underbrush.

Long ago separated, the bunk beds occupied opposite corners of the room. The beds were covered with piles of worn, wrinkled and wadded clothing, game cartridges, soda cans, blankets and CD covers. If the piles moved as I entered the jungle, I knew my sons (or a reasonable facsimile thereof) were in there, sleeping. If the piles didn't move, I'd poke the broom handle at the mass on the bed to disturb whatever jungle beast hid beneath. The beasts would growl and snap at me.

"What? Whadaya want? I'm sleepin!"

"Smells like you're dead. Get up."

"Let me sleep a little longer."

"Okay." Prepared to leave the jungle, I take one step then a deep breath. The smell makes my eyes water. I spin on my heels. "Changed my mind. Get up."

"God, Mom you're such a bi…"

"*Excuse* me?" I give him The Look.

"Nothin. Never mind. Sorry. I'm gettin up."

I assume the classic, 'Don't *even...*' pose. He knows it. He sees it. The jungle beast rises from his nest and half-smiles at me. "I, um, sorry, I'll be back up to help after I go to the bathroom, okay?"

"Okay." He will live to die another day.

No wonder teenagers are strange and angry beasts. The chaos in the room is overwhelming. I close my eyes and shake my head at the skull and cross bones painted in black and red, on the white walls. Even the colors are combative. I turn the stereo on so angry music can blast me through the cleaning job no one in the tiny bedroom wants to do.

I console myself with the fact that this is their space. Looking around the jungle, I hope their fascination with dead rappers and violent music will pass. I hope they'll outgrow their sullen, bipolar personalities. I hope their hormones will settle down. More than anything, I hope I'm not housing two serial killers.

Over time, my sons *do* take responsibility for the care and feeding of their own space.

"Do you have any candles, Mom?"

"For *your* room?"

"Yeah. Some that smell good. Like air fresheners?"

"Uh… sure!" I do the happy dance behind his back.

As my sons mature, *they* decide to redecorate. They repaint the walls, shampoo their own furniture, make their own beds, do their own laundry and take out their trash. They clean their own space, but not because I instilled them with great moral values, a sense of responsibility, or a solid work ethic. My teenage boys simply don't want any teenage girls (who might visit the premises) to know that they are piggies.

Had I known clearing the jungle was *that* simple, years ago I would have rented some firm, young thing to stand in the hallway, bat her eyelashes and smile every ten minutes. It could have spared me numerous treks into the jungle, and saved hours of cleaning time.

Emptying The Nest

It took a few years for our oldest son to leave the nest. When Kelby moved to Texas for college, I had time to adjust before he came back. When Kelby moved to Illinois for college, I had time to adapt before he came back. When Kelby went to Florida for a visit, found a home, made new friends, embarked on a new career and started an independent, adult life there, I waited. I spent time adjusting and adapting. I waited, but he didn't come back.

I was proud of him. I was happy for him. I had more free time to… I had more time to… I had more time. I missed him so much I thought I'd swallow my tongue every time the phone rang. *Is it him?Is it him?Could be him!Did he call?It's not him?*

I missed Kelby terribly but as long as *he* was happy, I would try to be content. I would be optimistic. I would be optimistically content with my nest, not half empty, but half full.

Bailey was content with his own room and happy to redecorate *his* space. The lone bunk bed made it's way to the dump when Bailey purchased new furnishings for *his* digs, with money *he* earned delivering pizzas.

"Hey, this is nice, B," I said.

"Yeah it is, isn't it?"

"The aquarium looks great over there. It's nice and quiet up here, too."

"Yeah. It can be."

"You can close the door and have privacy and peace and quiet to watch the fish."

"Yeah. I could if…"

"Oohh, I like this couch. It rocks? Cool. This is comfy. I could get used to sitting up here."

"Mom?"

"Uh huh?" Eyes closed, I rocked back and forth on my son's new sofa/glider, enjoying the quiet space.

"Could you go away? I mean, could you, ah, no offense but…"

"Oh. Yeah. Sorry, B."

"You can come back some other time, Mom. It's just that I kinda wanted to enjoy my new room by myself for awhile."

"No. I mean, yeah, I understand. I'll just go, ah, downstairs to, I'll just go." I stood, straightened and smoothed the cushions on the new sofa then ran down the steps. Kindergarten Deja Vu – he doesn't need me anymore!

Actually, he needed me for at least another year. Bailey was still in high school. He needed me to coordinate his schedule and remind him of his appointments so I could wave good-bye as he left the house. He needed me to buy massive quantities of food so he could consume it all before he left the house. He needed me to make sure he was clean and pressed, prepped and ready to leave the house.

"Pleaseplease, pa-leez Mom, I'll love you for-ev-er."

"You already love me forever. I'm The Mother. It's the law."

"Well, yeah, but I'll love you *more* if you'll iron my shirt." He kissed the top of my head and gave me a wide-eyed pleading look, "Pa-leez, Little Mommy?"

"Didn't your mother teach you to take care of yourself?"

"Yeah, but she does it so much better than I do."

I rolled my eyes as he handed me the shirt. "Gawd, you're such a flirt."

He needed me to make sure he was organized, fed, pressed, prepped, and loved so when the time came for him to *really* leave the house, he could leave the house. Job well done.

Move The Fish

⚡

Following Bailey's graduation and the subsequent two-day party (spouse and I spent a month in preparation for the bash, stayed awake for forty-eight hours during the party, then sat exhausted trying to visit with our sons the day after), I found a comfy chair. I closed my eyes for what I thought was a split second, opened them and commented, "Those were nice shoes. I asked if I could have them."

Everyone but me, burst into laughter. "That was, like, fifteen minutes ago, Mom. HaHa we were talkin about shoes fifteen minutes ago. What the hell? Are you losin it?"

"Already lost, honey. I think I'm already gone." I dozed off in the chair.

My sons waited a few days for me to regain my strength and vacate the recliner. When I was well rested, Bailey announced he was moving to Florida with Kelby.

When my sons were younger and violence escalated between them, I'd make them sit together on the couch and hug until they calmed down. For the first few minutes they'd beat the tar out of each other. Slugging and punching until the novelty wore off, my young men would inevitably decide to be pleasant so they could leave the sofa. They would be friends, and I never had to take bandages to more than one location.

When Bailey made his announcement, I began to play out various 'moving' scenarios in my head. If Bailey moved to Florida with Kelby, they could sit together on their *own* sofa to slug each other. They could buy their *own* bandages. *They* could decide when it was time to make nice and get off the couch.

I was happy my sons would be together again, but I was not feeling warm and fuzzy about emptying our nest. If the move was inevitable, I would try to be optimistic. I reminded myself they would love me forever - from wherever. I'm The Mother. It's the law. As long as they were happy, I would be supportive. I would be optimistically supportive. If I stayed busy making moving arrangements, filling the garage with new (and gently used) furnishings, spending our life savings on packing material, filling coolers with dry ice and sides of beef so my sons wouldn't go hungry so far away from home... if I stayed active, packing, carrying, cleaning and scheduling, maybe my heart wouldn't break when they left. Maybe heartbreak is inevitable. Maybe, because I'm The Mother, it's the law.

Food, furniture, boxes, bags and an ingenious aeration system my men designed to keep Bailey's fish swimming during the trip, were in the truck, ready to go. I stood, 'optimistically supportive', repeating my empty nest mantra, "They'll love me forever - from wherever. They'll love me forever - from wherever.'

I was okay when they backed the U-Haul up to the front door. I maintained composure, while double-checking the inventory, loading boxes and bags, until Bailey hooked up the aquarium pump. When the water began to burble, so did I.

"He's moving the fish! He's moving the fish! He's *really* leaving. He's moving the fish!"

I couldn't watch as my sons drove away. Everything I valued in life was on the front seat of that truck. I waved, turned my back, went into the house and cried.

My sons called every few hours from the road. "We're in Illinois. We're hungry. How are you? Are you still crying? We're in Georgia.

The Incontinental Divide

We're tired. Are *you* tired? Are you gonna lose it again and start talking about shoes?"

I was in mourning for days. I had horrifying visions of myself... *wearing polyester, sitting alone in my decrepit old house. Before heading out for Tuesday night bingo at the VFW Hall, I would share my Hamburger Helper dinner with my only friends – four ugly cats and dusty, old Bud-D, (stuffed and mounted on a taxidermy stand) propped up against the front door to ward off intruders. The phone wouldn't ring. There'd be no cars in the driveway. There'd be no gigantic shoes in the middle of the living room rug. I would be old and alone.*

When it began to dawn on me that my housework load was nearly nonexistent, the bathroom was mine uninterrupted, there was ice cream in the carton and juice in the fridge when I came home from work, and I did not have to listen to rap music while I tried to meditate, I dried my tears.

My sons called, often to remind me they would love me forever, from wherever. I adjusted to the altered activity / noise levels in my home then spent the next few months trying to decide if I liked my husband enough to spend any more time with him. The jury was still out deliberating when we took my vacation of choice, but I returned home determined to make my little house on the prairie as comfortable as possible so I could take my time deciding if I *wanted* to spend my time being comfortable with my husband in the little house on the prairie.

Now, I stand at the door to the empty bedroom prepared to be overwhelmed with memories. I'm not. I open the door to an empty room in an old house. That's it. That's all. Empty room. Old house.

I check out the closet. The bunk bed ladder is propped against the inside closet wall, with the white stilettos I wore at my wedding, hanging by their heels, from the top rung. No matter that my feet have grown over the years and the shoes no longer fit, I leave them hanging, untouched. A girl can't have *too many* shoes, and it's some sort of sacrilege to throw perfectly good ones away. Bailey's cap and gown from graduation hang on the closet rod. Beneath the ladder sits a box of baseball cards, Kelby's old chemistry set, and a chicken bone.

This redecorate the room thing isn't exactly going as planned. So far, I've identified six, serve-no-purpose, non life-enhancing items that, for the most part, remain undisturbed. I'm afraid to touch the chemistry set lest I accidentally redecorate the Midwest with a mushroom cloud, so I work around the box of questionable chemicals. Who knows what sort of booby trap the little buggers rigged the time they were angry with me for ending their chemical gopher bomb business before it had a chance to take off.

I am here to redecorate! I have to get tough! I can do this. I can!

With no tears and little ceremony, I use the Kleenex from my pocket to pick up the chicken bone, toss both into the trash and proceed to redecorate the bedroom.

A few weeks later I step back to admire my handiwork. With all of the eucalyptus leaves I've hung in swags around the room, I can't decide if it smells like an arts and crafts shop or a funeral parlor, but I like it. The room is full of new candles I'll never burn. They match the new furniture, curtains, pillows, color, texture and personality — all mine. I position my exercise bike (the one I hang the ironing on) at just the right angle in front of the new TV (which I've programmed to broadcast only chick flicks 24/7) and stand, satisfied. TaaDaa! "I claim this space in the name of the MA Queen!"

Now, *I* have a space with a door that closes and locks. It's the only room in the house with the potential for privacy (unlike the bathroom) I won't have to share. If I feel the need to do a secret, 'Bill Nye The Science Guy' experiment with new makeup, or try on clothes I *know* won't fit, this is where I'll do it. I need privacy to try on tight clothes. Should spouse see me struggling to pull on or zip up ill fitting garments, there would be comments about the Lay's Potato Chips I ate for breakfast, obligating me to defend my morning menu - not because chips for breakfast is a good idea, but because, a stressed-out, whiskey-drinking, chain-smoking man who had his first heart attack at the age of forty-six, doesn't get to choose *my* poisons for *me*. The no longer empty bedroom is *the* place to be.

I enjoy my new space. Months later, when my sons call to tell me they're coming home for a visit, I get all excited - until they mention they would like to sleep in their old room. *Nuh-uh! Give Way. This space belongs to the Queen.*

Happy Holidays

Every holiday since my sons moved away I've tried to convince myself I have this middle aged, empty nest thing, all under control — which I do, until I don't.

It broke my heart to hear Kelby describe his first Thanksgiving in Florida, eating turkey dinner alone at a Denny's restaurant, so I made sure Kelby's first Christmas in Florida was spent in Wisconsin. With his car keys, clothing and suitcase accidentally locked in the rental car (parked in a snow drift in the driveway) on Christmas Day, Kelby was *thrilled* to be home for the holidays.

He whined, "I mean it. I'm not coming here in the winter anymore. It's too cold. It hurts. No, don't laugh at me. I'm serious. It hurts to be this cold. This is painful."

"What? Are you taking blood thinners?" I teased him for losing the, 'brat-eating-beer-drinking-Cheeseheads-can-handle-it' temperament, that allows Wisconsinites to survive the brutal winters. The hearty, buck-up or freeze to death attitude he was raised with apparently melted in the Florida sun.

"So, after dinner, do you want to go snowmobiling? How about ice fishing? I heard they're pulling big walleyes out of Koshkonong."

"Ha. Ha. Aren't you funny? I'm just not used to this anymore. I'm *so* cold. I think my bone marrow is frozen."

"Big baby. Big, wimpy, Florida baby." I gave my son a hard time, but I jacked up the heat and kept the wood burner stoked so Kelby would be comfortable. Bailey, spouse, the dog and I were roasting, panting and dehydrating, looking for *any* opportunity to run outside naked to roll in the snow, but Kelby was comfortable. I wanted him comfortable, so he would *want* to visit.

Any visit from our son was cause for celebration, thin blood or not. I cleared my work schedule so we could spend quality time together. I cleaned and sparkled the house. I cleaned and sparkled the dog. I cooked my son's favorite foods in mass quantity, convinced he couldn't possibly get enough to eat in Florida. Kelby would arrive, tanned and healthy looking, visit for awhile, overeat, play with the dog, punch his brother in the shoulder, then just like when he lived here, go out with his friends.

I would turn the porch light on to spend quality time in my clean, sparkled space, munching leftovers, petting the dog, celebrating my son's homecoming - without him. When Bailey moved to Florida, I left the porch light on for months. The bulb finally burnt out and my sons did not come home, so I took comfort in the fact that they were taking care of each other in the Sunshine State.

Bailey's first Thanksgiving in Florida was spent, with his brother at a Denny's restaurant. Laughing about their own quirky, new holiday tradition, they thought it was hilarious to call me on Thanksgiving Day to tease me. When I took the bait they reeled me in like a big ol' catfish.

"Happy Thanksgiving, Mom!"

"Same to you. What are you guys doing today? Where are you going to…?"

"We're cold and shivering, waiting outside, in line."

"It's cold in Florida? In line? What are you waiting in line for?"

"We're in line at a soup kitchen with other homeless boys whose Mom's won't make them Thanksgiving dinner!"

"What?"

The Incontinental Divide

"Strangers took pity on us, because you kicked us out and made us move away."

"I did not! I did no such thing!"

"HaHaHa. Settle down, Little Mommy. We're just teasin'. So, what are you and Dad doin' today?"

"Eating too much and watching football. You're *not* funny, by the way."

"Yes we are and you love us."

"Forever, from wherever." Demon Seeds.

I wasn't about to give my sons the opportunity to call and tease me through another holiday so Bailey's first Christmas in Florida was spent with spouse and I arguing on our sons' sofa, in Florida. We flew in from the frozen North for a few days with our family in the Sunshine State. I cleaned *their* house, cooked the customary two tons of food in *their* kitchen, played with *their* dog and met *their* friends. With little variations thrown in for excitement, I followed the customary, holiday routine.

We made plans to spend Christmas day with our sons, on the beach. I dressed in my little tank top and coral capris. Wearing my pretty sandals, I stepped out onto the white sands and began an effective new weight loss program. As I walked the shores in my cute little Florida ensemble, I froze my big, white Wisconsin ass off. I dropped ten pounds, right then, right there, on the beach. When I caught a cold the likes of which I hadn't experienced since my hunting trip with spouse, back at the front – and I couldn't breathe, eat, sleep, swallow, (couldn't wait to get home where I knew how to dress for the weather) I lost another ten pounds, right then, right there, on the beach. The boys called me a baby. 'A big, wimpy, Holiday baby.'

Correct.

Perhaps, if I appeared pathetic enough around the holidays, my sons would invite me to visit so I could fill their nest and abandon my own.

The Thought That Counts

I whined and bawled through the next Christmas season. Work schedules could not be rearranged. Last minute travel plans fell apart. Spouse had a staph infection threatening his life and limb, and I was crazy upset. *Okay, so, if they amputate your leg, then can we go to Florida? I don't understand why you're being so stubborn. You've got another leg.* I would not be with my children for Christmas.

Mid-December, I arrived at some strange middle-aged, middle ground where Frosty the Snowman met Salvador Dali. Like using my internal weather radar to predict a storm, I couldn't pinpoint exactly *what* was wrong, but everything about the holidays without my sons was — off. The first Christmas I spent without my children was awful.

I made a feeble attempt to decorate our home by pulling random ornaments from the Rubbermaid in the garage and then tossing them in the direction of the Charlie Brown Christmas tree I had propped up in a corner. I had no incentive to clean (no one was going to see my house) or cook. Try as we might, spouse and I could not consume the customary two tons of lasagna without the assistance of our sons and their friends. Our friends (afraid of my dog) wouldn't be dropping by for an egg nog. (Which, I wouldn't serve a guest, even if I understood why any one would purposely swallow raw egg. Eeww.) When

The Incontinental Divide

I managed to shake the holiday blues long enough to head out to the mall, Christmas shopping was painful.

If you're already depressed, holiday shopping - alone - is miserable, so I borrowed a child to ease my pain. You can't have a nervous breakdown in front of some random child. You'd miss out on all of those fun, intensive, family therapy sessions following your meltdown. I borrowed a child like my own, who knew me and loved me anyway. Sherri's tweenage daughter, Cortney was young enough to claim no embarrassment being seen with me in public and old enough to be entertaining company. We had been hanging out, shopping and giggling together since Cort was a week old. Ours was a symbiotic relationship. I drove and Cortney provided the necessary adult supervision.

My young friend was a stabilizing force during the holiday trip to the mall. I wanted to throw myself into traffic, but Cort would then have to wait in the cold while they scraped me off the pavement, so getting run over was not an option. Expecting Cortney to hang around inside the mall, while I found a way to impale myself with a complimentary candy cane, would be inconsiderate. Asking her to use *her* Christmas money to post *my* bail if I head-butted the overzealous Santa's Helper who twice, grabbed my hand to give my already impeccably manicured nails a 'miracle makeover' with the seventy five dollar emery board he was trying to sell, would be rude. I was depressed - not crazy. If anything happened to Cortney, during the course of *my* demise, Sherri would disturb my peace — for all eternity. Falling off my nut in front of strangers was still an option, but I didn't want to spoil Cortney's fun.

We'd already followed the, tweenage-girl/bipolar-woman-probably-shouldn't-shop-together trail, into the checkout line at Wilson's Leather. I forked over two weeks pay for a fur-lined, pink suede coat for myself. Maybe if I looked great wearing my impulse purchase, I'd feel better immediately.

"You look really pretty in pink Chris, and you saved a lot of money not buying plane tickets this year."

"Oh, don't remind me Cort. What about the hat?"

"No. Not the hat."

"But I kinda' like it. It's very Dr. Zhivago."

"Who?"

"Dr… Never mind. No hat?"

"It's more like Dr. Seuss than doctor, whoever you said."

"Eewe, *that* bad?"

"Like a furry pink pumpkin."

"Okay. No hat."

"Like the Easter Bunny exploded on your head."

"Yeah. Okay. No hat."

"Like a polar bear stuck his tongue in a light socket."

"Yeah, yeah, no hat. I get the point. Do you want anything in here or are we done?"

"I'm done in here but we're not even close to *Done*, done, are we?"

"No. We're not even close."

We'd ravaged the clearance rack at a shoe store, where I purchased boots and shoes for Cortney. We found an incredible sale on jewelry around the corner, where I purchased earrings for Cortney. We poked fun at fellow shoppers as we ate Chinese noodles at the food court. We had our picture taken in a curtained booth near the electronics store, played with all of the, you-break-it-you-buy-it-toys and gadgets on display, then realized we hadn't purchased anything for anyone, but us.

"Maybe we should shop for something like, *gifts for other people?*"

"Now, there's a concept, Cort." I let my adult supervisor pull me deeper into the mall.

Teeming with activity; happy tunes, twinkling lights, and hopeful souls maxing out their credit cards, a busy shopping center can be Hell on Earth for the clinically depressed. I knew I was in Hell when I located Sherri's favorite candy, but had to take-on the Daughter of Lucifer to get it. This 'Evil One' was an infant, doe eyed, angora sweater-wearing clerk at the Fannie May candy shop. To the unsuspecting MA Queen, the Evil One appeared to be harmlessly sweet, soft and innocent. Caveat Emptor. She was wicked!

"I'd like a pound of the peppermint ice, please." I smiled.

The Incontinental Divide

"Oh, okay." The Evil One twirled a strand of plastic pearls around her finger until they tightened and left a spotted, crimson track across her neck. She made no move to assist me, but turned to stare vacantly out into the crowded mall.

"Excuse me?" I leaned closer.

"Oh, okay." She petted and stroked her sweater.

"A pound of peppermint ice, please."

"Oh, okay. How much?"

"A pound."

"That's like, a lot." She turned to the shop manager, "How much is a pound? I um, how many pieces of this make a pound?"

He smiled at his temporary Christmas help, "A pound is a pound. Weigh it."

"Oh, okay." She turned to me and smiled sweetly. She batted her eyelashes and twisted her necklace. "Do you, uh, don't you maybe qualify for the senior discount?"

Ouch! Stab me in the eye with a peppermint stick why don'tcha? Ow. Ow, ouch!

On a really bad day, I *might* look my age, but even in my worst nightmares, I don't look twenty years older than I am. I was dumbfounded. "Uh, a senior discount?! No." I experienced a momentary lapse of sanity, thinking, *You never will either, Little Debbie, because you won't live that long.*

My mini grown-up placed her hand on my sleeve and shook her head, no. *No, Chris. You don't look that old. No, Chris. You shouldn't strangle seasonal employees.*

I acknowledged Cortney's Christmas spirit, but responded to the Evil One in queen-speak. "You don't need to wrap that candy because I'm going outside now to sit in the parking lot, and eat all that chocolate before I kill myself."

Her doe eyes grew larger as I spoke. The Evil One batted her lashes, "You're kidding, right?"

Yeah. Just kidding. Seasonal depression is one big joke. Instinctively, I knew parking lot suicide wouldn't be any fun. I'd get my new pink coat dirty, and if she had to drive my car home, Cort would mess with the seat adjustment and tune the radio to some twangy country music station, for spite. "Can we be done now, Cort?"

Cortney patted my shoulder. "Yeah, I think you're done, but don't forget Mom's candy."

Justifiable homicide and Seasonal Sepaku were not really options, just items on my Christmas wish list.

At home, Ric made a valiant effort to brighten my holiday, because he loved me 'no matter what'. No matter, that I wandered around the house in my bathrobe, crying, mumbling the lyrics to White Christmas, shoving the last of the five dozen sugar cookies I'd baked for the holidays, into my mouth. He braved the cold and crowds, on a gimpy leg, without adult supervision, for the third time in thirty years, to shop for me. My husband bought me a present!

"It's your favorite color, right?"

Some generously proportioned pink stones surrounded by diamonds, sparkled from three tastefully shiny boxes. "Yes, pink is my favorite color to wear. Diamond is my other favorite color. These are beautiful. What kind of stones are these?"

"I don't know, but the sales girl had nice cleavage."

"Whatever."

"Topaz. They said something about Topaz."

"They? Her breasts spoke?"

"Yeah. I mean no. There were two of them. Sales clerks, I mean. I might have taken a quick peek. I was thinking of you, though. You have nice cleavage too, honey."

"Are you making this up?"

"No. You've always had nice cleavage."

"I mean about the stones, jeez. Topaz is my birthstone. Did you know that?"

He smirked, and lied outright. "Well, sure honey."

"Nice save, Ric." It's the thought that counts. Smiling, I held the necklace up to my throat then turned my attention to the gigantic stone on my finger. "Ooh, look, one of the diamond chips is missing. We should have this repaired or replaced before I wear it, huh?"

"Yeah, but you better do it soon. I think you're paying interest on it."

"*I'm* paying interest on what? What do you mean?"

"I didn't have enough cash with me. I put it on *your* credit card."

It's the thought that counts.

Christina Crall-Reed

Think Again

⚡

Any woman under the impression she can coast through middle age, needs to think again. Middle Age is not for sissies. No *wimpy* woman could be happy with her middle age body, knowing she may have to lift her breasts up and out of the way to buckle her own belt. But, an MA Queen has what it takes. If a middle aged body is what you have to work with, then work it honey! Just don't do it in front of your children.

Balanced human beings are genetically hard wired *not* to associate lust with family. If not, we'd be a planet full of half-wit-cross-eyed-second-cousins, playing *Happy Birthday Uncle Daddy* on our dueling banjos. My sons are balanced human beings. My sons are sooo balanced, they don't want to hear, know or see anything about the physical body to which I (Little Mommy) am attached.

Having survived Black Christmas by exercising, dieting, tanning and toning my way through the long winter, I thought a trip to Florida to visit my sons would be a breeze. Think again. I forgot they were men. In the company of those men I am not a grown woman in a grown woman's body, being her grown woman self. I am their Mom.

Their Mom is a different creature.

Their Mom has no body; no hormones, no sex, no drinking, drugs,

The Incontinental Divide

carousing, farting, burping or bodily functions. She has no physical abilities, no mental incapacities, and she doesn't behave in a raucous or rowdy manner. They prefer to think of *Their Mom* as the born again virgin, who enjoys the occasional Friday Night Fish Fry or a spirited evening of Bunko with her other MA friends. I've never met *Their Mom*, although I'm sure she's very nice. *Their Mom* didn't meet them in baggage claim at the airport, but I did.

I spotted Bailey, smiled and waved, then trotted down the aisle for a hug. He was grinning as I approached, but looked stricken by the time I wrapped my arms around his massive shoulders. He hugged me tentatively then held me at arms length. "Wow, Mom, I hardly recognized you. You look great."

"Thanks. You're kinda' pale. What's the matter?"

"I saw some hot chick running toward me and I was excited until I realized it was you. I oggled my Mom. I think I threw up in my mouth a little."

"Okay, that's gross. And if that was a compliment you might wanna work on your delivery. I am lookin' good, though."

"Yeah, you are, but I don't want my Mom to look hot."

"Too bad, so sad. Don't call me a chick by the way. I'm not poultry."

"Sorry." Bailey gave me a real hug and kissed the top of my head. "It's good to see you Little Mommy."

"It's good to be here." My overstuffed bags slid down the chute to the carousel. "Those two are mine – the big black ones."

"That doesn't exactly narrow it down Mom. They're all black."

"Mine are black and red. I painted them."

He easily snatched my overweight bags from the carousel and held them aloft. "These?"

I marveled at the iron-man, holding my suitcases as if they were pieces of paper. My tiny baby had filled out a bit since that Sunday morning in the living room so many years ago.

"Mom? These? They *are* painted! What, you run out of canvas? Paper shortage in Wisconsin?"

"It's so my sky cap knows which bags to grab. I'm not gonna tip you by the way."

"You can pay my rent."

"Lucky me. So, is your brother lost in traffic?"

"Outside, on the phone. He's got a new girl."

"A secret girl? She doesn't want Kelby's Mom to eavesdrop?"

"No, Kelby doesn't want Kelby's Mom to hear. He's probably singin' to her or licking the phone. I think he really likes her."

"Is she nice? Not a psycho or a lush?"

"I haven't met her yet, but Kelby's been nice since they met. Driving here, he only swore at two people and didn't even flip anybody off."

"Wow. Maybe he's in looove."

Outside, I couldn't tell if Kelby was in love or lust, but he was definitely in heat. We all were. The moment the exit doors slid open I was pasted with a sheet of hot, sticky air. Like the menopausal hot flashes after my hysterectomy, my body bypassed the lady-like glisten, and went straight to making rivulets of sweat run down my torso. By the time Kelby snapped his phone shut and wrapped his arms around me, I was dripping wet.

"Eewwe, welcome to Florida sticky Mom."

"Hi Honey. Florida's awesome. I can swim right here at the airport - in my own perspiration."

"You look great. You been workin' out?"

"No, I sweated off twenty pounds when I walked out here. Good Gravy Marie, it's hot!"

"You'll get used to it. Maybe. Or you'll just melt and we'll mail you back to Dad in a Zip-lock bag. Ready to go?"

"How far is it to your house, again? How long does it take?"

"About an hour."

"Do you still drive like a maniac?"

"I get around just fine. It's the fricken Snowbirds. They're old. They're lost and they can't see for shit. They come down here and drive like morons."

"I'm a snowbird."

The Incontinental Divide

"Yeah, but you won't be driving."

Then, I've gotta' pee first. If there are crazy Snowbirds on the highway they'll be lookin' for an exit to a bathroom. I don't want to get stuck in traffic."

I left my boys standing on the sidewalk, pretending to be annoyed with *Their Mom*, as I wheeled my carry-on into the washroom to freshen-up. I changed into the skort and T-shirt I had tucked in my oversized purse. In case the airline lost my luggage or I flew across the Incontinental Divide, *this* MA Queen was prepared.

Back outside, it took approximately two seconds for my fresh clothing to wilt and stick to my skin.

"It didn't get any cooler while I was inside, huh?"

Eyes agog, jaw dropped, Kelby said, "God Mom, nice legs!"

"Thanks honey. I kinda like em too. They get me from one place to…"

"Eewwe! Mom has nice legs! You're not supposed to have nice legs, you're a Mom! Here take my shirt. Cover yourself!"

"Very funny. I'm not covering any more skin. It's a thousand degrees out here. You guys act like you've never seen me before."

"The last time we saw you, you were normal looking."

"What?"

"And rounder."

"You probably should stop talking now, before a round, normal woman smacks you."

"We're just teasing you, Little Mommy." Bailey patted the top of my head.

Kelby maneuvered my luggage over the curb. "We think you're beautiful no matter what you look like, Mom."

"Nice cover, guys. Now, feed me, or I'll spend your inheritance on some boy-toy who appreciates my old legs. Or better, I'll go find the guy who told me I had hot wheels and a fine chassis."

"What guy?" Bailey paused mid-stride.

Kelby stopped in traffic. "Inside? Just now? What did he look like, this guy?"

209

"Oh, put your swords away Samurai. He was an old guy. It was last month. And it was a compliment."

"Some old guy was hittin' on you?"

"He wasn't hittin' on me. I was helping Aunt Vickie at a gun show, a military show and…"

"You were at a gun show?"

"Yah."

"And some jerk from the NRA made a pass at you? Charelton Heston was hittin on our Mom?"

"Yah. NO. Stay with me here, guys. Aunt Vickie caters the trade shows at the fairgrounds. I was helping serve coffee and this old - older - veteran came back for his third cup, pulled me aside and …"

"He touched you!?" Kelby steamed.

"Yes — And after we had hot monkey sex on the display table he said…"

"Okay, that's not funny Mom." Bailey protested.

"Any–way… he said, *'I don't want to offend you, maybe you shouldn't tell your husband, but, I've been all over the world and I've known hundreds of beautiful women – I just have to say, you have the hottest wheels on the finest chassis I've ever seen!'* It made my day. I thanked him and told him I most certainly *was* going to tell. I was going to run home and remind my husband what a fine vehicle he gets to drive."

No longer interested in pummeling an old veteran, Kelby was placated, but Bailey looked confused. "*You* were at a gun show?"

Kelby punched Bailey in the shoulder, "She was collecting pickup lines for you to use, so you can finally get laid."

Bailey slugged Kelby in the shoulder. "Oh, is that how it's done? A corny pick up line?"

"No. I rely heavily on natural charm, good looks, and an unhealthy dose of Captain Morgan's." Kelby punched Bailey.

Bailey slugged Kelby.

"Stop touching each other. God, what are ya, twelve?" I said.

"Just tryin to make you feel at home, Mom."

"I don't want to feel at home, I'm on vacation." Strolling as we talked, we were still in the street. "So tell me about this new Captain Morgan's girl, Kelby. I take it you met in a bar?"

"A Club. Yeah."

"What's her name?"

"Krystal."

"And?"

"And I really like her."

"And?"

Bailey jumped in, "And, what does she look like, and what does she do, and is she filthy rich, or dirty rich, or maybe just dirty? If she's dirty does she have a sister for me?"

"No."

"What, no? No job? No teeth? No sister for me?" Bailey asked.

"No sisters, lots of brothers. She's gorgeous. Owns her own home. Works at a trucking company."

"She's a trucker?"

"No! That's it! I'm not telling you guys anything."

"Wha-ut? If she drives a big rig I wanna know. I might want a ride." I said.

"You see, that's what I'm talkin about. I really like her, and you two are gonna' tease the shit out of me."

I smiled sweetly and batted my lashes. "No we won't. I just want what's best for you. I want you to be happy, honey."

Bailey said, "Yeah Kelby, we'll be nice."

"No you won't. I know you two."

"We'll be nice to *her*. When can we meet her?" I giggled.

"A week from later. Way later. I have to get her to like *me* before I let the family loose on her. You guys are nuts."

'Nuts' was our cue.

Bailey struck a hunchback pose and drooled, "Me want meet girl! Me like girl! Bring girl me!"

I pretended to scratch my butt and pick my nose, "Well you oughter brang er home tah Mama! She kin hep me skin sum roadkill fer supper."

Kelby rolled his eyes and shook his head.

A Snowbird in a shiny Cadillac pulled up next to us, cracked his window and yelled, "Get outta the road!" Kelby flipped him off as we crossed the street.

In the parking lot, a black SUV rolled past, bass thumping, as the driver whistled, "Caliente Mamasita!"

My sons bristled.

"Pick your battles." I cautioned.

Eyeing the tinted windows and covered license plate, and considering hairnets and bandanas were all that we could see of the vehicle's occupants, Kelby said, "No problem."

"No joke." Bailey whispered as we piled into Kelby's truck.

"So, if you're not going to engage in gang warfare, and you're not going to introduce me to Krystal, will you at least feed me?"

"Yes, Little Mommy."

"That's Hot-Little-Mama to you, homeys."

"Eewwe! Stop saying Mom and hot together! Moms can't be hot." Bailey said.

"Too late. We're in the Everglades."

Kelby laughed, "Not exactly the swamps Mom, but how 'bout cover your legs with that car blanket anyway, then we'll take you to the drive-thru at McDonalds. After that you have to go in the house and stay put. We can't protect you from pervs twenty-four/seven."

I reached over the seat and patted the tops of their heads. "Welcome to *my* world, boys."

Looking hot and feeling good for an old broad, I rolled down the window to rest my arm on the frame. I mumbled and hummed along with the radio. Tilting my head back I caught a glimpse in the side mirror of what looked like an airport wind sock flapping in the breeze.

It was the underside of my upper arm.

I slid my flabby limb into the truck, pressed my elbows to my ribs and folded my hands in my lap, hoping no one had noticed — I was "Their Mom" after all.

I'm The Mother. It's The Law

Since my sons worked together at a landscaping company located across the street from the house they shared, from work they could see any and all activity at their home. There wasn't much to see. I sat on the front stoop with my morning coffee and waved to my men across the street. Mid-morning, I let their crazy dog Cassius pull me on a 'walk' around the block. Before noon I was back on the stoop, plucking sand spurs from my feet and searching for something to do. I poked around the crushed shell pathway, hunting for shark's teeth. I threw tangerines for the dog to fetch, then picked sand spurs out of her feet.

When Bailey crossed the street for lunch, I asked him why two hard-working landscapers had a sickly looking tree dropping fruit on their thistle-infested lawn.

"Genetics."

"Weed genetics?"

"No, people genetics. Dad's a dairy farmer, but there's never any milk in the fridge, and you're an artist, but you don't display your art at home. We're wired, genetically wired, to do things for other people that we don't do for ourselves. Like a mechanic who drives a crappy car. Besides, this place is a rental."

I stooped to pick up a tangerine for the dog.

"You might not want to bend over like that Mom."

"Like what?"

Bailey blushed. "Like you just did. They can see you."

"Who can see me?"

"The field crews."

"Oh, for chrissake. I'm playin' fetch with a dog! Changes the game if I can't bend over, don'tcha think? Maybe you should talk to your crew if they're having problems with my activities."

"I will, but they're still laughing at me from this morning. I was trying to tell them to lift this big rock, only I spent ten minutes telling them to lift my leg. The Spanish words for rock and leg are almost the same."

"Okay, *that's* funny. But, 'Knock it off, that's my mother,' is the same in Spanish or English."

"I'll talk to them. Just wanted you to know they're watching."

"I don't care. It's not like I'm making porn over here."

Across the street a door slammed followed by angry, bilingual chatter. "… Mi Madre!… Si hermosa… But that's MY Mother!"

"TU Madre!?… lo siento, jefe… sorry."

Kelby stormed across the street mumbling in Spanglish. "Hey Bailey, your crew is done with lunch! They just told me they were ready to go back to work. And, you're beautiful by the way, Mom!"

I went indoors to pick sand spurs out of the rug.

Day two, I caught up on my reading and my sleep. I cleaned the house, painted my nails, played a racing game on an old Nintendo, and I took my untrained 'grand-dogger' on four more tug/walks around the block. I spent so much time bonding with Cassius the Boxer that by day three of my vacation, she was ready for the Westminster Dog show and I was ready to climb a clock tower to pop off a few rounds at passersby.

"Can we *DO* something tomorrow?" I asked.

"Like what?"

The Incontinental Divide

"Like anything. Don't you Floridians have one of those big ponds around here? I think they call them oceans."

"Should we take a day off to spend with our Little Mommy?" Kelby puckered and kiss-kissed the space in front of my face."

"Yes you should. And as long as I'm fantasizing you should call Kevin Costner and tell him to meet us at the beach so he can rub sunscreen on my back."

"That's not fantasy. Well, Kevin Costner is, but we can take a day off. Boss won't care."

"Both of you? A whole day?"

"Sure. Maybe we'll drive down to Sanibel and check out the beach. We haven't been there since before Charley."

"Charley who?"

"Hurricane Charley."

I moaned, "Nooo, if the beach is all messed up, let's not go. I don't want to visit another wiped out island. After hurricane Ivan, Grand Cayman was like a war zone. It was too sad. No trees or flowers, trash everywhere, they had to rake the beach. It broke my heart."

"First World problem, Mom. No whining on vacation."

"That's a rule for you guys. Moms *should* whine. We have more to whine about."

Bailey snuck up behind me and pulled me into a breathtaking hug. "Did you bring your water-wings Little Mommy? You'll need em' so you don't drown in all that wha-wha."

"Nope. I'm an excellent swimmer. All I need is a string bikini."

"Oh, no you *aren't* wearin' a bikini out in public!"

"Teasing. But if I went swimming wearing armor and a chastity belt, I'd sink, so we'll compromise. I'll wear what I want, where I want and you two will stop patronizing me. Sound like a plan?" I gave them The Look.

"Sorry, Mom."

"Yeah, sorry."

"Someday you'll have to introduce me to the nun who raised you.

She sounds quite pious — and pitiful. Maybe I could teach her a few things about a few other things."

"Please don't."

This was my first trek into their adult territory, but I'd let my sons rein me in about as far as I would go. If these grown men were having difficulty accepting their MA Mom - body, brawn and brass - it was my duty as a good Little Mommy to prolong their suffering. Because I'm the Mother, it's the law.

After finding a dog sitter for Cassius, our beach day began with a long drive down the Gulf coast. If you can't sit for a two-hour ride, you're too old. If a sea breeze is too windy, you're too old. If the music's too loud, you're too old. I wanted to whine about the rap and hip-hop making my ears bleed, and the leg cramps torturing me while stuffed into the jump seat in Kelby's truck, but no one would hear my complaints over the gale force wind blowing through the open windows. I tried not to be too old to enjoy the ride.

Laughing, singing, checking out points of interest enroute, my tour guides grew quieter the closer we got to Sanibel and Captiva. They wanted to show me their paradise, but vast swatches of nature were gone.

"Wow, that's sad. The trees are all topped."

"Look over there, that whole beach is under water. People used to have picnics there."

We toured the island, assessing damage. Passing one landmark after another, my sons tried to describe the beauty that used to be. I could only imagine the coconut palms swaying where bare sticks and trunks now jutted from the sand. Scrub brush and sea oats peppered the beaches. From the truck, I photographed the only splash of color on a denuded landscape. In a roped off reconstruction site, surrounded by stacks of lumber and rolls of plastic sheeting, the giant red petals of a lone hibiscus waved. Nature was reclaiming Her territory, but Man wasn't faring so well. Windows were boarded, foundations cracked, piers and fences toppled, and the tiled roofs had collapsed or disappeared in the mighty winds. Once-manicured lawns were ragged and patchy. Carefully tended foliage lay dead, dying, or had been washed away by the rushing flood waters.

The Incontinental Divide

"Hey, stop the truck! Go back. Back up." Bailey said.

"What? No, I can't. That car's right on my ass."

Bailey laughed. "Did you see that sign back there?"

"Which sign? There's about a hundred signs on this street." In traffic, Kelby lost what little patience he had.

"The signs at that hotel. Mom should get pictures of 'em."

"Fine. I'll go around the block — again."

Once we circled the block, I couldn't get out of the truck fast enough or stop laughing long enough to snap a clear picture of the hotel's street placards:

"RESORT CLOSED - NO REAR ENTRY" next to **"HOAR CONSTRUCTION."**

I didn't need blueprints for the building project, but I *had* always wondered about the origins of loose women. Evidently, they're built in Florida.

The beach had been decimated by the hurricane. We jabbered and joked like crazed tourists as if nothing was wrong because that's what tourists do. It was after all, a beach, where the waters of the Gulf rolled in to lick and slobber on the sand like grand aqua-colored tongues.

Each new wave left a ribbon of white foam stretched and bubbling along the shore. Gulls hopped into the surf to squabble over gooey morsels of shellfish. I teased the birds by screeching and flapping my imaginary wings because I didn't like seagulls, but I *was* excited to be out of the house in the company of two handsome men. Those men were overly cautious escorting *Their Mom* across the sand, watching me like I was a toddler at the playground. *Not so fast. Okay, that's high enough. Don't put that in your mouth. Be careful.* If I was a toddler I might have paid attention to their warnings. Instead I touched and poked and prodded and fondled every interesting bit of organic matter I found. Dead fish, driftwood, shells, jellyfish, some slinky-like plant skeletons, I saw art projects and jewelry supplies everywhere I looked. My sons saw debris.

After the fifth or fiftieth warning about red tide, killer algae, I'd had my fill of adult supervision.

"Let's go swimming!"

"Too cold." Bailey said.

Kelby frowned, "No way. Why don't we go get something to eat?"

I bent to retrieve an interesting shell and both of my sons shouted, "Stop!

"Really, guys? I thought we had an agreement."

"Yeah, but that algae…" Kelby saw the look on my face and stopped speaking.

On a devastated beach, we came to a new and awkward family understanding about our evolving roles in this world – I was Their Mom. Their Mom wore silk because it felt good, because she was a physical being. My sons would deny that fact as long as they drew breath. Their Mom also was going to touch and experience and taste and question and revel in whatever she chose. I'd arrived in Florida an MA Queen. I planned to leave the beach the same way. My sons would have to comply, because I'm the Mother and I write the laws.

Plague! You're It!

A person need not swim *in* polluted water to contract the plague. Simply petting and sniffing debris washed ashore *from* polluted water can yield Ebola-like results. For months after my Florida visit, I responded to every bodybug encountered, by breaking out in hives and burning up with fever. Had I respected the wisdom of my grown sons or listened to their warnings about killer algae, I may have been healthier, but I would have missed the opportunity to crawl room to room pondering the universe. If the heaving, sweating, doubled-over-in-pain filled hours I spent palming the bathroom floor were part of my karmic adjustment plan, in a past life I must have been one evil Bitch.

Ric tentatively eased the bathroom door open. "Chris? Are you sleeping in here again?"

"Yes. Leave me alone. If you need to use the toilet go back to the farm."

"But, it's two in the morning."

"So? Lemme die in peace."

"But..."

"Go away!" I kicked the door shut on his fingers. I was a bitch in every life.

After a few more miserable weeks, when the water-born pathogens in my system were nearly done with me, Ric brought home a random virus to share. He contracted pneumonia while I received a generous portion of double pneumonia. We took turns coughing, sleeping or trying to convince our dog to feed us.

"Bud-D bring me some soup. Bud-D? Bud? Stupid dog."

Dying was another option, but the first time I slipped out of consciousness into fever induced hallucinations I stopped considering my options. I couldn't tell the difference between reality and some imaginary planet on Star Trek. *Where did it go? Too hot in here. It's kibbles and bits. I'm gonna get me some kibbles and bits. Can I have a blanket? It slices! It dices! It's Ronco's handy... I can't find it. I can't...*

"Yes you can honey."

"What? Leave me alone." *If not for the courage of the fearless crew the Minnow would be lost. The Minnow would be lost.*

"No Chris, you're not lost. You have to get up. We're going to the hospital."

"Stop talking to me. I'm sleeping."

"You're delirious and talking in your sleep. C'mon honey. You know if I have to carry you we'll both end up on the floor. Let's go. I'll help you get dressed."

I whimpered, "I don't wanna go to the hospital. I'm sick."

Ric smiled as he stroked my damp hair away from my forehead. "I know you're sick, honey. We have to go. You're too hot, you're singin' TV songs and you sound crazy."

"So? I do that when I'm not sick." I sat up to cough. "Sherri said I looked awful. Was that today?"

"Yes. She took one look at you and started crying. She thought you were dead."

"Maybe I am."

"We'll try not to let that happen. C'mon let's get you dressed."

Bacterial infection coupled with viral pneumonia saves money, time and energy. If you're too ill to vacate the sofa you needn't spend your cash on groceries, you won't waste hours commuting to and from work, and you don't have to turn the lights or shower on to

The Incontinental Divide

primp and preen around your space. You're dying. You're not going anywhere for a while.

But - while you're dying on the sofa, and your spouse (who relapsed as you rallied) is in bed, also dying and then your oldest son calls to announce that you (his parents) will be meeting the love of his life (Krystal) within the week – you drag your sickly self away from death's door to turn the lights on. Family pride is an effective motivator.

I wanted to clean the house, polish the dog and prepare the customary feast but one whiff of bathroom cleanser left me balled up in a corner hacking and coughing. Kelby was forced to introduce his parents to his beloved like this:

"Krystal, this hovel is my childhood home. This lump? I think this specimen is my Dad, and the puddle on the sofa is my Mom. They used to speak English and smell better but they're sick. We warned Mom about the algae, but she went in the water anyway. As far as I know they won't get much worse, so if you can tolerate them in this condition – you'll really like them after we hose them down and fluff up the straw in their stalls."

Krystal didn't hesitate to hug me before she cozied herself into a spot on the love seat next to my sickbed. Between my coughing jags and her convulsive shivering caused by the seventy-degree temperature difference from Florida to Wisconsin, we giggled and ate grapes.

Somewhere between family photo albums and a penguin documentary on TV – I fell in love with my new daughter. If things didn't work out between her and my son, I planned to keep her anyway. More people to love gave me more reasons to survive the plague. Surviving any trauma is always cause for celebration.

Christina Crall-Reed

Cashing A Reality Check

⚡

For a year, I drove miles out of my way to avoid the ugly construction site where prairie grass once danced. When 'it' was up and running I ignored it. I paid no attention to the ads in the paper or the radio come-ons hyping jumbo bottles of this or that. I didn't need a pallet of paper plates. A ten-pound box of bacon would be wasted on me, and I refused to patronize the mega-corporation. Until I did.

Curiosity is a tempting mistress.

This MA Queen sauntered across the parking lot I swore I would never set foot on, just to satisfy my curiosity. Because I'm a rock star, an icon, and a legend in my own mind when I'm in MA Queen mode, I can make an entrance! *Silk gown, stilettos, and a flash of leg, I exit the stretch limo and step onto the red carpet. A slow motion breeze blows my hair away from my face. Camera shutters click and hum recording my every move. Horns trumpet my arrival. Fans cheer, "It's her! She's finally here!"*

Just as curiosity is a tempting mistress, reality is an evil bitch.

Wearing flip-flops, Bermuda shorts and a tank top, I stumbled out of my ten year old Ford. I immediately copped an attitude when my sandal stuck to a pinkish gray wad of gum melted on the pavement. I hobbled across the parking lot, dragging my foot behind to scrape my shoe. Standing on a strip of red Astro-turf at the entrance, a blast of hot air from an overhead vent made my eyes water. As I rummaged through my purse hunting for a tissue, security cameras recorded my every move. A generic Musak medley twittered from surround-sound speakers, announcing my arrival.

"Welcome to Sam's Club. May I see your membership card, please?" A two-hundred year old Wal-Mart Greeter blocked my path.

"What?"

"Your membership card?" His dentures clacked.

"I don't have one. I'm just looking."

"This is a 'members only' club."

"Yes. This is my first…"

"You have to have a membership to shop here."

I assumed any creature that had spent eons on the planet would recognize the danger of laying a gnarled hand on the shoulder of an MA Queen he'd never met, but my assumption was incorrect. The fossil's "Welcome! My Name Is Ray" tag, was markedly larger than his brain. I over-estimated the volume of his gray matter.

He pointed his free hand at the customer service desk as he curled his lips away from his false teeth in a patronizing smile. "You can apply for membership at the desk."

"I tell you what Crypt Keeper, if you don't take your hand off me, you'll be applying for disability."

His fingers crumbled into a shower of dust as I gave my shoulder a hard shrug. I spun out of reach, stumbled when the gum on my flip-flop stuck to the floor, then I caught my balance, and trotted off down the gigantic center aisle. I figured I had about an hour to wander before Crypt Keeper Ray would focus his one good eye on the spot I no longer occupied, and call security. I had no intention of making a purchase, but I wasn't about to let an uppity zombie turn me away from some store I considered to be a 'members-only' corporate flea market. I was uppity too.

I skittered down the barrels-of-coffee-aisle, peeked around the mattresses-stacked-sixty-feet-high-corner to make sure Crypt Keeper Ray wasn't trailing me, then stopped to catch my breath. As

I wandered I wondered why anyone would purchase a fifty-gallon drum of ketchup that required an additional ten feet of garden hose and a sump-pump delivery system. Who had breath so stinky that they might use a case of mouthwash before it aged and fermented into some sort of hooch? And when would the average person have occasion to slide around in a five-pound jar of petroleum jelly? I found no ready answers in the "Buy-One-Hundred-Get-One-Free-aisle, but when I happened upon the free food samples, I thought I'd uncovered the secret to a great day at Wally World.

In any other location, if a man wearing a stained apron and an unfashionable hairnet waved a bit of sausage at me, I'd mace him. At a grocery store, I hold out my beggar's hand or open my beak like a baby bird, to let a stranger feed me. Here, I ate what was offered, bird-hopped table to table, then peep, peep, peeped for more. When I chomped into a cookie laced with peanuts, I begged for a beverage sample before an allergic reaction could swell my lips together. Rinsing my mouth might slow the inevitable throat bloat. Directed beyond the grocery aisles I found my Nirvana.

Liquor and cigarettes at Rollback Prices?!

Separated from the rest of the store by glass partitions, various beers, brews and beverages had special status at Wally World. Behind the counter a woman stood at attention fixing her dark-eyed gaze on me. Her movements were as stiff as a rusted tinman. The black bangs slicing across her pale forehead appeared painted-on, and her thin slit of a mouth barely opened when she said, "Can I help you?"

"I sure hope so. I need a drink."

That's what they all say after the AA meetings," she deadpanned. "You've come to the right place."

Great. A cyborg comic. "Do you have water?"

"Yes I do. I will sell you something else, however."

"Water's fine. I just need something to rinse my mouth. I ate some peanuts. I'm allergic."

"Why would you eat a thing if you know you have allergies to it?"

"I didn't eat them purposely. They were in a cookie sample. Where is the water?"

The Incontinental Divide

"They're not supposed to give samples containing nuts. People are allergic."

"Yes. I know. The water?"

"We don't sell water in here."

"But, you just said…"

"I said I have some. I didn't say you could purchase it. We *sell* beer, wine and tobacco products here."

"But I…"

"Colas can be used to degrease automotive parts. Perhaps you could purchase a soda to cleanse your system?"

"And perhaps you are trying to kill me?" *Stepford Clerk.*

"That would be a violation of our customer service policy." The corner of her mouth twitched. I wasn't sure if she had just smiled at her own warped joke, or if there was a short-circuit in her robotic wiring. Either way, if I was about to go into anaphylactic shock I would go with a smile on my face. The LiquorBot *was* funny.

"Fine. Where's the soda?"

"Out in the main store near the bottled water." The clerk's pupils fixed and dilated on a spot on my forehead.

My tongue swelled as small blisters bubbled in my mouth. "Good Gawd woman, gimme a break! I don't have a membership."

"At this location, a membership is not required in order to purchase tobacco or alcohol at everyday low prices." She stared straight ahead.

The LiquorBot was beginning to annoy me. "So, if I buy something in here — anything in here — will you give me a frickin drink?"

"Yes."

"Great. Right after you give me a drink, I'll buy something."

The clerk unceremoniously plunked a bottled water and a paper cup on the counter. I poured a shot, took a swig, swirled it around my mouth, then spit it back into the cup. One of her penciled-on eyebrows rose ever-so-slightly as I gently placed my cup of drool on the countertop. I smiled. "I'll have a carton of Marb reds and a 12-pack of Bud Light. Bottles, please."

Unwilling to pick up my paper cup gauntlet, LiquorBot closed her eyes in an attempt to reboot her customer-service-skills-system. Either that, or she was trying to choose the most efficient way to hurl me out of the airlock of her spaceship. She slid the water aside, making room for the carton of cigarettes she placed in front of me. "May I see your identification please?"

"Excuse me?" I giggled.

"Your identification?"

"My ID? What for?" I laughed at her jest.

"You are attempting to purchase tobacco products. I am required to confirm your age."

"You're funny. Which cooler is the Budweiser in?"

"To your left. I need your identification."

If the LiquorBot's eyes had laser capabilities, her stare would have burned a hole through my skull. "You're serious?"

"Quite."

"Oh – kaay." I slid my driver's license out of my wallet and laughed. "You can't possibly think I'm under-age."

"It is company policy to confirm the age of any customer who appears to be under the age of forty."

Under *forty was* over *a decade ago! I love you LiquorBot!* "Wow! Thanks. Can I kiss you?"

"Just your ID please."

Until that moment, I hadn't considered a physical relationship with a Wal-Mart clerk, but when she sold me beer and cigarettes at reduced prices *and* gave me ten years, I wanted to give her tongue — maybe a kidney, or one of my kids.

To thank LiquorBot, I tossed my own spittoon into the trash bin near the exit. I swear I heard ungreased gears turn and squeal as she blinked her appreciation. With my twelve pack of brew, carton of smokes, and a revitalized ego, I flip-flopped out to my car, nodding goodbye to Crypt Keeper Ray as I passed.

Curiosity is a tempting mistress, and reality *can* be an evil bitch, but those girls got nothin' on this MA Queen. I write my own reality checks and cash them whenever, wherever I can — without a membership.

Buy One Hundred - Get One Free

⚡

Once I was buckled in and ready to roll, I chose not to fish around in my pants for my buzzing cellphone. I simply enjoyed the vibrations. With both hands locked on the wheel and a dopey grin plastered on my face, I drove home hoping my caller would ring again. And again and again and…

Hands full, I held the front door ajar with my hip so Bud-D could lumber outside to sniff around and lift his leg on the whitewall tires. Seconds after my pocket stopped humming, the house phone rang. The heavy door spanked my backside as I lunged into the kitchen to grab the phone. *Alright, already, I'm coming. I'm,* "Helllooo?"

"Hi Mom, Where you been? I've been tryin' to get ahold of you."

"Oh, that was you? Thanks for the buzz, Kelby."

"What?"

"Never mind." I giggled. "So, what's up pup?"

"Not much. I just have a quick question for you."

"Maybe I've got a quick answer for you."

"Okay, what would you say if I told you I was going to be a Dad?"

"I'd say, Who is this?" The kitchen walls moved closer. *How odd.*

"Very funny."

"And then I'd ask if you were teasing me."

"No joke, Mom. You're gonna be a Grandma. What do ya thinka that?"

"Uh, that thought hadn't crossed my mind today. Until — wow Kelby, um, wow." The phone gained weight in my hand. Memories swirled as *my* youth morphed, and melted into snapshots of Kelby's childhood. *He's going to be a Dad? What am I supposed to say? Oh yeah, I'm supposed to be happy. If he says it's a good thing, then this is a good thing.* "I'm happy if you are Kelby. I'm uh, how's Krystal? If you two are good, then I'm…"

"Hey Krystal's beeping in. Can I call you right back?"

"Yah." The phone went dead. I whispered into space as I lowered myself to the middle of the kitchen floor. "Sure. Call me back." Sprawled around the twelve-pack on the cool tile, my bare legs went numb. My mind tried to do the same. As I tore at the carton to rip open a pack of smokes, white sticks flew, scattered and rolled around the room. I snatched a cigarette mid-air, shoved the unfiltered end into my mouth and let it dangle while I waited for the phone to ring. When it did, I jumped.

"Shit! Hello? Wrong phone – shit!" Pushing buttons on the land-line receiver, I barely managed to pluck my vibrating cellphone from my pocket before it went to voicemail.

"You're not gonna believe this, Mom!"

"Believe what? I believe you're setting me up for the punch line to one of your off-the-wall jokes, Kelby. That's what I believe."

"I'm serious Mom! Twins! We're having twins!"

"That's nice, honey. That's…"

Holy Shit! Twins? Two times a Grandmother!?! A Grandmother? Me? Grandma? Grandmas are old. Sounds old. Granny? Like the Beverly Hillbillies? No. Kelby called my Mom Granny when he was little – when he was a baby. My baby. My baby's having babies? Am I old enough to be a grandma? I'm older than Mom was when she got this call from me. He can't be old enough to be a Dad. How old are dads? He's almost thirty. They're not married. Are they ready? No one's ready. Am I ready to be a grandma? Hell no! YES! How the hell would I know? Of TWINS? Grand MA?

"Mom? Are you there? Mom? — Ma!"

"Don't call me Ma, you sound like a sheep."

"Gets your attention every time." Kelby laughed.

"Oh, I heard every word you said. Maybe not in the order you said them — but I heard the words."

"So, whatcha think Mom? Or should I say, Grandmom?"

"I think…"

I think I'll go make nice with Crypt Keeper Ray. I think this future grandmother of twins will stock-up on valium and tequila at everyday low prices. I think a Buy-One-Hundred-Get-One-Free-Sale on diapers is looming on my horizon. I think this MA Queen just got a sparkling new jewel in her crown.

I think I'll go call your Dad.

Gramma Kiss

I fell off my nut long before Krystal's scheduled C-section. I was crazy with worry about a pregnancy I didn't control. Twin to twin transfusion, erratic heartbeats, premature labor, contractions, contradictions, in the hospital, out of the hospital, yes they're fine, no they're not, and *Dammit!* I'm no help to anyone fifteen-hundred miles away. By the time my plane touched down at the Tampa airport the day the babies were born, I was bouncing around in a mosh pit of emotion, too tired to cuss.

"Hi honey." I cried when Bailey kissed the top of my head.

"Hello little Mommy. How was your flight?"

"Good. I think. I don't know. I slept."

"You look tired, like you should sleep some more."

"Yah. No. I've been worried about Krystal. And your Dad is losin' it, and I had to have another autopsy last week."

"What? You had what? Aren't you 'sposed to be dead first, Mom?"

"Huh? Why would you say *that*? That's not nice." My eyes welled up.

Bailey smiled as he drew me into a hug. "I'm not being mean, Mom. You said autopsy."

"Oh. I did? Oh." Tears fell to the rhythm of my giggles. "I meant biopsy."

"Yah. I figured. So how did that go?"

"I don't know. Every time is scary, every…" I squeezed my eyes shut to search the back of my lids for a pleasant thought. My test results were inconclusive, so breast cancer and my own mortality were on my mind — again. Ric's out-of-control addictions and our failing marriage were two more un-fun realities to ponder. But babies? Yes! Babies! I concentrated on the 'new people' reason for this trip. "So have you heard from Kelby? How's everybody doing?"

"Fine I guess. I talked to him right after the babies were born. They're tired, but happy."

"And?"

"And they're fine. Stop worrying. We'll get there as fast as we can. Didn't you already talk to them?"

"Yeah, but."

"They're fine, Mom."

"But."

"They. Are. Fine." Bailey grabbed my luggage from the carousel, placed his free hand across the small of my back and gently ushered me outside. To confirm all was well, we hurried to wait in the hospital lobby.

"Is it weird for you Mom, thinking about one of your babies having babies?"

"Surreal is more like it. I have a hard time picturing you and Kelby as adults, let alone as parents." Bailey turned to walk away from me mid-conversation. "Where are you going?"

"To sign in."

"To sign in what? Why?"

"We have to sign in to let them know we're here."

"They know we're coming. We'll just knock on the door."

"We have to get a visitor's pass."

"From Kelby?"

"No. At the desk."

"What desk?"

"That one. Turn around Mom."

I spun and smacked into the rib-high reception desk where a chinless giant smiled down at me. I signed the visitor's log, surprised the behemoth clerk didn't pat the top of my head. Nodding and patronizing he could have pinned an envelope with bus fare and an, *"if-found-please-return-to-sender"* address label to my shirt. Instead he gave me a "Visitor" sticker. Because I'm special.

Bailey suggested I take a seat in the waiting room, but I plastered my Visitor tag to my chest, and wandered off to visit the drinking fountain, the gift shop, and the bathroom, before I revisited the reception desk to ask the Giant how much longer I'd have to wait to visit my family.

"We'll call you."

"You don't have my number."

The Giant rolled his eyes and gestured in the direction of the waiting room as he slowly, clearly enunciated each word. "Have — a — seat. I'll — announce — your — name."

Chastized and embarrassed, but too tired for a snappy comeback, I plopped down on a chair next to Bailey. He gently patted my shoulder. "It won't be long."

Bailey was correct. It wasn't long — before I dozed off. Head bobbing, I snoozed...

"It's just the inside of a plant, Kelby. Pumpkin guts won't hurt you."

"It's gross. I'm not touchin' it."

"How are you gonna' change a diaper when you're a dad?"

"Maybe I won't have to. Maybe my kids won't pee."

I jerked myself upright, and popped my eyes open. "Whoa!"

"You okay?"

"Yeah. Pretty sleepy I guess." I smiled at Bailey. *He's so handsome. He looks like his dad.* I closed my eyes again. *They have some of the same mannerisms, not the mean ones though.* I drifted off. *Bailey and Kelby aren't mean like their dad ...*

"You called him stupid, Ric. You told our child he was stupid now he's

upstairs crying, saying he won't be like you, and he doesn't want to talk to you."

"Oh for Christ sake, he can shake it off."

"A nine year old should 'shake-off' a broken heart? Shame on you! You belittle him, but it's Kelby's problem, Kelby's fault now? Shame. On. You."

"Talk to him."

"I can't fix this Ric! And you can't unsay something ugly. At best, you showed him what a good man, a good dad, shouldn't do..."

"Mom." Bailey tapped my shoulder. "Mom? You in there? Hello?"

I tried to shake the sleep from my head as I sucked in a spot of drool that had pooled at the corner of my mouth.

"They were calling our name. Are you sure you're alright? You were scowling and mumbling."

"I was thinking about your Dad and Kelby. Old wounds, you know?"

"Yeah. We've got some scars." Bailey gathered our belongings and ushered me to the elevator bay. "Speaking of, try not to make that sleep-zombie face at the babies. You'll scar them for life."

"I look that bad?"

"I'm teasin'. You're beautiful, Little Mommy. Little Grandmommy."

"*That* sounds weird. I'll have to let the name simmer. Krystal asked me what I wanted to be called, like Grandmother or Nana or whatever. I kinda liked the Grammy/Gramma Kiss nickname. Sounded cute. Kiss is way better than Aunt Piss —like Lauren used to call me."

"What?" Bailey laughed.

"Don't you remember? Lauren couldn't make that hard C-H-R sound in Chris, so she called me Aunt Piss?"

"At least it rhymes. She was close."

We lurched when the elevator slid to a not-so-smooth stop at the fourth floor maternity ward. "And by the way Bailey, to scar a kid, an ugly face isn't enough. You have to teach them the, 'if-I-should-die-before-I-wake' prayer or sing that 'rock-a-bye-baby-and-cradles-fall-out-of-the-tree' song. Those are awful."

"Then read Mother Goose to them? Where they throw cats in the well, and chop up blind mice, and whip kids 'til they cry? The ones you read to us when we were little?"

"Yeah. Exactly."

"You're sick. I like that in a parent."

Laughing at our twisted plans to warp the little minds of our newest family members, the instant we entered the birthing suite — plans changed. Life as I knew it, changed.

Pale, swollen and tethered to an IV and monitor, Krystal struggled to reposition herself to visit. Kelby sported a two day beard and dark circles under his bloodshot eyes. Yawning and smiling as he fussed over the bassinet, I'd never seen him look so tired or so blissful.

"Look Mom, we made people."

"Yes you did. Congratulations Daddy." I held my firstborn in a long embrace while choking back emotion. "Congratulations Daddy *and* Mommy." Hugging Krystal would only cause her pain so I chose instead, to blow her a kiss. The second I touched my fingers to my lips my eyes welled-up. As I spun around to turn my attention to the babies, I lost control of my tears. "Wow, you two do nice work!" I cried as I lifted the corner of one of the swaddling blankets. "Which one is this?" The little guy wiggled and passed gas.

Kelby laughed. "Apparently, that is PoopyBaby. You already scared the shit out of him Mom. Way to go."

"Ha-ha. You're sooo funny, Demon Seed. Are there diapers so I can change him?"

"No!" Kelby's face flushed red.

"No what? No diapers?"

"No – I'll change him. This is my family. I'll take care of them!"

"Ohh-kay. I was only going to change his pants Kelby, not steal him and harvest his organs. Can you say, over reaction? Jeesh." Hurt that he'd snapped at me without cause I surrendered my hands to the air and backed away from the bassinet. "Sorry."

"It's not. It's, it's just that this… Look at them Mom. This is *my* family. Mine. If I don't take care of them who will?"

Grateful he was honoring his paternal instincts, I smiled and nodded in understanding. "No one will, Honey. You're right." My smile widened to a grin. "Welcome to parenthood. May I at least hold one of your children while you change the other? It's nice that you made spares for the grandparents to hug."

Kelby relaxed as he unwrapped the gassy baby-bundle. "Okay, but don't try to stuff him in your purse to take him. I'm watchin you. And I'm keeping all of 'em."

Bailey glanced over Kelby's shoulder, said "Eewe" then quickly turned his attention back to a magazine. Before dozing off, Krystal explained which baby wore what color hat, but it didn't matter. Decked out in stocking caps, booties and mittens with only their pink cheeks exposed to the elements, they both looked like virgin longshoremen.

I lifted the baby from his bed, nestled his warm, tiny body into the crook of my arm, and took a seat near the window. Sunlight danced through the miniblinds. I peeled back the wrappings and pushed back his stocking cap to say hello to — Kelby. My child's child looked just like him.

The flood gates opened and tears streamed down my cheeks. Instantly, there wasn't an illness or marital problem that mattered as long as I had this child and his brother to love. Like Bailey and Kelby before them, holding the baby centered me. He wouldn't care if I was an MA Queen or a roller derby queen. It wouldn't matter if I wore red silk undies, or red pantaloons on my head. I could be fat or ugly or sing off key and the babies wouldn't know the difference. I could be – Me. These babies would know my love, and I would continue to get my identity from the people in this room.

With his smooth head tucked under my chin I whispered, "Tis Himself. Welcome to the world little man. I'm your Gramma Kiss."

The baby jerked, frowned and puckered his lips. "Eewe" he said.

Figures.

Move The Body

A friend will help you move. A good friend will help you move a body. If I ever leave my starter house my pals will probably help me pack and carry, but only my buddy Sherri has agreed to drag my sorry corpse down the steps if I should die in my sleep.

Some people hope to check out of this life while they wander dreamland. Not me. I might welcome a peaceful cross over into the white light, if the logistics and 'what-ifs' of death-in-my-sleep didn't already keep me awake at night.

I sleep naked. I'm comfortable in the buff, but I know full well I'm better looking if I'm strapped in, trussed up and covered with fabric. If I died in my sleep I wouldn't have the energy to dress myself. When the EMTs came to haul my body away I would be dead *and* embarrassed.

On cold winter nights I wear socks to bed. Just socks. If I died in my sleep on a cold winter's night, without Sherri there to supervise the pick-up for the morgue, it would go something like this:

"Where's the body?"

"Upstairs." A grizzly old farm-hand points his gnarled finger at the ceiling.

"Where's the light switch?"

The Incontinental Divide

"There is no light. The bulb blew years ago, but she was afraid to replace it."

A gurney won't fit in the narrow stairway so the veteran EMT and his rookie partner will have to bump and feel their way up the steps — unarmed and unprepared.

"Jeez, this is an old house. It's freezin' in here."

"I've heard stories about this place. My grandmother was an EMT in the eighties. She helped deliver a baby here."

"Oh yeah. This place was struck by lightning like a thousand times. Saw it on the news. And didn't they have a big watchdog? Wouldn't let anybody get near the lady who lived here?"

"Hope *he's* not here."

The EMTs stumble over the clean clothes stacked in front of the dresser then bump into the open drawer of a nightstand. The rookie cusses. "Ouch. Shit! Hey, I think I found a flashlight." An amber light glows as a 'flashlight' hums and buzzes. "There's a couple of em' but they don't give off much light, oh, wait, feels like a lampshade, and a — What the!?"

"Oh Man! You wrapped your hand around *that*!?"

"How was I supposed to know? Who the hell bronzes a dildo to make a lamp?"

"Apparently, *She* does — did." The veteran smiles and points. "What's that little plaque say?"

Big Boy, My Friend... You Light Up My Life.

"They're not gonna believe this back at the station."

The rookie cocks his head, "Did you hear that?"

"What?"

"Sounded like a leprechaun."

"I didn't hear anything. Let's get movin'. It's freezing in here."

"How we gonna lift her? She's naked."

"No. She's wearing socks."

"What's that in her underarm?"

"Her breast, I think. Boy oh boy, gravity's *mean* to big breasted women."

237

"Where's the other one?"

"The other what?"

"Boob."

"I don't know. Maybe she only had one."

The rookie freezes. "Did you hear *that*?"

"Hear *what*?"

"The leprechaun! I swear to God, I just heard an Irish voice whisper, 'It's in the drawer.'"

"What's in the drawer?"

"How should I know? You didn't hear anything?"

"No."

"This place is startin' to freak me out. When we came in, did you notice all of the paintings - but none of them are hung up…or the books and notebooks? There must be a thousand of them."

"Yeah. So, maybe she was moving. The guy downstairs, the hired man said this woman was a writer. Used to be an artist. Maybe she was packing to move."

"I didn't see any boxes."

"They said she died in her sleep. Maybe she didn't have time to get boxes."

"Yeah, well, it's still freaky. So how we gonna do this? Lift her by her socks?"

"Don't be an ass."

The rookie flinches. "Ouch! Knock it off, man!"

"Knock what off?"

"You hit me."

"I didn't touch you. I'm on the other side of the room for chrissakes! What? Are you losin' it? Job stressing you out?"

"I swear! Something just smacked the side of my head and I heard that leprechaun again!"

"Sure. Okay. And what did Mr. Lucky Charms say this time?"

"It's not a man. It's a woman. An Irish woman. She punched me and called me an idiot."

"You are an idiot."

"She said, *Eejit!*"

"Yeah. Okay. So, you're an 'eejit' and you pissed off some Irish No-See-Um. Can we move her now so I can go home and watch the game?"

"Fine by me. Let's get outta here."

The EMTs wrap me in my sheets, slip my corpse into a black body bag, then fold up the paperwork they can't finish in the dimly lit room.

"You've gotta shut off that lamp."

"I'm not touchin' it again."

"Just unplug it. Could be a fire hazard."

The rookie reaches for the cord. "Ouch! Shit!"

"What now? You boxing the ghost of Muhammad Ali?"

"No, Man! I got a shock. Spark just shot right outta the outlet!"

"Yep, probably a fire haz…"

"Look at this!"

"For chrissakes, what? Look at what?"

"A breast. Half a breast. It's a fake one, in the drawer, bouncin' around by those… Oh, man, those aren't flashlights!"

⚡

Sherri knows where my real flashlights are stored.

If I die in my sleep my friend will give me a few days to cool down and settle into my new routine. The first morning, she'll call and leave a message, knowing I seldom answer my phone. "Hey Sunshine! Just calling to see what you're up to. Talk atcha' later."

Day two will begin with the message, "Oh, where is my little friend, Chrissy? She didn't call me back. She should." On my cell phone there will also be a message to lure me from the house. "I'm going for ice cream. Call me if you want to come."

On the third day my answering machine will record the messages in quick succession:

"Did you move? Are you on vacation again?"

"Answer your phone or I'm comin' over. Call me when you get this message."

"That's it, I'm comin' over! And if you had another sex accident with a household product I'm laughin at your dumb ass before I take you to the hospital."

When I don't return her calls or show up for ice cream, Sherri will discover my corpse. She'll cuss, wail, and scream into the abyss, then my friend will keep her promise to move my lifeless body to an acceptably pleasant location closer to the ground.

Sherri will tuck my girls (and the spare) into a lacy Victoria Secret bra then dress me in a favorite pink suit. After shoving accessories into a laundry bag, which she will proceed to kick and roll down to the kitchen, my friend will pause to take a deep breath. Like a boxer preparing to step into the ring, she'll shake the kinks out of her limbs, bounce on the balls of her feet, take a few air-punches at her invisible opponent - then grab the cuffs of my wool socks to drag my inanimate self downstairs.

I'm sure I won't mind my head bouncing on the steps because my pal has already promised to rearrange my hair once she has me propped up in the recliner.

She'll peel my socks away then do her best to squeeze my feet into four-inch stilettos. She won't be able to see through her tears to pencil-in my eyebrows, but she'll make sure I'm wearing some sparklies like the pink topaz rocks Ric gave me for Christmas.

She'll call my kids, notify the coroner, then lay Big Boy and his less talented relatives to rest in the kitchen trash bin. Sherri will pour herself a cup of my thick, black, brewing-for-days-coffee, light a cigarette, plop down on the sofa across from my chair — and wait. She'll wait and she'll mourn, but she will keep her promise. No more, 'God Save The Queen.' When this life is done with me, my lady-in-waiting will help me make my next move.

Lights Out At The A.L.

At the Front, we were taught not to speak to strangers. During our MA years we chat up the weather and current events with people we don't know because those are safe subjects for idle prattle. By the time we reach the Back part of life, we've already covered every topic of conversation imaginable, so we begin to give voice to the totally inappropriate. In The Back, we should be reminded not to talk to strangers.

I may not understand where The Front went, nor can I pinpoint the start date of The Middle, but I know *MY* Back officially begins the moment I subject a stranger to tales of my bodily functions. It is unfortunate that old people ache and wheeze and get blocked up and locked up and can't get up when they fall down. Even worse, if they don't get enough fiber but they get too much salt and somewhere in between the two there is a space for chit – chat, old people will find the words to describe, in great detail, the goop, soup and poop their bodies produce to fill the voids.

The word phlegm for instance, is composed of leftover letters that stick in your throat when you try to cough them out. Phlegm sounds like what it is. Although it is an interesting word, phlegm is not to be used in casual conversation with a stranger nor in public. I don't want to get so old that I start talking about my phlegm. If I have some, people around me will know soon enough, so I don't need to tell them about it. Ever. Eewwe.

If the girl behind the counter at Walgreens has to hear any talk of my fluids, flow or internal pressures, I hope she will proceed to club me over the head like a baby seal so the phlegmy, Back part of my life will be brief. If a heavy blow to the temple doesn't permanently shut my lights off, perhaps a blunt force trauma will secure a room with a view, for me, at a fine Assisted Living Center. My reign as M.A. Queen will come to an inglorious conclusion when I am crowned Supreme-Omnipotent-Empress of Capital A, Capital L, - Assisted Living.

A.L. is my ticket outta here.

A.L. will be my last home.

At Assisted Living, once I've settled-into my new digs, someone will be paid to care for my phlegm, and other bodily malfunctions. My gross conversations will be appropriate because I'll be able to compare horror stories with other old folk. If the old people don't want to talk, I can always ask the orderly, "Do you want to see my ass?"

I'll smile, hike my snap-on house dress (with the Kleenex in the pocket) up to my wrinkled thigh and show them my faded tattoo.

When visitors come to see what's left of the Electric Woman, I'll giggle and shuffle off in my fuzzy cow slippers. The static created may discharge a few pacemakers enroute, but at least the guests will have a memorable visit.

Before falling asleep in the chair by the window, I might consider the body of a twenty five year old. Fondly, I'll remember, reminisce and recall my own curved and polished steel beauty...

Or, I won't.

Maybe my twenty five year old will be one who graduated with my great-grandsons. He could feed me, wipe my chin, or clean me if I cross the Incontinental Divide. When he turns the lights off as he leaves the room there'll be no tears from me.

The only sound will be my ancestors cooing. *"Tis Herself, reloxan ahn glad tah have been here."*

Acknowledgements

For all of my Queens and Princesses: I love you. Thank you for talking me off the ledges and pushing me over the edges. My little life is big and juicy because all of you are in it.

To my first true loves, my sons Kelby and Bailey - Gungee pee me bombees. Gungee pee. If you read this book, remember, unconditional love endures. And I'm not paying for your therapy.

For Carter and Dylan – Count every leaf on every tree and add one – That's how much I love you.

For saving and enriching my life, dissecting, and always protecting my soul — my friends Anne Luiting and Sherri Heth Dampier sustain me with their love. Okay, love, a little tequila and some 'purse chicken' also help. You have my heart. Keep it always.

To my friend and mentor, Lorin Oberwerger – Editor/Agent/Woman Extraordinaire - I am grateful for your professional expertise, but more so for your incredible friendship and support. By welcoming me into your life and home you've helped me find my own. Your brilliance lights my path. Shine on, my sweet friend. Shine on.

To Brenda Windberg For insight, editing skills and for infusing my life with the stardust that is you - Thank you.

To Roman White for understanding the pain at the core of comedy and for making sure I don't linger too long at that core. For hugs, giggles and for changing that blue door picture, I thank you Ro.

To my kindred spirit, friend, author Janet Chapman, I am grateful you didn't have me fit with a straightjacket when first I contacted you. Crows, cranes, flashes of insight - thank you for sharing your world with me. You gave me back my magic, urging me to write on. I shall.

Thanks to Jason Sitzes, the Pope of the old WRW, for special dispensation to use MY voice MY way. You gave me an instruction manual to this writer's life and I am eternally grateful. Grazie Padre.

For life support, my love and thanks go to my siblings Vickie, Steve, Mat and Liana; friends Jo Cooper, Janice Croom, Kai Towles, Wendy Daugherty, Rita Rosin, Peggy O'Leary, my osmosis daughter CortneyDampier-Miles, my Stepdad Vern, and our amazing Scribble Katz writing group: Lorin Oberweger, Larry Kay, Liz Sentz Horvet, Brenda Windberg, Usman Tanveer Malik, Kelsey Tressler, Adam Carter, Geodie Baxter Padgett, Gemma Cuomo Kay, and the late Tom Towles We did it! WooHoo!

About the Author

Struck by lightning at the age of twelve and again as an adult, author/artist/humorist, Christina Crall-Reed lived on a Wisconsin dairy farm, in a house zapped by lightning more than twenty times. Today she lives in a metal-framed house, in the lightning capitol of the USA (Tampa, FL) - because she can.

In addition to creative pursuits, Christina worked in child abuse prevention, taught mural painting, was design director at a new age magazine, and is a Certified Laughter Leader through the World Laughter Tour.

Writing about the absurdities of life, lightning, and the healing power of laughter, Christina's AMISH CRACK HOUSE SERIES, (including PET MY PRETTY LIZARD; MAYBE SPINACH DOESN'T LIKE YOU EITHER; and her own coming-of- middle-age story, THE INCONTINENTAL DIVIDE) launches in 2017.

Contact her at:
www.facebook.com/crallspace
www.facebook.com/Christina Crall-Reed
Twitter @lightningccr
www.thecrallspace.com (under construction)

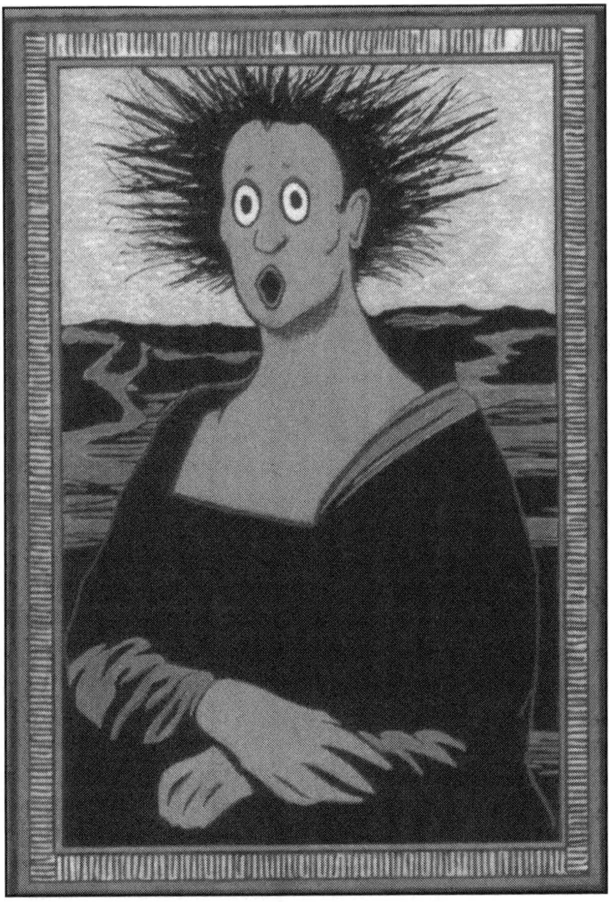

Coming Soon

From Author Christina Crall-Reed, and TheCrallspaceCreative

The Amish Crack House Series

"Any message written on liver pate' is probably a bad omen. It doesn't matter if the dips are colored, frosted, and formed into the shape of wedding bells. Heartfelt sentiment could be painstakingly written on every edible on the buffet table, but it makes no difference. The bride's mom may giggle as she snaps Polaroids of the hors-de-vours, and the groom's mother can run table to table scraping words off the food with a butter knife, but if the bride is Christina and the groom's name is Ric—then, 'Best Wishes Chris and Mark' is bad luck."

Pet My Pretty Lizard

"Eyes swollen, snot dripping, I drew a jagged breath, and grabbed the stock of the shotgun. I was all done praying."

Maybe Spinach Doesn't Like You Either

"Oops, I stabbed you. Fourteen times. I don't think they'd believe me. No random act of violence was ever committed with a knife."

Made in the USA
San Bernardino, CA
02 January 2018